Primary Care
of the Newborn

Primary Care of the Newborn

Ronald W. Coen, M.D.

Associate Professor of Pediatrics,
University of California, San Diego,
School of Medicine, La Jolla, California;
Chief, Neonatal Medicine,
University of California, San Diego,
Medical Center, San Diego, California

Herbert Koffler, M.D.

Associate Professor of Pediatrics,
Obstetrics, and Gynecology, University
of New Mexico School of Medicine;
Director of Newborn Services,
University of New Mexico Hospital/
Bernalillo County Medical Center,
Albuquerque, New Mexico

Little, Brown and Company
Boston/Toronto

Contents

Preface   vii

Acknowledgments   ix

1. History and Initial Assessment   1

2. Admission Procedures and Routine Evaluations   19

3. The Physical Examination   27

4. The First 24 Hours: Common Problems   65

5. The First 24 Hours: Special Problems   111

6. Beyond the First 24 Hours   139

7. Nutrition   153

8. Discharge   167

9. Organization and Management of the Nursery   179

Appendixes   193

Index   255

Preface

Almost four million infants are delivered annually in the United States. More than 90 percent of these infants have an uncomplicated perinatal course. Yet the major focus of newborn care during the past 20 years has been on the compromised infant. This interest also has spawned a voluminous amount of literature pertaining to neonatal physiopathology.

In teaching nursing and medical students, house officers, and graduate nurses and physicians about the newborn infant, we realized that a single, current reference source on the management of infants in a level I nursery was not available. A classic text, *Management of the Newborn* (2nd edition), by Dr. A. H. Parmelee (Chicago: Year Book), was last published in 1959, before the concept of regionalized neonatal/perinatal care. Parmelee's book remains pertinent today because it provides excellent descriptions and discussions of common problems. However, there are issues that require restatement and others that have come to light only recently because of new research.

Our book is intended to be comprehensive but not encyclopedic. It has been designed to present the newborn infant as the physician might encounter him* in daily practice. It addresses situations that may be encountered during or shortly after the period of initial hospitalization. The normal state and its variations are emphasized, and summaries of common problems and references for more intensive evaluation are provided.

Initial chapters address the methods used by the nurse and doctor to assess the most important adaptation process the human makes, namely, the transition from intrauterine to extrauterine existence. The prophylactic procedures necessary to protect the infant also are discussed. Subsequent chapters present a system by system commentary on common problems encountered during the first 24 hours and thereafter. Special emphasis is placed on the assessment of gestational age and the understanding of jaundice, sepsis, and nutrition. The final chapters discuss discharge procedures and the function and design of a level I nursery. The appendixes contain information on the technical aspects of neonatal care and dosages for commonly used drugs.

We hope this book will contribute to the reader's appreciation and understanding of the nuances of the newborn infant. If that is so, then we have repaid our debt to those who have taught us.

R. W. C.
H. K.

---

*Throughout the text we have chosen to use the male pronoun rather than "he or she" or "his or her." This convention is not meant to be sexist or discriminating.

Acknowledgments

There are many individuals who encouraged and assisted us in the completion of this book. We pay special thanks to Drs. Jon Aase, Dale Alverson, Charles Anderson, Phil Anderson, Kurt Benirschke, Kyung Chung, Terrence Dillon, Kenneth Lyons Jones, Ann Kosloske, Mel Levine, and Carl Weihl, and nurse practitioners Pat Mooney and Ruth Wester. Our secretaries Bernadette Armijo, Carol Heil, Laura Kane, Perlinda Lujan, Linda Carreon Matthes, Anne Reid, Jean Sennet, and Debbie Wogenrich deserve special mention for the amount of time spent at the computer keyboard. And finally, we thank Gail Flax for doing an excellent job on the medical illustrations.

Our gratitude is extended to Curtis Vouwie, formerly of Little, Brown and Company, for not giving up! Without his encouragement, the early manuscripts might still be sitting on a shelf somewhere. Elizabeth Willingham and Chris Davis of Little, Brown and Company helped bring the book to completion.

Finally, we dedicate this book to our families and Drs. Robert Tully of Albuquerque, New Mexico, and James M. Sutherland of Cincinnati, Ohio. The Koffler and Coen families deserve special merit awards for being so patient with us during the many times we were working on the book. Their encouragement and comments like "Not again!" were invaluable. We want to specifically praise Esther and Merrille Koffler (Herb's mother and sister), who spent time editing many "final" editions. Dr. Tully was especially helpful in reviewing the early and final manuscripts, contributing valuable criticism, and sharing his copy of the out-of-print Parmelee textbook. Dr. Sutherland played a pivotal role in the evolution of our careers as neonatologists. During our pediatric training program at the University of Cincinnati, he taught us the fundamentals of neonatal care. Later, he provided the milieu in which we, as postgraduate fellows, furthered our understanding and pursued our curiosity about the physiology and pathology of the newborn infant. We are grateful to Dr. Sutherland for taking time to fly to New Mexico and assisting in the review and editing of the text. He enthusiastically shared his wisdom and experience with us. We both admire his continued dedication to our field. Without him, this book would not be a reality.

Special gratitude is extended to Florence and Marvin Dollin, whose residence in Angel Fire, New Mexico, was used to start the writing on a cold wintry day.

Primary Care
of the Newborn

1. History and Initial Assessment

THE NEWBORN HISTORY

The first comprehensive medical evaluation of the newborn infant should be performed as soon after birth as possible and no later than 24 hours following delivery. The examination begins with a thorough review of the history of the pregnancy, labor, delivery, and the medical histories of the parents and their families. This information usually is included in the obstetric record, a copy of which is sent routinely to the nursery with the infant. When complete, the record should contain the following information:

1. Mother's and father's ages
2. Marital status
3. Mother's obstetric history, number of previous pregnancies, birth weight and gestational ages, and outcome
4. Last normal menstrual period (LNMP) and expected date of confinement (EDC)
5. Prenatal care during the current pregnancy
6. Prepregnant weight and weight gain during the current pregnancy
7. Medications (prescription and nonprescription)
8. Exposure to infectious diseases
9. Habits (drugs, alcohol, smoking)
10. Family and genetic diseases
11. Maternal systemic diseases
12. Maternal blood type and serology
13. Mode of feeding preferred (breast or formula)
14. Circumcision (yes or no)

If any of this information is missing or incomplete, it is necessary to question the obstetrician or interview the parents. The medical history of the newborn infant is complex because it encompasses genetics, embryology, obstetrics, and the developmental physiology of the fetus and newborn.

THE PREGNANCY [9, 21]

The gestational period of the human infant is approximately 266 days from the time of fertilization. However, the expected date of confinement (EDC) or delivery is estimated for clinical purposes from the onset of the last normal menstrual period (LNMP) because that event may be determined more precisely. Because the last menstrual period begins approximately 14 days before ovulation and fertilization, the calculated gestational period is approximately 280 days. This is equivalent to 10 lunar months or nine calendar months.

An error in the calculation of the EDC, based on the LNMP, occurs in approximately one out of five pregnancies, most commonly because vaginal bleeding occurring in early pregnancy is mistaken for a menstrual period. When the EDC is uncertain, fetal age may be estimated using other clinical criteria [4], plus sonographic, biochemical, and radiologic techniques. The common clinical assessments of fetal age and their estimated accuracies are shown in Table 1-1.

The gestational timetable is divided into the period of the embryo and the period of the fetus [3]. During the period of the embryo there is rapid tissue growth and organ differentiation. These processes are completed by the eighth week after conception. Organogenesis spans the embryonic and early fetal growth periods and is completed by the twelfth week. During the remainder of the period of the fetus there is continued

Table 1-1. Range of accuracy for obstetric estimates of gestational age

Estimating gestational age	Range for 95% of cases
In vitro fertilization	< 1 day
Ovulation induction	3–4 days
Recorded basal body temperature	4–5 days
Ultrasound crown-rump length	+/− 0.7 wk
First trimester physical examination (normal uterus)	+/− 1 wk
Ultrasound BPD before 20 wk	+/− 1 wk
Ultrasound gestational sac volume	+/− 1.5 wk
Ultrasound BPD from 20–26 wk	+/− 1.6 wk
LNMP from recorded dates (good history)	+/− 2–3 wk
Ultrasound BPD 26–30 wk	+/− 2–3 wk
LNMP from memory (good history)	3–4 wk
Ultrasound BPD after 30 wk	3–4 wk
Fundal height measurement	4–6 wk
LNMP from memory (not good history)	4–6 wk
Fetal heart tones first heard	4–6 wk
Quickening	4–6 wk

Key: BPD = biparietal diameter.
Source: J. D. Bowie and R. F. Andretti. Estimating Gestational Age in Utero. In P. W. Callen (ed.), *Ultrasonography in Obstetrics and Gynecology*. Philadelphia: Saunders, 1983, P. 34. With permission.

differentiation, evolution, and maturation of each organ system. During this time the placenta provides total sustentation for the fetus.

Gestation is divided into three 3-month trimesters [15]. The first trimester consists of the first 14 weeks of pregnancy and includes the periods of embryogenesis, organogenesis, and early fetal growth. The period of the fetus continues through the second and third trimesters. Changes in embryonic and fetal development are shown in Appendixes 1 and 2.

In the first trimester the developing organism faces a number of intrinsic and extrinsic hazards. Intrinsic risks to a normal pregnancy include: (1) defects in the egg or sperm producing genetic or chromosomal abnormalities; (2) defects in the fertilization process with formation of an abnormal zygote; (3) faulty progress of the ovum through the fallopian tube, resulting in an ectopic pregnancy; and (4) failure of normal implantation, ending in spontaneous abortion. Extrinsic risks include exposure to infectious organisms and chemicals such as tobacco, alcohol, and prescription or nonprescription drugs.

The second trimester is the fifteenth to the twenty-eighth week postconception. *Quickening,* or fetal movements felt by the mother, and fetal heart tones heard with a fetoscope are first detected at 17 to 20 weeks' gestation. During the second trimester, normal fetal growth and development may be disturbed by conditions affecting (1) the mother, such as chronic hypertension; (2) the placenta, such as retroplacental hemorrhage (abruptio placentae); and (3) the fetus, such as hemolytic disease with anemia secondary to blood group incompatibility.

As the pregnancy progresses into the third trimester, prenatal care usually includes more frequent assessments of the mother's general health and uterine size, and an evaluation of fetal activity and heart rate. At approximately 36 to 38 weeks, pulmonary maturation occurs, enabling the infant to make the transition to an extrauterine existence. Thus, the most important distinguishing feature between fetal development in the second and third trimesters is the maturation of the fetus into a viable infant.

The third trimester culminates with the birth of the infant.

NORMAL LABOR
Labor is divided into three stages [11]. The first stage begins with the onset of regular contractions and concludes when the cervix is completely thin (effacement) and dilated to the diameter of 10 cm. This stage progresses through a latent and active phase (Fig. 1-1). The second stage of labor is the time from complete cervical dilation to delivery of the infant. In the primigravida, the normal duration for the second stage is no more than 45 minutes. The third stage of labor concludes with delivery of the placenta.

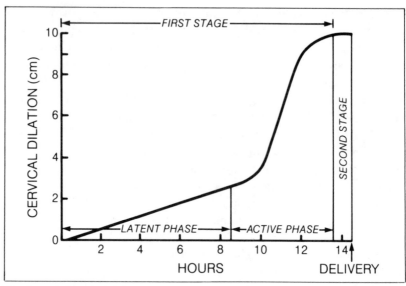

Fig. 1-1. Labor and delivery curve. (Adapted from E. A. Friedman. The labor curve. *Clin. Perinatol.* 8 : 15, 1981. With permission.)

Most pregnancies progress normally, and nearly all fetuses enter labor in a healthy condition. However, intrapartum complications must be anticipated if appropriate therapy is to be rendered. Currently, the preferred technique for assessing the fetus during labor is electronic monitoring of fetal heart rate activity [14]. Normally, early decelerations and beat-to-beat variability of the fetal heart rate occur (Fig. 1-2). In addition, the fetal scalp pH remains above 7.25, and no other evidence of fetal compromise or asphyxia is present (e.g., passage of meconium). Figure 1-3 shows fetal heart rate variability and late deceleration, conditions associated with a compromised fetus.

NORMAL DELIVERY
In the majority of cases, delivery of the term infant occurs vaginally. Almost all infants deliver in a vertex position; approximately 3 percent deliver breech [6]. The infant's delivery may be assisted electively with forceps, vacuum extractions, or both. In recent years there has been an increasing number of cesarean section deliveries [19].

The color, odor, and volume of the amniotic fluid should be noted at delivery. Amniotic fluid is clear, colorless, and usually nonmalodorous. The volume, normally about 1 liter, is rarely measured. However, it is very important to note a paucity or marked excess (greater than 2 liters) of fluid at delivery.

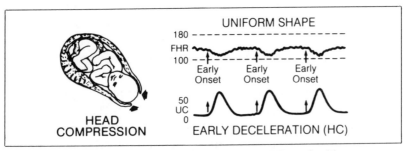

Fig. 1-2. Early fetal heart rate decelerations. (Key: FHR = fetal heart rate; UC = uterine contraction; HC = head compression.) (From E. H. Hon. *Fetal Heart Rate Deceleration Patterns. An Atlas of Fetal Heart Rate Patterns.* New Haven, CT: Harty Press, 1968. With permission.)

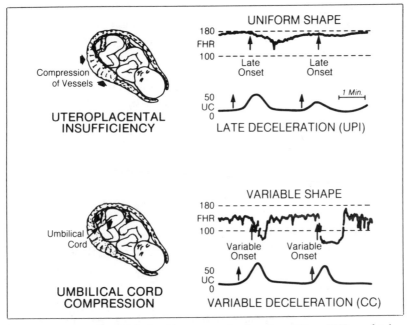

Fig. 1-3. Late and variable fetal heart rate decelerations. (Key: FHR = fetal heart rate; UC = uterine contraction; UPI = uteroplacental insufficiency; CC = cord compression.) (From E. H. Hon. *Fetal Heart Rate Deceleration Patterns. An Atlas of Fetal Heart Rate Patterns.* New Haven, CT: Harty Press, 1968. With permission.)

The average length of the umbilical cord of the term infant is 50 to 60 cm [20]. In approximately 20 percent of deliveries it is wrapped around a fetal part, most commonly the neck. This entanglement may compromise the fetal circulation during labor and delivery. There should be a notation of the time the umbilical cord was clamped and cut and if it was stripped of blood before clamping, because these procedures will affect the infant's hematocrit.

Infants should be delivered in a facility in which all maternal, fetal, or newborn complications can be managed. Unfortunately, up to 40 percent of the problems for which infants are admitted to special care units are not expected or detected before labor and delivery. Although it is not the intent of this book to emphasize the recognition and management of the high-risk infant, it is important to stress that the perinatal team must be attentive and prepared for crisis intervention during labor and delivery. Every hospital that provides maternal and infant care should have written and approved plans to manage both healthy and stressed infants.

NEONATAL ADAPTATION
Following delivery, the full-term infant makes numerous physiologic adjustments that are geared toward survival. A successful transition depends primarily on the transfer of respiratory function from the placenta to the newborn's lungs in concert with changes in the cardiovascular system. Although each component of the adaptation process is discussed individually here, these changes occur in a coordinated fashion, minutes to hours after birth.

PULMONARY ADAPTATION
The anatomic and biochemical status of the fetal lungs at birth are the primary determinants of independent survival. At term, the lungs consist of major and minor bronchi, respiratory bronchioles, alveolar ducts, and alveoli in grapelike clusters.

Fetal lungs are filled with a fluid that differs chemically from amniotic fluid [5] (Table 1-2). Pulmonary fluid has a lower pH, protein, and bicarbonate concentration than amniotic fluid, and the osmolarity, sodium, and chloride content is higher in pulmonary fluid. During gestation, the pulmonary fluid from the fetal lungs contributes to the volume of amniotic fluid. With vaginal delivery, fluid in the airway is squeezed out through the infant's nose and mouth. The *thoracic squeeze* does not occur or occurs only minimally with cesarean delivery. Any remaining lung fluid is resorbed into the circulation.

Although sustained rhythmic breathing does not occur in utero, mechanical movements of the fetal chest and diaphragm have been verified

Table 1-2. Composition of body fluids

Subject	Fluid	Osmolarity (mosm/liter)	Sodium (mEq/L)	Potassium (mEq/L)	Chloride (mEq/L)	HCO$_3$ (mEq/L)	pH	Protein (gm/dl)
Fetus (term)	Pulmonary	300.00	142.00	5.00	144.00	4.00	6.40	0.30
Fetus (term)	Amniotic	265.00	126.00	4.00	100.00	18.00	7.10	0.30
Newborn (term)	Plasma	290.00	145.00	5.50	103.00	21.00	7.40	5.50

Source: Adapted and reproduced by permission from: June P. Brady. Homeostatic Adjustment of Fetus and Neonate. In Silvio Aladjem, Audrey K. Brown, and Claude Sureau (eds.), *Clinical Perinatology* (2nd ed.), St. Louis, 1980, The C.V. Mosby Co.

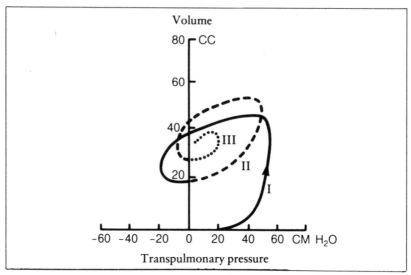

Fig. 1-4. The onset of respiration. Roman numerals indicate the first, second, and third breaths. (From C. A. Smith and N. M. Nelson. *Physiology of the Newborn Infant,* 1974. Courtesy of Charles C. Thomas, Publisher, Springfield, Illinois.)

with sonography and are termed *fetal breathing.* In a healthy fetus, breathing movements increase with maternal hyperglycemia and when there is fetal distress. They decrease in the presence of nicotine and with the use of medications, such as meperidine [8].

Immediately following delivery, the newborn infant's first inspiratory effort generates a very large transpulmonary pressure (40–100 cm of water), thereby overcoming increased pulmonary tissue resistance, alveolar surface tension, and fluid viscosity within the lung. When mature lung surfactants are present, each succeeding breath requires less distending pressure.

By approximately one hour after birth the healthy infant will generate a transpulmonary pressure of 20 cm of water and a tidal volume of 5 to 10 ml/kg (Fig. 1-4).

Normally, surfactant matures at 35 to 36 weeks' gestation, as reflected by an increasing ratio of amniotic fluid lecithin (phosphatidylcholine) to sphingomyelin (L/S ratio). Other components of the amniotic fluid surfactant profile also change: as phosphatidylinositol decreases, phosphatidylglycerol concurrently appears and increases [17]. Phosphatidylglycerol in the amniotic fluid is the single most important indicator of pulmonary maturity (Fig. 1-5).

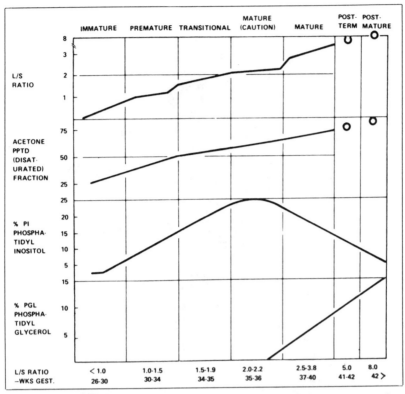

Fig. 1-5. Lung profile. (Copyright © 1977 by the Regents of the University of California. With permission.)

CARDIOVASCULAR ADAPTATION

In the fetus the organ of gas exchange (respiration) is the placenta rather than the lungs. Consequently, the course and distribution of the fetal circulation (Fig. 1-6) differs from that of the newborn infant. In the fetus, blood with the highest oxygen content courses from the umbilical vein through the ductus venosus and across the foramen ovale into the left side of the circulation. Blood with a lower oxygen content in the right side of the circulation bypasses the lung through the ductus arteriosus and returns to the placenta through the umbilical arteries.

At birth, clamping the umbilical cord eliminates blood flow through the lower resistance placental circuit. A series of changes then occur. As the lungs fill with air, pulmonary vascular resistance drops and pulmonary blood flow increases. Subsequently, left atrial pressure increases and exceeds right atrial pressure, thereby functionally closing the fora-

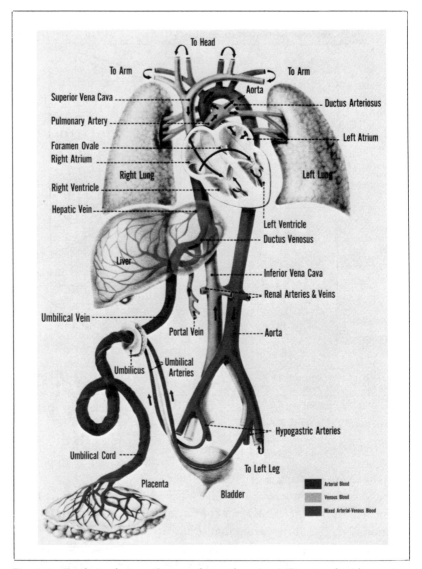

Fig. 1-6. Fetal circulation. (See text for explanation.) (Reprinted with permission of Ross Laboratories, Columbus, OH 43216, from Clinical Education Aid #1, © 1963 Ross Laboratories.)

men ovale. In the term infant, the ductus arteriosus closes by two to three days. The ductus venosus begins to close with cessation of umbilical venous blood flow.

ROLE OF OTHER ORGAN SYSTEMS IN ADAPTATION

Following birth, survival critically depends on the integration of cardiac and pulmonary functions. However, these adaptations are influenced by other organ systems. Abnormal development of the gastrointestinal system, kidneys, or brain may contribute to faulty neonatal adaptation. During gestation, the fetal gastrointestinal tract and kidneys regulate the volume and composition of amniotic fluid. Renal agenesis or obstruction of the fetal urinary tract results in a paucity of amniotic fluid (oligohydramnios) and its consequences [22] (Fig. 1-7): pulmonary hypoplasia, late intrauterine growth retardation, deformities of the extremities, and abnormal facies (oligohydramnios tetrad). Pulmonary hypoplasia results in early acute pulmonary failure since hypoplastic lungs are difficult to aerate. Excessive amniotic fluid (polyhydramnios) results from (1) upper gastrointestinal tract obstruction, such as esophageal or duodenal atresia; (2) dysfunctional sucking or swallowing arising from abnormalities

Fig. 1-7. Mechanisms and consequences of oligohydramnios. (From D. W. Smith. *Recognizable Patterns of Human Malformation* (3rd ed.). Philadelphia: Saunders, 1982. With permission.)

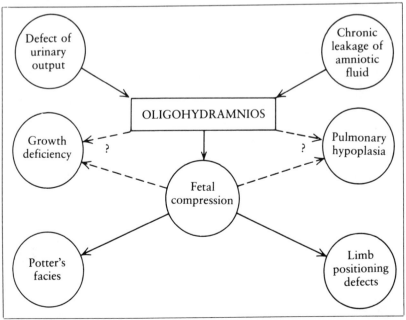

of the central nervous system; (3) fetal heart failure secondary to anemia, myocardial abnormalities, or other abnormalities; (4) multiple fetuses; or (5) congenital chylothorax [16].

Other impairments to the adaptation process may be due to heart failure, aspiration pneumonias, lung compression, anemia, or polycythemia.

ASSESSMENT OF ADAPTATION

The Apgar score is the clinical standard for evaluating the newborn's response to labor and delivery and his early adaptation to extrauterine life [2]. The Apgar score consists of five categories that are assessed at one and five minutes following birth. The components include skin color, two vital signs, and two neurologic signs (Table 1-3). The infant's adaptation is considered normal when the total score is 7 to 10. A score of 10 at one minute rarely occurs because virtually every infant has *acrocyanosis* (blueness of the hands and feet). A score of 4 to 6 indicates moderate depression, and a score of 0 to 3 reflects severe depression.

RESUSCITATION

Immediately after birth the newborn infant should be dried with a warm towel and kept warm; the nasal and oral air passages should be cleared of secretions, the vital signs monitored, and the Apgar scores recorded. These basic techniques will suffice for infants with Apgar scores between 7 and 10. Those with scores of 4 to 6 may require additional stimulation and supplemental oxygen. Apgar scores between 0 and 3 indicate the need for immediate intervention. When an infant presents with apnea, generalized cyanosis, bradycardia, and hypotonia (Apgar score of 3 or less), intervention must begin immediately with simultaneous attention to ventilation and perfusion. Respiratory depression may result from maternal anesthesia and analgesia, obstetric trauma, fetal airway abnormalities,

Table 1-3. Apgar score

Sign	0	1	2
Heart rate	Absent	Below 100	Over 100
Respiratory rate	Absent	Weak cry, hypoventilation	Strong cry
Color	Blue, pale	Body pink, extremities blue	Pink
Muscle tone	Limp	Minimal flex	Active motion
Reflex response	None	Grimace	Response

Source: V. Apgar. A proposal for a new method of evaluation of the newborn infant. *Curr. Res. Anesth. Analg.* 32 : 260, 1953.

or asphyxia [1]. Although the etiology of the respiratory depression must be determined eventually, immediate action should be taken to establish a patent airway and adequate ventilation [13]. Infants with Apgar scores less than 3 require immediate assisted ventilation, which may be accomplished with a mask and infant resuscitation device [10, 18]. However, the insertion of an endotracheal tube is preferred, followed by assisted ventilation with an infant breathing bag (Fig. 1-8). During hand bagging, the chest should be auscultated to determine if air entry is equal on both sides. Simultaneously the expansion of the chest with each insufflation and whether the cyanosis is abating should be observed. Ideally, the inspiratory pressure being applied should not exceed 30 to 40 cm of water at a rate of 40 to 50 breaths per minute. If the infant remains cyanotic and air entry is absent or unequal, the position of the endotracheal tube should be checked to determine that it is not in the esophagus or in a mainstem bronchus. If the endotracheal tube is in proper position, it may be necessary to adjust the ventilation pressure or rate. Pulmonary blood flow may be dampened by positive pressure that is either excessive or is applied in the presence of a low circulating blood volume. The latter should be corrected with appropriate blood volume expanders. A No. 8

Fig. 1-8. Resuscitation bags. Mapleston bag with Norman elbow and Laederal infant mask (top); Laederal and Hope self-inflating ventilation bags (middle and bottom).

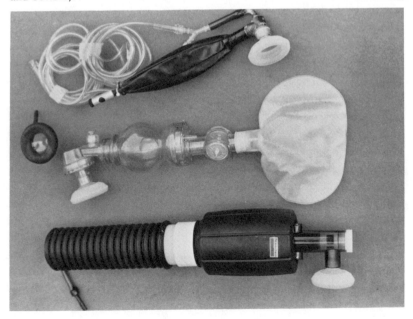

suction catheter should be passed into the stomach to prevent gaseous distention of the abdomen if ventilation is provided with a mask and bag.

The immediate application of positive pressure ventilation is contraindicated in the depressed infant who passed meconium into the amniotic fluid during labor [7, 12]. It is imperative that the person delivering the infant suction the meconium-stained fluid from the nasal and oropharynx before the thorax is delivered. Following delivery, the larynx should be visualized with a laryngoscope and the trachea cleared of meconium by suctioning with an endotracheal tube or a large suction catheter attached either to a DeLee suction trap or directly to low pressure wall suction. The airway should be cleared quickly because hypoxemia and acidosis increase with prolonged suctioning and airway manipulation. Sometimes an infant who passed meconium in utero and was suctioned on the perineum at delivery is crying and is vigorous. In this situation, the risk of iatrogenic trauma during intubation must be balanced against the risk of leaving meconium in the upper airway.

External cardiac massage should be started if a heart rate greater than 100 beats per minute is not established after five to ten breaths. A second person is required to assist in this procedure. To achieve successful cardiac massage, one hand should be placed around the infant's chest with the thumb over the middle to lower third of the sternum. The chest should be compressed one-third of the distance to the spine during cardiac massage. Most general manuals on resuscitation state the peripheral pulses (femoral or brachial) should be palpated to evaluate the cardiac output produced by the compression. However, in the newborn, even under normal circumstances, it is difficult to feel femoral pulses. Therefore, the best assessment of the infant's response to resuscitation is a resolution of cyanosis and an increase in heart rate. The following guidelines should be considered: (1) during cardiac massage the sternum should be compressed, not the ribs; (2) cardiac massage should be performed at a rate of 100 to 140 times per minute; and (3) the cardiac massage should be coordinated with ventilation in a sequence of three chest compressions followed by a single insufflation (cardiac/ventilation ratio of 3 : 1). If external cardiac massage is applied during a period of positive pressure ventilation, the resuscitation will not only be ineffective, it may result in a pneumothorax.

Medication may be necessary in patients refractory to ventilation and cardiac massage, especially in cases of narcotic depression or hypovolemia. The infusion of alkali for the treatment of initial acidosis is seldom necessary. Unless adequate ventilation (elimination of carbon dioxide) is established, the infusion of bicarbonate may increase respiratory acido-

Table 1-4. Medications used in resuscitation of the newborn

Medication	Dosage	Indications
A. Epinephrine	0.1–0.3 ml/kg of 1 : 10,000 solution Repeat every 5 min Given: Intravenous or into endotracheal tube	Asystole, heart rate < 80 beats/min despite adequate ventilation with 100% oxygen and chest compression
B. Volume expanders		
1. Type O negative blood (cross-matched with mother's blood)	10 ml/kg	Pallor, weak pulse, poor response to resuscitation
2. 5% albumin/saline or other plasma substitute	10 ml/kg	
3. Normal saline/Ringer's lactate	10 ml/kg	
C. Naloxone hydrochloride (neonatal— 0.02 mg/ml)	0.01/mg/kg Repeat every 2–3 min Given: Intravenous, endotracheal tube, subcutaneously, or intramuscularly	Respiratory depression secondary to narcotics

Source: Reproduced with permission. © J.A.M.A., June 6, 1986. American Heart Association.

sis. Thus, the major resuscitative effort is to establish ventilation. If necessary, diluted sodium bicarbonate should be infused, but very slowly. The most commonly used resuscitation medications with indications and doses are given in Table 1-4.

DELIVERY ROOM PROCEDURES
Every infant should have a brief examination in the delivery room to ensure that extrauterine adaptation is occurring without compromise and to ascertain that no major anomalies exist. Once stable, the infant should be weighed. An identification band stating the mother's name, her hospital number, the infant's sex, and the time and date of birth should be placed on both an ankle and a wrist in the delivery room. Subsequently, the infant's identification should be rechecked on admission to the nursery.

Foot printing, palm printing, or finger printing are difficult to do accurately and may unnecessarily prolong the time the infant is exposed to cold stress in delivery room [23]. If foot printing is done, the results should be good enough to permit identification.

Before the infant is taken to the nursery, the parents should have an opportunity to spend time with their infant. If the admitting nursery is a distance from the delivery suite, the infant should be taken to the nursery in a warmed transport incubator rather than being carried in an attendant's arms. Each infant should leave the delivery room with the following:

1. Proper identification
2. A completed maternal history chart
3. The delivery record, including one and five minute Apgar scores
4. An explanation of perinatal complications
5. A recorded temperature
6. A recorded brief physical examination
7. A secured cord clamp

In general, prophylactic procedures in a busy delivery room are performed perfunctorily. The administration of vitamin K and prophylactic eye care should be done in the newborn nursery.

After the placenta has been examined to determine if there are any gross changes or abnormalities, it should be labeled and stored in the refrigerator until the infant is discharged or transferred.

REFERENCES

1. American Academy of Pediatrics Committee on Drugs. Effect of medication during labor and delivery on infant outcome. *Pediatrics* 62 : 402, 1978.
2. Apgar, V. A proposal for a new method of evaluation of the newborn infant. *Curr. Res. Anesth. Analg.* 32 : 260, 1953.
3. Arey, L. B. *Developmental Anatomy: A Textbook and Laboratory Manual of Embryology* (7th ed.). Philadelphia: Saunders, 1965.
4. Battaglia, F. C., and Hellegers, A. E. Status of the Fetus and Newborn. In F. C. Battaglia and A. E. Hellegers (eds.), *Report of the Second Ross Conference on Obstetric Research.* Columbus, OH: Ross Laboratories, 1973.
5. Brady, J. P. Homeostatic Adjustment of Fetus and Neonate. In S. Aladjem, A. K. Brown, and C. Sureau (eds.), *Clinical Perinatology* (2nd ed.). St. Louis: Mosby, 1980.
6. Braun, F. H. T., Jones, K. L., and Smith, D. W. Breech presentation as an indicator of fetal abnormality. *J. Pediatr.* 86 : 419, 1975.
7. Carson, B. S., et al. Combined obstetric and pediatric approach to prevent meconium aspiration syndrome. *Am. J. Obstet. Gynecol.* 126 : 12, 1976.
8. Chernick, V. Fetal breathing movements. *Semin. Perinatol.* 1 : 339, 1977.
9. Creasy, R. K., and Resnik, R. *Maternal Fetal Medicine—Principles and Practice.* Philadelphia: Saunders, 1984.
10. Finer, N. N., et al. Limitations of self-inflating resuscitators. *Pediatrics* 77 : 417, 1986.

11. Friedman, E. A. The labor curve. *Clin. Perinatol.* 8 :15, 1981.
12. Gregory, G. A., et al. Meconium aspiration in infants — a prospective study. *J. Pediatr.* 85 : 848, 1974.
13. Hildebrand, W. L., Schreiner, R. L., and Stephens, D. C. Endotracheal intubation of the neonate. *Am. Fam. Physician.* 26 :123, 1982.
14. Hon, E. H. Fetal Heart Rate Deceleration Patterns. In E. H. Hon (ed.), *An Atlas of Fetal Heart Rate Patterns.* New Haven: Harty, 1968.
15. Hughes, E. C. *Obstetrics and Gynecology Terminology.* Philadelphia: Davis, 1972.
16. Koffler, H., Papile, L. A., and Burstein, R. L. Congenital chylothorax: Two cases associated with maternal polyhydramnios. *Am. J. Dis. Child.* 132 : 638, 1978.
17. Kulovich, M. V., Hallman, M., and Gluck, L. The lung profile I. Normal pregnancy. *Am. J. Obstet. Gynecol.* 135 : 57, 1979.
18. McPherson, S. P., and Spearman, C. B. *Respiratory Therapy Equipment* (3rd ed.). St. Louis: Mosby, 1985.
19. Monheit, A. G., and Resnik, R. Cesarian section: Current trends and perspectives. *Clin. Perinatol.* 8 : 101, 1981.
20. Naeye, R. L. Umbilical cord length: Clinical significance. *J. Pediatr.* 107 : 278, 1985.
21. Pritchard, J. A., MacDonald, P. C., and Grant, N. F. *Williams Obstetrics* (17 ed.). Norwalk, CT: Appleton-Century-Crofts, 1985.
22. Smith, D. W. *Recognizable Patterns of Human Malformation* (3rd ed.). Philadelphia: Saunders, 1982.
23. Thompson, J. E., et al. Footprinting the newborn infant: Not cost effective. *J. Pediatr.* 99 : 797, 1981.

2. Admission Procedures and Routine Evaluations

Once the infant's vital functions are evaluated and the parents have had initial contact with their infant, the newborn may be transferred to either a transition (observation) or newborn nursery. There the processes of physiologic adaptation will be completed as admission procedures and other routine evaluations are accomplished.

THE TRANSITION PERIOD [4, 7]
The medical and nursing staff should keep in mind that the newborn infant continues to make physiologic adjustments during the first postnatal day. The period of initial transition is well defined (Table 2-1). In general, the infant remains alert in the first hour after delivery, whereupon a period of quiet sleep ensues if he is not disturbed. A second period of reactivity then follows, during which meconium may be passed, excess oral secretions may cause gagging and vomiting, and respirations may become irregular.

THERMOREGULATION [13]
Immediately following birth the infant's rectal temperature is the same as or slightly greater than that of the mother. Since the infant is wet and the delivery room is cool, the infant's body temperature begins to fall immediately. Cold stress evokes a series of events that will compromise the infant's adaptation significantly. Unfortunately, there are no specific guidelines for delivery room temperatures other than what is comfortable for the adults in the room. A delivery room temperature of 75°F to 80°F is recommended to reduce cold stress to the infant. Following delivery the infant should be dried with a warm towel and placed in a warm environment. He should be wrapped in a warm blanket during transport to the nursery.

Upon admission to the nursery, the infant should be unwrapped and placed in a supine position for observation. Temperature stability should be maintained because the infant's metabolic rate increases as he adapts to wide swings in environmental temperature. A neutral thermal environment (NTE), the environmental temperature at which oxygen consumption is minimal, will ensure an efficient adaptive response.

The mechanisms by which heat is transferred between the baby and the environment are (1) evaporation, (2) conduction, (3) convection, and (4) radiation. Evaporative heat loss occurs predominantly in the delivery room, but it may occur in the nursery when the infant is bathed.

20

Table 2-1. Newborn adaptations following birth

	Birth	15 Min	1 Hr	2 Hr	3 Hr	4 Hr	5 Hr	6 Hr
Cardiovascular system								
Heart rate	Rapid Irregular / Loud and forceful	Decreasing Regular	Visible apical impulse		Labile			
Cord pulsation	Present	Absent	Present		Cord oozing			
Color	Transient cyanosis/acrocyanosis		Flushing with cry		Swift changes in color			
Respiratory system								
	Rapid, shallow / Rales and ronchi / Flaring alae, grunting, or retraction		Clear	"Barrelling" of chest		Variable rate, related to activity		
Mucus	Thin, clear small bubbles					Thick, yellowish		
Temperature	Falling			Low		Rising		
Neurologic system								
Activity	Eyes open		Intense alerting behavior		First sleep	Variable		
Reactivity	First reactivity period		Relatively unresponsive		Second reactivity period		(Gagging, swallowing)	
Tonus	Increased tonus					Variable		
Posture	Upper extremities flexed, lower extended				Relaxed in sleep			
Bowel function								
Peristalsis	Bowel sounds absent / Abdomen filling / Bowel sounds present		Bowel sounds	Visible peristalsis		Variable		
Stools	Present at delivery				Meconium passage			
Age	Birth	15 Min	1 Hr	2 Hr	3 Hr	4 Hr	5 Hr	6 Hr

Source: M. M. Desmond, et al. The clinical behavior of the newly born. I. The term baby. *J. Pediatr.* 62 : 307, 1963. With permission.

Conductive heat loss occurs when the infant is placed on a cold surface such as a nursery scale or examining table. Conductive heat loss can be minimized by placing a warm blanket between the infant and the cold surface. Heat loss from convection results when air flows briskly across the infant as, for example, from ceiling air ducts in the delivery room and nursery. Radiant heat loss is the transfer of heat from a warmer to a cooler object when the two are not in contact. Radiant heat loss is common in the nursery when the infant is undressed, even if he is dry and on a warm surface. To counter this problem, the infant should be swaddled or placed under a radiant heater.

If the infant inadvertantly becomes cold, the rewarming process should be gradual and should be monitored closely to prevent warming too rapidly or hyperthermia. Gradual rewarming under a radiant heater can be accomplished by setting the control point of the heater 1 to 2°C above the skin temperature of the back or abdomen, whichever is closest to the heat source. When this skin temperature is reached, the control point then is raised another 1 to 2°C until the finally desired skin temperature of 35.5° to 36°C is attained.

If a convective incubator is used to warm an infant, consideration should be given to the infant's skin temperature, the ambient temperature, and the incubator's environmental temperature. The integration of these three temperatures is a better guide to the overall thermal-metabolic state of the infant than just the infant's rectal or core temperature [9]. Guidelines for achieving an NTE when using an incubator are provided in Appendix 7.

ROUTINE LABORATORY EVALUATIONS

The newborn infant is the only patient who enters the hospital without a required admission complete blood cell count (CBC), chest x-ray, and urinalysis. Some clinical conditions may warrant these procedures, but they should not be done routinely. Some routine screening procedures are more relevant to the newborn infant. These include a hematocrit, a glucose determination, a serologic test for syphilis, blood-typing, and a Coombs' test. In some nurseries, hemoglobin electrophoresis and the serologic determination of immunoglobulin M (IgM) levels are routine.

A serologic test for syphilis, blood-typing, and a Coombs' test, as well as hemoglobin electrophoresis and determination of IgM (see Chapter 5) levels, can be performed on umbilical cord blood collected at the time of delivery. The need for blood-typing every infant can be abrogated by checking the mother's blood type and indirect Coombs' test (antibody screening test) and performing a direct Coombs' test on the infant's red blood cells to screen for blood group incompatibilities.

If the serologic test for syphilis is positive on the cord blood specimen, a further assessment is needed. The management of this problem is discussed in Chapter 5.

Hematocrit and glucose levels are determined on capillary blood usually obtained from a heel puncture. The recommended site [1] for warmed heel punctures is identified in Fig. 2-1.

HEMATOCRIT [12]

A normal capillary hematocrit ranges from 45 to 60 percent and the hemoglobin from 15 to 20 gm/dl. Although peripheral capillary blood is used routinely to estimate the packed cell volume, capillary hematocrit values consistently are higher than those from veins or arteries. Thus, when levels determined from capillary specimens are more or less than the normal limits, the hematocrit should be performed again on blood from a venipuncture. Capillary hematocrits less than 45 percent should be rechecked to exclude the possibility of significant anemia. A central hematocrit value less than 40 percent indicates a moderate to severe anemia that often is secondary to hemolysis or acute or chronic blood loss.

Capillary hematocrits of 65 percent or more should be rechecked to ascertain that a polycythemic state exists before treatment is undertaken. *Polycythemia* is defined as a central hematocrit value of greater than 65

Fig. 2-1. Recommended sites (shaded areas) for warmed heel puncture. (From T. A. Blumenfeld, G. K. Turi, and W. A. Blanc. Recommended site and depth of newborn heel skin puncture based on anatomical measurements and histopathology. *Lancet* I : 230, 1979. With permission.)

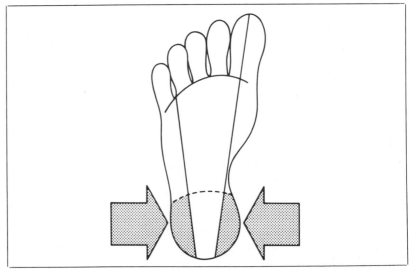

percent. It may be secondary to transfusion or hypervolemia on the one hand or chronic intrauterine stress and hypoxia on the other hand. Polycythemia may result in hyperviscosity and may subsequently compromise blood flow to several organ systems, including the central nervous system, cardiovascular system, intestines, and kidneys. The therapeutic approach to this problem is presented in Chapter 5.

GLUCOSE [3]

The fetal serum glucose concentration approximates that of the mother. After the umbilical cord is clamped, there is a rapid fall in the infant's serum glucose concentration to the mean value of 50 mg/dl during the first few hours. Subsequently, the blood glucose concentration rises and equilibrates at approximately 70 mg/dl by the third postnatal day. *Hypoglycemia* is defined as a whole-blood glucose concentration of less than 30 mg/dl (serum or plasma value less than 35 mg/dl) during the first 72 hours and then less than 40 mg/dl (serum or plasma value 45 mg/dl) after three days.

An assessment of the blood glucose concentration usually is done on every infant at the time of admission to the newborn nursery to exclude hypoglycemia. An approximation of the blood glucose concentration can be obtained rapidly [5] by using reagent strips for glucose testing in whole blood. The technique requires that the test instructions be followed precisely. Although the technical aspects of the procedure appear simple, sloppy techniques will produce an inaccurate result. Furthermore, the chemicals in these strips are sensitive to oxidation, so the container should be capped tightly. If the color reaction indicates a low blood glucose value, a blood sample should be drawn and sent to the chemistry laboratory for confirmation and documentation of the hypoglycemia. Therapy should begin immediately while awaiting these results (see Chapter 5).

ROUTINE ADMISSION PROCEDURES

VITAL SIGNS

The vital signs must be checked hourly for the first four to six hours to detect any aberrations.

The heart rate and respiratory rate are counted for a full minute while listening with a stethoscope placed over the precordium. The temperature is obtained with a mercury or electronic thermometer placed in the rectum or axilla. Measurement of the rectal temperature also confirms patency of the anus. Systolic blood pressure may be obtained with a Doppler flow probe and a newborn-size blood pressure cuff. As in the adult, the blood pressure is read when flow becomes audible as the blood pressure cuff is deflated [10]. Normal values for the vital signs are presented in Table 2-2. Any deviations from normal require continued close observation and thus preclude dressing or swaddling the infant.

EYE CARE

Ophthalmia neonatorum once was a major cause of blindness. However, with the introduction of prophylactic therapy the incidence of gonococcal ophthalmia has been reduced to much less than 1 percent. All infants should receive eye prophylaxis, including those delivered by cesarean section. Although all states have statutes or regulations regarding treatment, the guidelines are not clear as to when the treatment is no longer effective.

The eyes should be treated within the first hours after birth. The procedure should be done in the nursery rather than in the delivery room to ensure that it is done properly and consistently. Successful eye prophylaxis requires that the medication be instilled into the lower conjuctival sac. Agents that have been used include erythromycin, penicillin, silver nitrate, sulfacetamide, and tetracycline. Unlike antibiotics that have a direct effect on bacteria, silver nitrate produces its bactericidal effect by causing an excoriation of the superficial conjuctiva and secondarily evoking a neutrophilic inflammatory response. Therefore, if silver nitrate is used, the eye drops should not be rinsed out and the parents should be told an exudative response is expected. Erythromycin and silver nitrate currently are the agents most frequently used.

VITAMIN K PROPHYLAXIS [6, 8, 14]

None of the known coagulation factors cross the placenta. Hemorrhagic disease of the newborn, a diffuse bleeding diathesis that manifests between 18 and 80 hours after birth in breast-fed infants, is caused by a deficiency of vitamin K and can be prevented by the administration of vitamin K. Until recently, it was thought that vitamin K was necessary for the hepatic synthesis of factors II, VII, IX, and X. It now is recognized that these factors circulate in an inactive state and vitamin K, which is produced by intestinal bacteria, converts these coagulant proteins into an active form. Clinically, a single injection of either the natural fat-soluble vitamin K derivative (phytonadione 0.5–1.0 mg) or the synthetic water-

Table 2-2. Normal newborn vital signs

Heart rate	120–160 beats/min
Respiratory rate	30–60 breaths/min
Temperature	36–37.5°C
	96.8–99.6°F
Blood pressure	60–70 mm Hg (indirect systolic)

soluble form (menadione sodium bisulfite 0.1–0.2 mg) has proven effective and will not produce the hemolysis associated with excessive doses. The medication should be injected into a standard location such as the mid-anterolateral aspect of one thigh, so that in the event of a hemorrhagic crisis, the presence of a puncture mark on the thigh confirms that vitamin K had been given and that the hemorrhage may be of a different etiology. The oral administration of vitamin K may prove as effective as the intramuscular route [11].

BATHING

The infant may be bathed after the initial observation period during which the temperature has stabilized and the vital signs are normal and unchanging. The first bath is for cosmetic purposes and should be performed in a warmed environment to minimize cold stress. The practice of bathing an infant in a sink with running water is potentially dangerous. First, it violates the principles of keeping the infant warm, and second, there is a risk of scalding the infant. Blood and debris on the newborn skin and scalp that appear unsightly are removed easily with water alone or a mild soapy solution. Bathing the infant with soap containing hexachlorophene is controversial. Hexachlorophene is absorbed through the skin and is known to produce brain lesions. Hexachlorophene absorption is increased if skin injuries such as burns, large abrasions, or cracks are present. However, hexachlorophene baths are useful in preventing bullous dermatitis and periumbilical cellulitis secondary to staphylococcal infections.

The American Academy of Pediatrics [2] recommends a "dry technique" for initial and daily skin care for the following reasons: (1) heat loss is minimal; (2) skin trauma is diminished; (3) no exposure to agents with known or unknown side effects occurs; and (4) it is less time consuming. This technique acknowledges the bactericidal properties of vernix caseosa. Areas of the skin that become soiled may be cleansed gently with cotton or soft tissues (not gauze) and sterile water.

The umbilical cord stump deserves special attention. Normally, the Wharton's jelly and vessels of the cord dry and mummify. The inflammatory process accompanying healing may produce a minimal amount of erythema and nonodorous exudate. Infection of the umbilical stump delays healing and may lead to omphalitis, fasciitis of the anterior abdominal wall, and even vasculitis of the umbilical vein. Therefore, it is advisable to keep the umbilical area open to the air, clean, and dry. Although no single method is proven effective in limiting bacterial colonization, the umbilical stump and periumbilical tissues may be treated with triple dye, alcohol, or antimicrobial ointments. Wiping the cord area with an alcohol solution several times a day hastens healing. The infant should not be immersed in a tub of water for bathing until the umbilical cord remnant has fallen off and the umbilicus is healed.

Once bathed, the stable newborn infant is dressed with a diaper and shirt, wrapped in a blanket, and placed in an open crib. To prevent cross contamination, each crib should have a bin for a disposable suction bulb, hospital shirts, diapers, soap, lotions, pins, vitamins, and other necessities. The infant may be housed in the nursery and transported to his mother for feedings and visits. Alternatively, depending on local hospital regulations and facilities, the infant may room with the mother. The father may visit and hold the infant after carefully washing his own hands and covering his street clothes with a hospital gown. Siblings also may visit if the hospital has a policy that includes measures to protect the infant and the nursery population.

REFERENCES

1. Blumenfeld, T. A., Turi, G. K., and Blanc, W. A. Recommended site and depth of newborn heel skin puncture based on anatomical measurements and histopathology. *Lancet* I : 230, 1979.
2. Brann, A. W. Jr., and Cefalo, R. C. *Guidelines for Perinatal Care.* Evanston, IL/Washington, D.C.: American Academy of Pediatrics and American College of Obstetricians and Gynecologists, 1983.
3. Cornblath, M., and Schwartz, R. *Disorders of Carbohydrate Metabolism in Infancy* (2nd ed.). Philadelphia: Saunders, 1976.
4. Desmond, M. M., et al. The clinical behavior of the newly born. *J. Pediatr.* 62 : 307, 1963.
5. Herrera, A. J., and Hsiang, Y. H. Comparison of various methods of blood sugar screening in newborn infants. *J. Pediatr.* 102 : 769, 1983.
6. Keenan, W. J., Jewett, T., and Glueck, H. I. Role of feeding and vitamin K in hypoprothrombinemia of the newborn. *Am. J. Dis. Child.* 121 : 271, 1971.
7. Lagercrantz, H., and Slotkin, T. A. The "stress" of being born. *Sci. Am.* 254 :100, 1986.
8. Lane, P. A., and Hathaway, W. E. Vitamin K in infancy. *J. Pediatr.* 106 : 35, 1985.
9. LeBlanc, M. H. Skin, rectal or air temperature control in the neonate: Which is the preferred method? *J. Perinatol.* 5 : 2, 1985.
10. Lum, L. G., and Jones, D. M. The effect of cuff width in systolic blood pressure measurements in neonates. *J. Pediatr.* 91 : 963, 1977.
11. O'Connor, M. E., and Addiego, J. E. Jr. Use of oral vitamin K_1 to prevent hemorrhagic disease of the newborn infant. *J. Pediatr.* 108 : 616, 1986.
12. Oski, F. A., and Naiman, J. L. *Hematologic Problems in the Newborn* (3rd ed.). Philadelphia: Saunders, 1982.
13. Sinclair, J. C. *Temperature Regulation and Energy Metabolism in the Newborn.* New York: Grune & Stratton, 1978.
14. Sutherland, J. M., Glueck, H. I., and Gleser, G. Hemorrhagic disease of the newborn. *Am. J. Dis. Child.* 133 : 524, 1967.

3. The Physical Examination

The beginner's first attempt at examining a newborn usually is awkward. As confidence grows with experience gained from examining many infants, subtle variations between infants become evident. Thus, the physical examination becomes more fascinating as familiarity with anatomic and physiologic variations of the newborn infant increase [4, 34, 39].

Every newborn infant should have an initial assessment soon after birth and a thorough physical examination no later than 24 hours after admission to the nursery. Repeat examinations are suggested at least every three days during the hospital stay and are mandatory within six hours of the time of discharge from the nursery. An early discharge from the hospital (see Chapter 8) is no reason to omit the second examination.

A physical examination should be performed carefully and completely. The basic principles of the newborn physical examination include inspection, palpation, percussion, and auscultation. The examination begins with the careful inspection of the infant before undressing him or while he lies undressed beneath a radiant warmer. The infant's color, breathing pattern, morphology, level of activity, and responsiveness should be noted. After the initial general inspection is completed, the chest and abdomen should be examined rather than the head, since the evaluation of the ears and mouth may provoke the infant into an uncooperative state. To keep the infant warm during the remainder of the examination, he should be placed under a radiant heater or undressed and redressed in a stepwise fashion.

The examination is a step-by-step evaluation of each region of the body. The infant's spontaneous activity often provides clues to structural and functional deficits. An alert and experienced examiner takes advantage of opportunities provided by the infant. For example, when the infant cries, the examiner can easily inspect the oropharynx. It also is a good time to auscultate the chest to determine the quality of air entering each lung during deep inspirations. Similarly, when the infant is quiet, there is an opportunity to auscultate the heart, check the pulses, and gently palpate the abdomen. It is frustrating and difficult to examine these areas when the infant is fretful. Above all, if there is any portion of the exam that is inadequate or a problem, it is imperative to reexamine that portion until the issue is resolved.

CHEST
The chest is inspected for obvious deformities, particularly in the area of the nipples, the clavicles, and sternum. It should be noticed that the chest

normally moves upward and downward synchronously with the abdomen during inspiration and expiration. The normal respiratory rate ranges from 30 to 60 breaths per minute. Since the neonatal respiratory cycle normally is variable, counting respirations for 15 seconds, rather than a full minute, and multiplying by four may yield a falsely low or high result.

Percussion of the chest usually is nonproductive unless a tympanitic sound is being sought as evidence of air trapping.

Next, the chest is palpated. The positions of the nipples and the size of the underlying breast buds should be noted [43]. The point of maximal cardiac impulse (PMI) may be identified, but thrills, taps, and thrusts normally are not present. The entire length of the superior aspect of the clavicles should be palpated to ascertain that they are distinct and intact. A clavicular fracture is suspected if crepitus, swelling, or both is present. The infant may not cry when a fracture is palpated.

The quality of the breath sounds in the newborn is similar to that of an older patient. Bronchovesicular breath sounds are heard over the large airways, while vesicular breath sounds are heard more peripherally. Auscultation of the lungs shortly after birth often discloses the presence of adventitious sounds such as rales or rhonchi. These are produced by pulmonary fluid that has not been absorbed completely. In addition, noises made by secretions in the upper airway, especially the nose, are transmitted to the lung fields. Upper airway noise normally clears spontaneously within several hours after delivery or with nasal suctioning.

Auscultation of the heart begins with determination of the heart rate. Generally, the normal rate is from 120 to 160 beats per minute, but it may range between 80 and 180 beats per minutes. The rhythm may vary with the phase of respiration, increasing during inspiration and decreasing during expiration (sinus arrhythmia). In addition, the second heart sound splits during inspiration and closes with expiration. This splitting of the second heart sound is the best evidence of normal pulmonary circulation [32].

All heart murmurs [24] should be described according to their location, intensity, and timing, and according to whether they are transmitted to other areas of the chest. Heart murmurs associated with patency of the ductus arteriosus and changes in the pulmonary circulation often are heard during the first one to two days after birth and then disappear. Other murmurs of an innocent nature also may be heard and must be distinguished from murmurs of pathologic origin. In general, innocent murmurs will change in intensity and quality when the infant's position is altered. If there is concern that a murmur is pathologic, further evaluation of the peripheral pulses, blood pressure, skin color, and respiratory rate, in addition to specific laboratory tests, is needed.

ABDOMEN

The configuration of the abdomen is inspected to determine if it is symmetrical, distended, or sunken (scaphoid). Then the umbilical cord is examined to determine that two arteries and one vein show through the cut end. If the cord is dry and hardened, it still is possible to discern the number of vessels by soaking a segment of the mummified cord in water overnight.

Next, the abdomen is palpated gently but thoroughly. There are three hindrances to a successful examination: tense rectus abdominis muscles, normal abdominal distention during the first 24 hours, and the crib itself. The examiner should not let these interfere with the task at hand! If the infant is sleeping, the palpation should be attempted without waking him. If the infant is awake and fussing, he must be calmed before beginning palpation, either by being cuddled or allowed to suck on a pacifier or his own hand. During palpation, the examiner's dominant hand explores the abdomen. The opposite hand then either is placed over the flank and back for a bimanual examination or is used to flex the lower extremities to relax the abdominal musculature (Fig. 3-1). Diastasis recti or an umbilical hernia are readily noted on inspection and confirmed by palpation.

The liver edge may be palpated in the right upper quadrant approximately 2 to 3 cm below the right costal margin in the midclavicular line. The edge then is followed medially to the subxiphoid area. The superior border of the liver may be discerned by percussion technique or by using the "scratch test." The "scratch test" is performed by placing the stethoscope over the liver and scratching the skin lightly with a finger above and below the expected liver margin. The site at which there is a definite increase in the intensity of the sound referred to the stethoscope represents the liver edge. The percussion method is the more reproducible [52].

Only rarely is the normal spleen palpable.

Normal kidneys are not felt easily. They are palpable deep in the abdomen. Gentle but firm pressure must be applied to determine their presence and size. The left kidney is palpated easily unless the descending colon is distended with meconium. The right kidney is more difficult to palpate because it is partially covered by the liver. Both kidneys are difficult to feel in the crying or irritable infant because of abdominal guarding and movement. If the abdominal musculature is relaxed completely, normal fetal lobulations of the kidney may be identified. If kidneys are felt easily, the examiner should suspect that they are enlarged.

Femoral pulses are palpable in the femoral triangle when the infant is

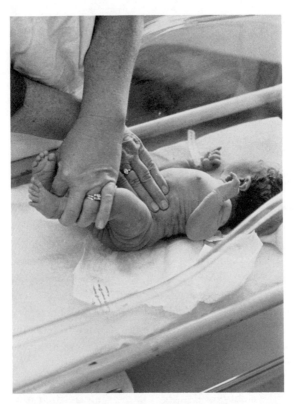

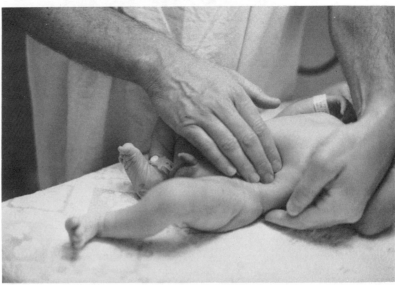

Fig. 3-1. Technique for abdominal exam. (See text for explanation.)

relaxed and not crying. It is impossible to detect femoral pulses in a squirming or kicking infant. If the pulses are not verified, a note should be made and it should be attempted again later. If pulses are not palpable, blood pressures should be obtained in both upper and lower extremities to rule out coarctation of the aorta.

GENITALIA

Examination of the genitalia requires only inspection and palpation.

FEMALE

At term, the labia majora completely cover the labia minora and clitoris. The vaginal tissue may be hypertrophied and may protrude through the labia majora as a tag (Fig. 3-2). The labia majora should be palpated for masses that may be hernias or ectopic gonads. The labia should be spread. An abundant grayish-white, mucoid secretion normally is present in the vaginal orifice. The labia minora, clitoris, and hypertrophied vaginal mucosa should be identified. Whether the vaginal orifice is patent or closed by hymenal tissue should be determined. It normally is difficult to determine the external urethral orifice.

MALE

The penis of the term male infant averages 3.5 cm in length when measured from the pubic symphysis to the end of the glans [17]. It also is ap-

Fig. 3-2. Vaginal tag.

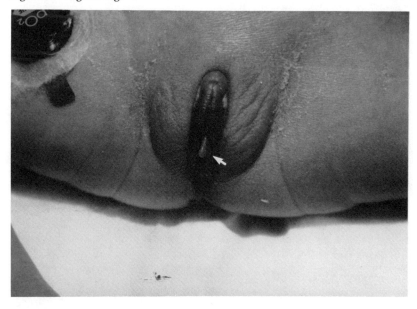

proximately 1.1 cm in width. Unless there is malposition of the penile urethra, the glans is completely covered with foreskin. The mature scrotum normally is wrinkled and should contain the testes. To prevent retraction of the mobile testes into the abdomen during the examination of the scrotum, each inguinal canal should be simultaneously blocked by the thumb and forefinger of one hand while the opposite hand palpates the scrotum. If the infant is cold, the testes may have already retracted into the inguinal canal. If the scrotum is empty, the testes may be in the inguinal canal or abdomen or be absent. Bilateral fullness of the scrotum suggests the presence of masses, which most commonly are hydroceles (Fig. 3-3). These are verified by transillumination (Fig. 3-4). A unilateral mass that does not transilluminate may be a tumor or testicular torsion of the testes.

ANUS [15]

The anus should be inspected to determine its patency, its position on the perineum, and the relationship of the sphincter to the anal orifice. The position of the anal sphincter can be determined by observing sphincter contraction (anal wink) when the perineum is stimulated.

As a general rule, the use of a digital examination should be restricted because it is traumatic, and noninvasive techniques may provide as much information. Combining abdominal palpation with a rectal examination sometimes is useful in locating and describing abdominal masses. A digi-

Fig. 3-3. Bilateral hydroceles.

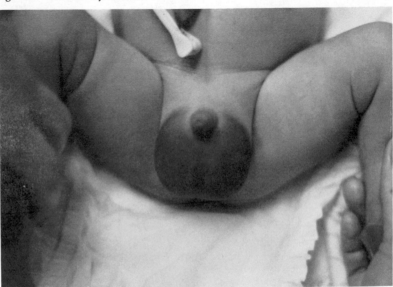

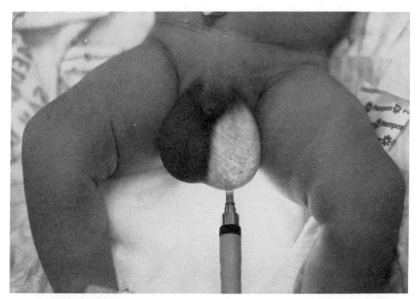

Fig. 3-4. Transillumination of bilateral hydroceles in the scrotum.

tal exam should be performed with the examiner's smallest finger. The perianal tissue is very friable and is subject to laceration during digital examination or overzealous wiping during diaper changes.

SKELETON

The posture of the normal term infant reflects a predominance of flexor tone. During the entire skeletal exam, the observer should carefully note whether the infant actively moves all extremities equally and symmetrically, both spontaneously and when stimulated. The passive range of motion of all extremities and hips is checked by flexing and extending each joint. The number of fingers and toes should be determined and particular attention paid to their length and formation and the color of the nail beds. The ridge pattern [29, 44] on the fingers and hands (dermatoglyphics) may provide clues to the diagnosis of chromosomal disorders and syndromes. Figure 3-5 shows the normal ridge pattern.

Intrauterine positioning may deform the lower extremities [45]. These deformations should not be confused with congenital malformations. For example, ankle and forefoot adduction (Fig. 3-6), a deformation, can be differentiated from congenital equinovarus malformation by positioning the foot passively in the midline and dorsiflexing it (Fig. 3-7). The equinovarus malformation will not yield easily to this maneuver and will require orthopedic correction. Another example is genu recurvatum associated with frank breech deliveries (Fig. 3-8).

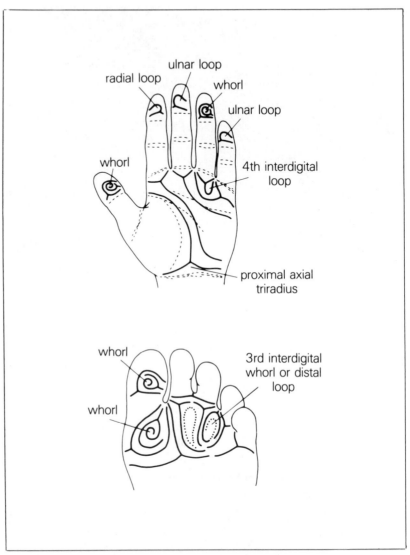

Fig. 3-5. Dermatoglyphics: normal hand and foot. (Adapted from D. W. Smith. *Recognizable Patterns of Human Malformation* (3rd ed.). Philadelphia: Saunders, 1982.)

The examination of the hips is critical [10, 20, 41]. Dislocations or potential dislocations may be diagnosed and treated early. Specifically, it is crucial to determine whether the femur subluxates or dislocates from the acetabulum. To accomplish this, two techniques may be employed: the Ortolani (reduction) test and the Barlow (dislocation) test (Fig. 3-9). Although disparities in the symmetry of the skin folds and length of the

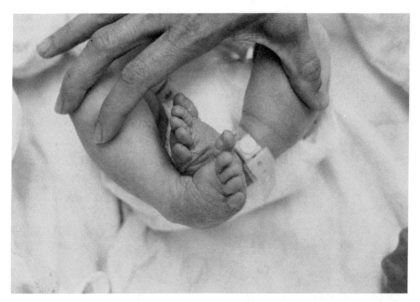

Fig. 3-6. Positional deformation of the ankle (forefoot adduction).

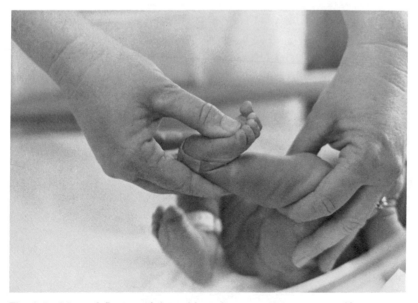

Fig. 3-7. Normal flexion of the ankle, ruling out equinovarus malformation.

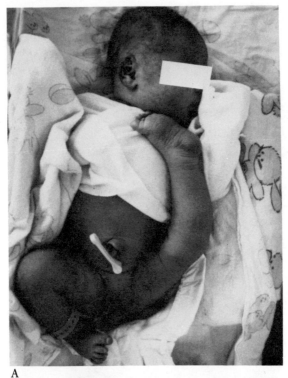

A

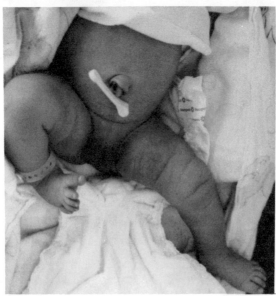

B

Fig. 3-8. Genu recurvatum. A. Natural position.
B. Extended position. Extra skin folds on the thigh
should be noted.

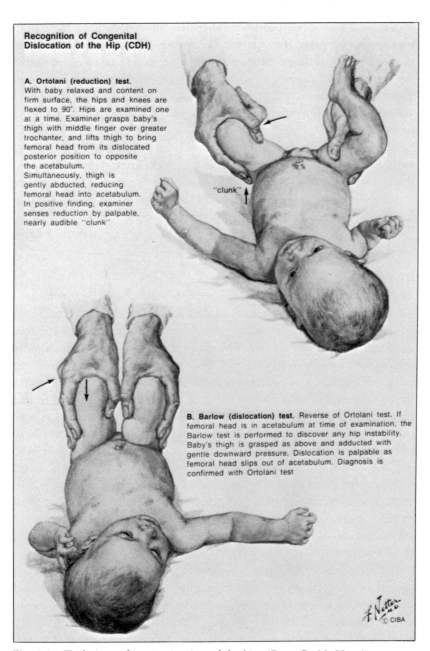

Recognition of Congenital Dislocation of the Hip (CDH)

A. Ortolani (reduction) test.
With baby relaxed and content on firm surface, the hips and knees are flexed to 90°. Hips are examined one at a time. Examiner grasps baby's thigh with middle finger over greater trochanter, and lifts thigh to bring femoral head from its dislocated posterior position to opposite the acetabulum.
Simultaneously, thigh is gently abducted, reducing femoral head into acetabulum. In positive finding, examiner senses reduction by palpable, nearly audible "clunk"

"clunk"

B. Barlow (dislocation) test. Reverse of Ortolani test. If femoral head is in acetabulum at time of examination, the Barlow test is performed to discover any hip instability. Baby's thigh is grasped as above and adducted with gentle downward pressure. Dislocation is palpable as femoral head slips out of acetabulum. Diagnosis is confirmed with Ortolani test

Fig. 3-9. Techniques for examination of the hip. (From R. N. Hensinger. Congenital dislocation of the hip. *Ciba Found. Symp.* 31 : 5, © copyright 1979. CIBA-GEIGY. Reproduced with permission from Clinical Symposia — by Frank H. Netter, M.D. All rights reserved.)

thighs have been described with congenital hip dislocations, these findings are not observed frequently in the newborn and may not appear until after the age of weight bearing. The "clunk" produced by relocation of
the femoral head slipping over the acetabular rim is the most important
finding in a dislocation. Clicks are not associated with hip pathology but
are produced by the movements of tendons, ligaments, or fluid in the hip
or knee joints.

The back is examined with the infant lying prone in the crib or held
suspended with the examiner's hand under the chest. The spine is inspected from the base of the skull to the coccyx in order to identify sinus
tracts that may connect with the spinal canal. The position of the scapu-
lae are noted to identify a winged scapula (Sprengel's) deformity. Next,
the entire length of the spine is palpated to determine the presence of dorsal spinal processes or scoliosis.

HEAD

The shape and contour of the head at birth is influenced by the mode of
delivery. The head that is free of molding and strikingly symmetrical usually has not been engaged in the pelvis; the infant usually will have been
delivered by cesarean section. The greatest molding will occur in those
infants who are delivered vaginally. Following a vertex presentation, the
head will be elongated posteriorly in the shape of a cone with the vertex
of the skull being at the apex of the cone. Some infants delivered from a
breech position will have a relatively unmolded head if the head has been
held in a flexed position [19]. If held in an extended position, the head
will have a flattened crown and a prominant overhanging occiput [45].

The position of the skull bones relative to each other should be noted
and recorded if one bone overlaps another. The ossification of the cranial
bones may vary. *Craniotabes* [18], an area of bone that is easily indented
by light pressure, is found most frequently in the parietal area near the
sagittal suture. It is usually benign and resolves spontaneously in two to
three months.

Lacerations, bruises, puncture marks, and petechial hemorrhages
should be noted during the inspection of the head. Soft tissue swellings or
bony prominences produce asymmetrical contours. These are differentiated by palpation. A common finding is soft tissue edema of the scalp, also known as *caput succedaneum.* This swelling is differentiated from a
cephalhematoma by its location and duration. The caput crosses cranial
suture lines and usually wanes by the second or third day. A cephalhematoma is a subperiosteal hemorrhage confined to a single bone and does
not cross the suture lines. Subgaleal hemorrhage is characterized by a
boggy, pitting swelling that crosses the cranial suture lines. It also may

appear as ecchymosis localized to the upper eyelids, mastoid area, and nape of the neck. Rarely is the hemorrhage severe enough to cause life-threatening blood loss. When this occurs, it may be associated with a hemorrhagic diathesis and if severe, may require transfusion of whole blood or specific coagulation factors and an extensive workup.

A network of cranial sutures and fontanelles is identified on further palpation (Fig. 3-10). The major sutures include the sagittal, coronal, lambdoidal, and frontal [46]. The sutures may be obliterated by overlapping bones. Occasionally, the skull bones are widespread, making the sutures more evident. Widened sutures should raise suspicion of intracranial pathology. The anterior fontanelle [16, 37] normally is diamond-shaped and is found in the midline at the junction of the parietal and frontal bones. It should be patent and soft and remain flat when the infant is quiet and held upright. Figure 3-11 shows anterior fontanelle size.

The triangle-shaped posterior fontanelle also is midline at the junction of the parietal and occipital bones. It frequently is difficult to discern the edges of the posterior fontanelle because it is obliterated partially by the overlapping of the juxtaposed skull bones. A "third fontanelle" [49] often is palpable along the sagittal suture between the anterior and posterior fontanelles.

Additional methods for examining the head include percussion, auscultation, and transillumination. Under normal circumstances, these procedures are not necessary, but they are employed on occasion and therefore require a description:

1. Percussion is performed with one finger tapped firmly but gently against the cranium. In the newborn infant with nonfused sutures, this maneuver normally elicits a dull thud, the "cracked pot" sign. Percussion has very little use in the newborn.

2. Auscultation of the head often is performed on infants with unexplained cardiac failure and neurologic symptoms. The procedure should be performed in a very quiet room since bruits associated with arteriovenous communications are of a low intensity.

3. Transillumination [12] is performed on infants with micro- or macrocrania or other neurologic signs and symptoms. It should be done in a completely dark room with a high intensity light source or with a flashlight and a light-occlusive gasket fitted between the light source and the scalp. Time should be allowed for the examiner's eyes to adapt to the dark so that the rim of transillumination may be observed. Questions concerning interpretation of transillumination can be resolved by cranial ultrasound, computed tomographic scans, and magnetic resonance imaging.

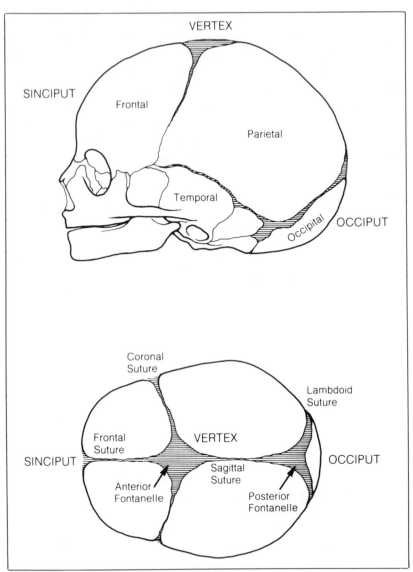

Fig. 3-10. Cranial bones, sutures, and fontanelles. (Reprinted with permission of Ross Laboratories, Columbus, OH 43216.)

EYES

The examination of the eyes begins with an evaluation of their position and size in relation to other facial structures. In general, the intercanthal distance approximates that of a palpebral fissure [22]. The lacrimal duct papillae may be seen near the medial junction of the upper and lower eyelid. Tearing is unusual. The normal cornea is clear, allowing visualization

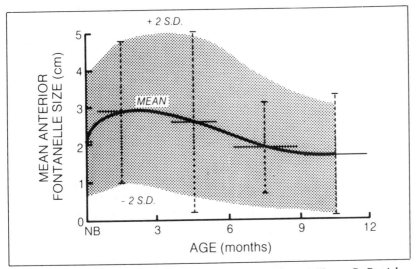

Fig. 3-11. Anterior fontanelle size. (Key: NB = newborn.) (From G. Popich and D. W. Smith. Fontanels: Range of normal size. *J. Pediatr.* 80 : 749, 1972. With permission.)

of the pupil and iris. The sclerae are bluish-white and are without hemorrhages. The pupils measure 2 to 3 mm and will constrict in response to light. The routine funduscopic examination is performed both to determine the presence of a red reflex and to rule out lenticular opacities or intraocular tumors. If a more extensive ophthalmoscopic exam is indicated, it is necessary to dilate [9] the pupils with a safe mydriatic and cycloplegic agent, such as a solution of Cyclogyl 0.5%, Mydriacyl 0.5%, and Neo-Synephrine 2.5%. The visual pathway from the cornea to the retina then may be observed by dialing the ophthalmoscope from + 12 to 0 diopters.

Visual fixation and conjugate eye movements are tested when the infant is quiet and alert by having the examiner hold the infant in front of him in a midline position at a distance of 18 in. After the examiner fixes the infant's gaze on his face, the examiner slowly moves the infant to the left or right. Normally, the infant will move his eyes in a conjugate fashion as he maintains his fixed gaze. As the infant is moved back toward center and beyond, the gaze is usually lost at the midline. The examiner should not talk to the infant during the procedure because the infant may react to the voice. The infant's visual attentiveness can be demonstrated to the parents.

EARS
The helix of the ear should be inspected, and it should be noted that it attaches to the scalp at a point horizontal to the lateral angle of the eye.

This landmark is important since it is used to determine the presence of "low set" ears. The length of the external ear is approximately 3.75 cm (the range is 3.5–4.25 cm [1]. The newborn's ear is distinct in that it is slightly lower set and its cartilage is less developed than the adult ear. During otoscopy [14], it may be noted that visualization of the tympanic membrane is blocked by vernix and other debris. The vernix will clear spontaneously in one to two days, whereupon the tympanic membrane is visualized as a gray-white, highly vascular tissue. The pinnae should be pulled inferiorly and posteriorly to straighten the external ear canal for optimum visualization.

Parents often ask if their infant can hear. Under normal circumstances the answer is yes [3]. This may be demonstrated to them by having the examiner hold the infant in front of him with the infant's ear about 6 to 10 in. from his mouth. With the infant in a quiet but alert state, the examiner speaks to the infant in a falsetto voice of normal intensity. The infant should turn his head toward the examiner if hearing is normal. If the examiner or the parents are suspicious that the infant's hearing is impaired or if there is a history of a high-risk factor (Table 3-1), the hearing may be tested with one of two techniques: the Cribogram [42] or the brainstem-evoked potential [40, 48]. With the Cribogram, a noise of approximately 90 dB is presented to the infant. His response is measured as a gross body movement. Auditory-evoked potentials are derived by applying clicking noises of varying frequency and intensity directly to the ears with headphones. The responses are electric potentials that are detected with scalp electrodes and amplified and averaged with a clinical computer. The Cribogram is the easier of the two auditory screening de-

Table 3-1. Risk criteria for hearing impairment

1. Family history of childhood hearing impairment
2. Congenital perinatal infection (e.g., cytomegalovirus, rubella, herpes, toxoplasmosis, syphilis)
3. Anatomic malformations involving the head or neck (e.g., dysmorphic appearance including syndromal and nonsyndromal abnormalities, overt or submucous cleft palate, morphologic abnormalities of the pinna)
4. Birth weight less than 1500 gm
5. Hyperbilirubinemia at level exceeding indications for exchange transfusion
6. Bacterial meningitis, especially Hemophilis influenza
7. Severe asphyxia, which may include infants with Apgar scores of 0–3, infants who fail to institute spontaneous respirations by 10 minutes, and infants with hypotonia persisting to 2 hours of age

Source: American Academy of Pediatrics Joint Committee on Infant Hearing. Position statement 1982. Reproduced by permission of *Pediatrics* 70 : 496, copyright 1982.

vices to use. Compared to brainstem-evoked potentials, it is less expensive. It can be performed by nursery personnel, and the test results are easier to interpret. Furthermore, the test results grossly reflect the infant's cortical function, whereas short latency brainstem potentials measure responses only at the level of the upper brainstem.

NOSE

The nasal passages normally are symmetrical, and flaring of the nasal alae should not be present. Patency of the nasal airway may be checked with the passage of a suction catheter, but this can be traumatic, producing swelling and partial airway obstruction. Since newborn infants primarily are obligatory nose breathers [30], any nasal obstruction causes distress. Partial nasal airway obstruction produces nasal flaring, snorting, and crying. The nature of the obstruction should be defined further by (1) selective auscultation of each nares, (2) holding a wisp of cotton in front of each nostril, or (3) observing the pattern of fogging of a cold metal surface held under the nares. Routine examination of the nasal passages with a nasal speculum is unnecessary.

MOUTH

The lips and mouth are observed for symmetry at rest and during movement. Using a bright light and tongue blade, the infant's gums and hard and soft palates should be inspected, and the buccal mucosa and parotid duct papillae should be visualized. The exam is completed with a visual inspection of the entire oral cavity. The infant often will open his mouth if the lips are spread gently with the tongue blade. As the mouth opens, the mass and symmetry of the tongue, as well as its protrusion forward and other general movements, should be noted. Epithelial rests, a normal finding, are frequently seen in the midline of the hard palate and are known as *Epstein's pearls*. Cysts found on the alveolar ridge and palate away from the midline are called *Bohn's nodules*. The tongue is depressed to visualize the *uvula*, a single unclefted structure hanging from the posterior of the soft palate in the midline. It is simultaneously noted whether the infant gags. If palpation of the oral cavity is needed, it should be done with a gloved finger.

NECK

The neck is extended to inspect it for symmetry, sinuses, and clefts, and to palpate the trachea in the midline. The thyroid isthmus may be palpable as a smooth, soft rim of tissue crossing the midline. The thyroid gland usually is not felt. No other masses should be present. The carotid pulses should be easily palpable.

NEUROLOGIC SYSTEM

The most important aspect of the neurologic exam is careful observation. The state of alertness appears to be the most sensitive of all indicators of neurologic function. Changes in the state of alertness depend on gestational maturity, chronologic age, feeding schedules, and environmental stimuli (see Appendixes 5 and 6).

The neurologic exam is influenced significantly by changes in the behavioral state. The newborn infant displays six behavioral states [8] (Table 3-2). There are two sleep states (quiet and active) and four waking states. The examiner, caretakers, and parents should learn these states in order to appreciate the infant's spontaneous behavior and response to varying stimuli or disease. The neurologic exam of the newborn provides information about the infant's alertness, coordinated muscle activity, tone, and basic reflexes. Specific deviations from the normal require more thorough evaluation.

CRANIAL NERVES

Cranial nerve functions were assessed during the examination of the head, eyes, ears, nose, and throat, and in the evaluation of the vital signs. Thus, it is unnecessary to retest these nerve functions unless a specific question about a deficit exists. The function and testing of each of the twelve cranial nerves are reviewed in Table 3-3. It is as important to assess the integrated function of these nerves as it is to assess their individu-

Table 3-2. Newborn behavioral states

State	Description	Characteristics
1	Quiet sleep	Regular respirations, no rapid eye movement, no muscular movement
2	Active sleep	Irregular respirations, rapid eye movement, occasional muscular jerks
3	Drowsy	Eyes partially open or closed, increasing movement
4	Quiet/alert	Quiet, eyes open and searching the environment
5	Active/alert	Eyes open, increasing movement, more vocal
6	Crying	Self-explanatory

Source: Adapted from T. B. Brazelton. Neonatal behavioral assessment scale. *Clin. Develop. Med.* No. 50. Spastics International Medical Publications. Philadelphia: Lippincott, 1973. With permission.

Table 3-3. Function and testing of the cranial nerves

Cranial nerve	Name	Function and testing
I	Olfactory	Smell—not tested. May use peppermint to stimulate sucking or an arousal-withdrawal response.
II	Optic	Vision—tested by blink response to light and by visual fixation with eyes following brightly colored object or examiner's face.
III	Oculomotor	Control pupillary response to light (III) and extraocular muscle movements (III, IV, and VI). Latter may be tested by observing spontaneous eye movements or movements elicited by turning head from side to side (doll's eye maneuver).
IV	Trochlear	
VI	Abducens	
V	Trigeminal	Sensory component displayed by rooting reflex and eye blink reflex. Strength of masseter and pterygoid muscles are best assessed by evaluation of suck and biting (motor V).
VII	Facial	Evaluated by carefully noting presence of nasolabial folds and position and movement of corners of mouth. Facial expressions are under control of VII.
VIII	Auditory	Vestibular component tested by rotating infant clockwise or counter-clockwise and simultaneously noting that eyes turn in direction of rotation. Auditory component may be demonstrated by startle response to loud sound or simply speaking into one ear and noting infant's head turn toward voice.
IX	Glossopharyngeal	Tongue movement and taste—tested by gagging infant with tongue blade and noting normal midline positioning of uvula.
X	Vagus	Evaluated by noting normal cry and autonomic visceral functions.
XI	Accessory	Controls sternocleidomastoid muscle. Can be tested by observing the head move from side to side.
XII	Hypoglossal	Controls tongue movement. Tested by simply observing tongue thrusting and tongue movements when inspecting oropharynx.

Source: Adapted from J. J. Volpe. *Neurology of the Newborn.* Philadelphia: Saunders, 1981.

al functions. The coordinated actions of the cranial nerves required in feeding are a prime example. Sucking requires the integration of cranial nerves V, VII, and XII, while swallowing involves nerves IX and X.

MOTOR FUNCTIONS

Basic motor functions involve tone, posture, and reflex activity. In the term infant, passive or resting tone is exhibited as flexion. Active tone is the infant's muscle response to gravitational changes. For example, when the infant is pulled to a sitting position, the neck flexors and extensors stabilize the head as the trunk moves forward. Similarly, when the infant is supported in a standing position, he will become erect if muscle tone in the trunk and lower extremities is normal.

REFLEXES

Deep tendon reflexes are spinal reflexes that involve peripheral sensory, motor, and proprioceptive nerve fibers. The biceps reflex and the knee jerk are two basic spinal reflexes that are tested to confirm depressed neuromuscular function or asymmetry in body tone. These reflexes are most active during the first two days after birth, while the infant is alert. They are elicited by tapping the tendon of the muscle group being tested. The response is graded as weak or strong.

Unsustained clonus of the ankle may be a normal response when the Achilles tendon is tapped or when the ankle is flexed rapidly.

Reflexes Associated with Feeding Behavior

Hunger is associated with three major reflexes: rooting, sucking, and the palmomental mandibular reflex of Babkin. These reflexes are present only when the infant is awake. The *rooting reflex* occurs when the corner of the infant's mouth is stroked gently. In response, the infant's head turns toward the stimulus and simultaneously the lips draw the stimulus into the mouth. This reflex is most evident in the hungry nursing infant who searches for the nipple of the mother's breast. The *sucking reflex* is elicited by placing a nipple or gloved finger in the infant's mouth. Characteristically, a negative pressure is created and there is movement of the jaw and tongue in a backward "stripping" action. Audible sucking noises may be heard in a quiet room as the infant sucks on his hand, protruded tongue, or pressed lips. Finally, the *Babkin reflex* consists of sudden mouth opening and forward extension of the head when the examiner firmly presses on the palms of the infant's hands.

Other Reflexes

Other primitive integrated responses characteristic of the newborn include the following reflexes [35]:

1. MORO REFLEX AND STARTLE. The Moro reflex is a response to the sensation of loss of support. When the infant's head is brought forward and then allowed to fall back suddenly, there follows abduction of the upper extremities at the shoulder, extension of the elbow, and opening of the hand. The startle reflex consists of flexion of the extremities and palmar grasping. The startle often is considered part of the Moro response. In fact, they are two distinct movements since one can occur without the other. Both reflexes are not inhibited completely during sleep. Although their intensity diminishes, they remain active in postprandial states.

2. PALMAR AND PLANTAR GRASP. Both the palmar and plantar grasps occur when a finger is placed in the palm of the hand or sole of the foot. The palmar grasp tightens in response to the examiner pulling slowly against the infant's grasp. If the palmar grasp is strong the infant may be lifted off the mattress.

3. STEPPING REFLEX. Alternating stepping movements may be observed if the infant is held upright and the soles of the feet touch a flat surface. It is helpful to move the infant forward to accompany the stepping. This reflex is more active 72 hours after birth and is absent in infants delivered by breech or depressed at birth.

4. CROSSED EXTENSOR REFLEX. The crossed extensor reflex is most active when the infant is alert and is usually older than two days. Extension and minimal adduction of one lower extremity occurs when the sole of the opposite foot is stimulated while that extremity is held in extension. Its absence suggests a spinal cord or peripheral nerve injury.

5. TRUNCAL INCURVATION (GALANT'S RESPONSE). When the paravertebral area is stimulated in a line about 3 cm lateral to the midline of the back, the infant's trunk becomes concave on the stimulated side. An absent response occurs below the level of a spinal cord lesion. Normally, the response is weak during the first four to five days.

6. BABINSKI REFLEX [38, 51]. While studies have shown the primary response to be plantar flexion, it is difficult to clinically isolate this reflex from a background of competing reflexes. Therefore, the Babinski reflex contributes very little to the neurologic examination.

SENSORY SYSTEM
The peripheral sensory system involving pain, touch, and temperature is tested specifically only when there is a gross neurologic lesion, such as a myelomeningocele or a suspected cervical cord transection, in order to

evaluate the level of healthy spinal cord function. Otherwise the function of the sensory system generally is assessed while performing the routine physical examination.

SKIN [21, 47]

The skin of the mature newborn is pink and feels soft and velvety. At delivery, the skin is covered with a white, greasy substance called *vernix caseosa*. *Lanugo* is downy hair covering the body, most abundantly on the back, forehead, and cheeks. The skin may become erythematous after birth, whereupon a desquamation of the stratum corneum begins.

There are a variety of self-limited benign cutaneous lesions that must be distinguished from those that have a pathologic connotation. The transient lesions include: (1) milia, (2) mongolian spots, (3) a variety of capillary hemangiomas, (4) sucking blisters, and (5) transient pustular melanosis. *Milia* are white, firm papules found on the nose, forehead, cheeks, and chin. They develop in association with pilosebaceous glands and clear spontaneously as the glands naturally involute. *Mongolian spots* are solitary or multifocal macular lesions of blue-gray color. They usually are located in the lumbosacral area although they may be widespread. They occur in over 90 percent of black, Oriental, Spanish-American, and American Indian infants. They are uncommon in white infants. Almost all of these lesions fade in the first years of life, but occasionally may persist indefinitely. *Capillary hemangiomas* are present in over 50 percent of all infants at birth. They vary in size and are distributed over the forehead (flame nevus), the nape of the neck (stork bite), the glabella, and the eyelids. They are macular patches, red to pink in color, and have diffuse borders. Their most distinguishing feature is that they blanch when direct pressure is applied. Most capillary hemangiomas, except those on the neck, fade or involute before age 1 year. *Sucking blisters* are isolated blisterlike lesions on the forearm and dorsal surface of the hands of infants who have sucked on these areas in utero (Fig. 3-12). They resolve spontaneously. *Transient pustular melanosis* [27] (lentigines neonatorum [36]) is present at birth and is found in both Caucasian and non-Caucasian infants (Fig. 3-13). The distribution is generalized, but the heaviest concentration is on the forehead, submental, and lumbosacral areas. When the characteristic pustular lesions desquamate, a freckle is left in the center of a shallow crater. Histologic examination shows debris, a large number of polymorphonuclear cells, a few eosinophils, and no bacteria. No systemic symptoms are present. The placenta may contain excessive squamous metaplasia. The freckles usually fade within three months.

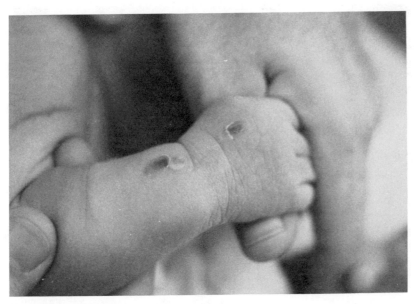

Fig. 3-12. Sucking blisters present at birth.

MEASUREMENTS

Examination of the infant must include the following measurements:

1. VITAL SIGNS. The heart rate, respiratory rate, temperature, and blood pressure are usually taken on admission to the nursery and recorded in the nurse's notes. They should be rechecked during the examination if there is a significant abnormality. The normal ranges for heart rate and respiratory rate are 120 to 160 beats per minute and 30 to 60 breaths per minute, respectively (see Table 2-2).

The core or rectal temperature ranges from 36 to 37.5°C (96.8–99.6°F). During thermal neutral conditions when metabolic expenditure is minimal, the temperature of the skin over the abdomen should be 1 to 2°C lower than the core or rectal temperature.

The blood pressure [25, 26] is assessed in the normal newborn infant by indirect, rather than direct or invasive methods. The indirect technique requires a method for detecting the pulse and a blood pressure cuff whose width is approximately one half of the extremity's circumference. After the blood pressure cuff is inflated on the extremity, it is then slowly deflated. The systolic blood pressure (measured with a stethoscope, a Doppler flow probe, or both) or a mean blood pressure (measured by direct palpation) is that point on the aneroid or mercury gauge at which the pulse is detected. The return of the pulse may be noted by direct palpation, auscultation with a stethoscope, or

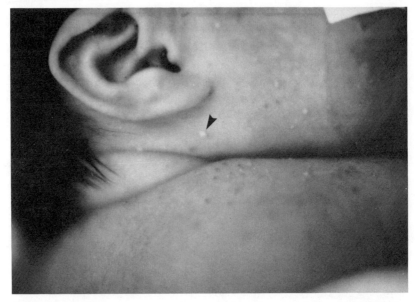

A

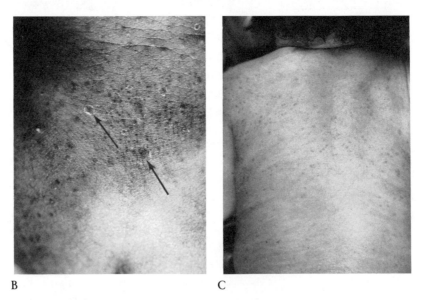

B   C

Fig. 3-13. Transient pustular melanosis. A. Arrow points to pustule. B. Arrows point to desquamated pustules and pigmented bases. C. Pattern of pigmentation over back.

a Doppler flow probe. The latter is the most sensitive of the three techniques.

The normal indirect systolic blood pressure for term infants delivered vaginally is 65 to 70 mm Hg; for those delivered by cesarean section it is approximately 60 mm Hg.

Normal peripheral perfusion is characterized by pink skin color, the presence of peripheral pulses, and rapid capillary refill after blanching. Low-flow states are characterized by cyanosis, mottling, thready weak pulses, and prolonged capillary refilling times greater than five seconds.

2. BIRTH WEIGHT. The birth weight should be measured on a metric scale and recorded in grams since vital statistics are based on the metric system, and drug dosages and fluid requirements are calculated on a gram or kilogram basis. Conversion of the metric weight to pounds and ounces is done for the convenience of the family who may not be conversant with the metric system (Table 3-4).

3. HEAD CIRCUMFERENCE. The head circumference or occipital-frontal circumference (OFC) should be measured in centimeters with a non-stretchable tape. The largest head circumference is recorded. The head circumference approximates the crown-rump length or the chest circumference measured at the nipple line and is about two thirds of the infant's total length. The head circumference also equals the infant's length in centimeters divided by 2 plus 10 cm (OFC = L ÷ 2 + 10) [11].

4. MEASUREMENT OF LENGTH. The measurement of length [28] is difficult because of the infant's tendency to maintain a flexed position. The measurement is facilitated by placing the infant in a supine position in the bassinet or on another measuring surface, and then marking where the top of the head and the bottom of the feet are posi-

Table 3-4. Conversion of common birth weights
in metric units to pounds and ounces

Grams	Pounds/ounces
2250	5/0
2500	5/8
3000	6/10*
3500	7/12*
4000	8/14*

*For each 500-gm increase, add 1 lb and 2 oz.

tioned on that surface while the infant is fully extended. The length then is determined by measuring the distance between the marks.

The crown-rump length is measured from the top of the head to the bottom of the buttocks. It is the sitting height. An additional measurement, the upper segment to lower segment ratio, is attained by measuring the distance between the crown and the superior edge of the symphysis pubis, and then from the superior edge of the symphysis pubis to the sole of the foot. In the newborn the upper to lower segment ratio normally is 1.7 : 1.

ASSESSMENT OF GESTATIONAL AGE [5, 13, 23]

By convention, gestational age is expressed as completed weeks from the last normal menstrual period. A term gestation is 38 to 42 completed weeks. A postterm infant is more than 42 completed weeks. A preterm infant is less than 37 completed weeks.

The assessment of gestational age is an important and integral part of the examination and evaluation of each newborn infant. Gestational age is a nomenclature based on time. As explained in Chapter 1, the calculation of gestational age is based on the time of the mother's last menstrual period or the time of conception. When these are unknown, the gestational age is inexact and must be estimated. In these situations, techniques for assessing fetal growth and fetal and neonatal maturation have been used to estimate gestational age. However, the timetable of both growth and maturation varies from individual to individual and is based on factors such as nutrition, heredity, metabolism, and acute and chronic stress.

The two most common clinical procedures for assessing the infant's gestational age are the maturational rating scores of Dubowitz or Ballard. The Dubowitz scoring system is comprehensive and considered the clinical standard (Fig. 3-14). The Ballard assessment is an abbreviated version of the Dubowitz score (Fig. 3-15). Either test should be administered within the first six to 12 hours following birth since drying of the skin and other changes effect the scoring of the physical criteria. The neurologic criteria remain consistent over many days. The assessment also may be incorporated into the admission procedures performed by the nursing personnel.

Using the Ballard assessment, a typical mature infant is fully flexed and has opaque skin with few visible veins, scanty lanugo, plantar creases that cover the entire sole of the foot, full areolae and prominent breast buds, stiffened ears, and mature genitalia. These characteristics add up to a total score of 40, which equals an estimated maturational age of 40 weeks.

External (superficial) Criteria

External sign	SCORE				
	0	1	2	3	4
Edema	Obvious edema of hands and feet; pitting over tibia	No obvious edema of hands and feet; pitting over tibia	None		
Skin texture	Very thin, gelatinous	Thin and smooth	Smooth; medium thickness; rash or superficial peeling	Slight thickening; superficial cracking and peeling, especially hands and feet	Thick and parchment-like; superficial or deep cracking
Skin color (infant not crying)	Dark red	Uniformly pink	Pale pink; variable over body	Pale; only pink over ears, lips, palms, or soles	
Skin opacity (trunk)	Numerous veins and venules clearly seen, especially over abdomen	Veins and tributaries seen	A few large vessels clearly seen over abdomen	A few large vessels seen indistinctly over abdomen	No blood vessels seen
Lanugo (over back)	None	Abundant; long and thick over whole back	Hair thinning, especially over lower back	Small amount of lanugo and bald areas	At least half of back devoid of lanugo
Plantar creases	No skin creases	Faint red marks over anterior half of sole	Definite red marks over more than anterior half; indentations over less than anterior third	Indentations over more than anterior third	Definite deep indentations over more than anterior third
Nipple formation	Nipple barely visible; no areola	Nipple well defined; areola smooth and flat; diameter <0.75 cm	Areola stippled, edge not raised; diameter <0.75 cm	Areola stippled, edge raised; diameter >0.75 cm	
Breast size	No breast tissue palpable	Breast tissue on one or both sides <0.5 cm in diameter	Breast tissue both sides; one or both 0.5–1.0 cm	Breast tissue both sides; one or both >1 cm	
Ear form	Pinna flat and shapeless; little or no incurving of edge	Incurving of part of edge of pinna	Partial incurving whole of upper pinna	Well-defined incurving whole of upper pinna	
Ear firmness	Pinna soft, easily folded; no recoil	Pinna soft, easily folded; slow recoil	Cartilage to edge of pinna, but soft in places; ready recoil	Pinna firm; cartilage to edge; instant recoil	
Genitalia Male	Neither testis in scrotum	At least one testis high in scrotum	At least one testis right down		
Female (with hips half abducted)	Labia majora widely separated, labia minora protruding	Labia majora almost cover labia minora	Labia majora completely cover labia minora		

Fig. 3-14. Assessment of gestational age: Dubowitz exam with instruction on neurologic examination. (From L. M. S. Dubowitz and V. Dubowitz. *Gestational Age of the Newborn*. Menlo Park, CA: Addison-Wesley, 1977. With permission.)

Neurological Criteria

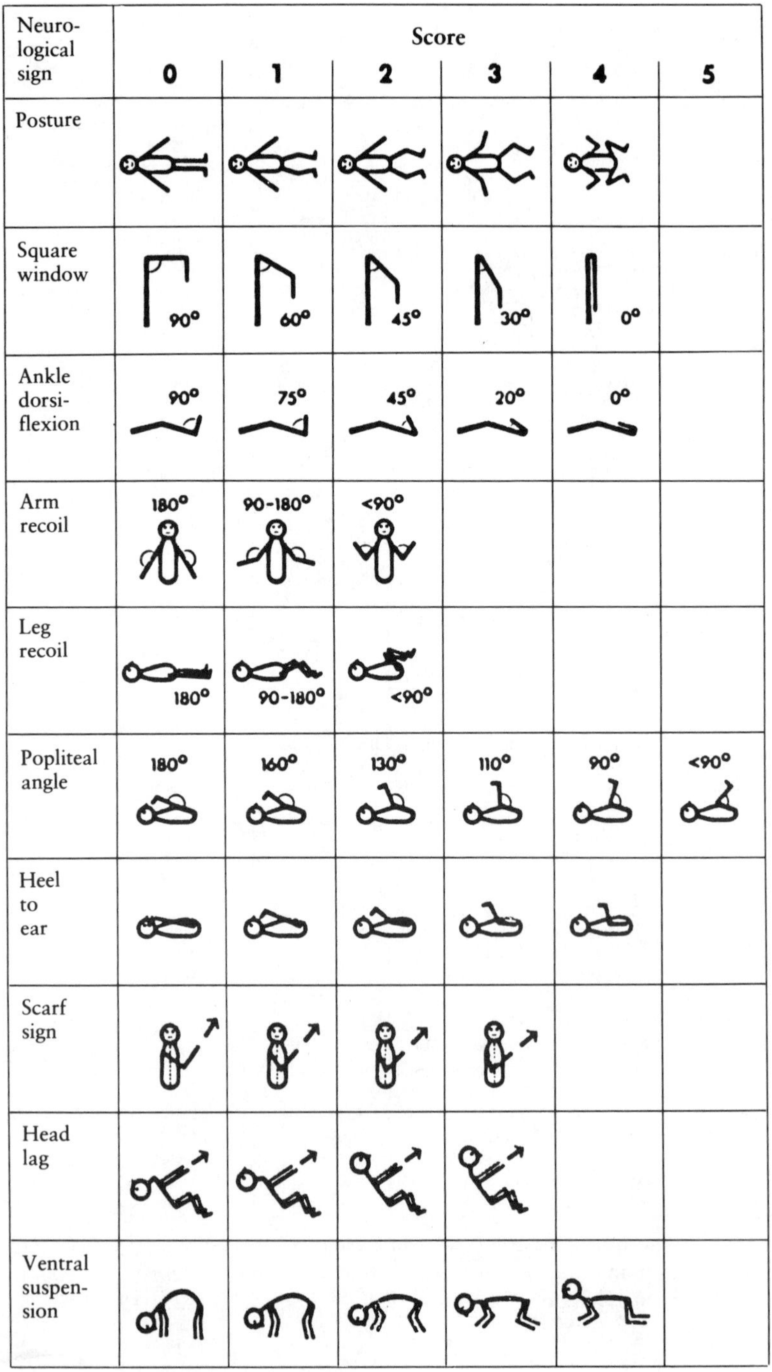

Neuro-logical sign	Score					
	0	**1**	**2**	**3**	**4**	**5**
Posture						
Square window	90°	60°	45°	30°	0°	
Ankle dorsi-flexion	90°	75°	45°	20°	0°	
Arm recoil	180°	90-180°	<90°			
Leg recoil	180°	90-180°	<90°			
Popliteal angle	180°	160°	130°	110°	90°	<90°
Heel to ear						
Scarf sign						
Head lag						
Ventral suspen-sion						

Fig. 3-14 (continued).

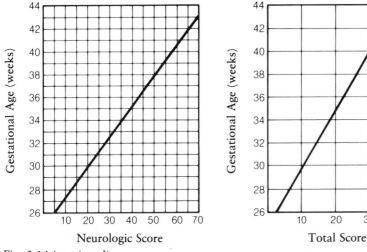

Fig. 3-14 (continued).

Some Notes on Techniques of Assessment of Neurologic Criteria*

Posture: Observed with infant quiet and in supine position. Score 0: Arms and legs extended; 1: beginning of flexion of hips and knees, arms extended; 2: stronger flexion of legs, arms extended; 3: arms slightly flexed, legs flexed and abducted; 4: full flexion of arms and legs.

Square window: The hand is flexed on the forearm between the thumb and index finger of the examiner. Enough pressure is applied to get as full a flexion as possible, and the angle between the hypothenar eminence and the ventral aspect of the forearm is measured and graded according to the diagram. (Care is taken not to rotate the infant's wrist while doing this maneuver.)

Ankle dorsiflexion: The foot is dorsiflexed onto the anterior aspect of the leg, with the examiner's thumb on the sole of the foot and other fingers behind the leg. Enough pressure is applied to get as full a flexion as possible, and the angle between the dorsum of the foot and the anterior aspect of the leg is measured.

Arm recoil: With the infant in the supine position the forearms are first flexed for 5 seconds, then fully extended by pulling on the hands, and then released. The sign is fully positive if the arms return briskly to full flexion (Score 2). If the arms return to incomplete flexion or the response is sluggish, it is graded as Score 1. If they remain extended or are only followed by random movements, the score is 0.

Leg recoil: With the infant supine, the hips and knees are fully flexed for 5 seconds, then extended by traction on the feet and released. A maximal response is one of full flexion of the hips and knees (Score 2). A partial flexion scores 1, and minimal or no movement scores 0.

Popliteal angle: With the infant supine and his pelvis flat on the examining couch, the thigh is held in the knee-chest position by the examiner's left index finger and thumb supporting the knee. The leg is then extended by gentle pressure from the examiner's right index finger behind the ankle and the popliteal angle is measured.

Heel to ear maneuver: With the baby supine, the baby's foot is drawn as near to the head as it will go without forcing it. The distance between the foot and the head is observed as well as the degree of extension at the knee. Grading is according to diagram. The knee is left free and may draw down alongside the abdomen.

Scarf sign: With the baby supine, the infant's hand is taken and attempted to be put around the neck and as far posteriorly as possible around the opposite shoulder. This maneuver is assisted by lifting the elbow across the body. It should be seen how far the elbow will go across and graded according to illustrations. Score 0: Elbow reaches opposite axillary line; 1: Elbow between midline and opposite axillary line; 2: Elbow reaches midline; 3: Elbow will not reach midline.

Head lag: With the baby lying supine, the infant's hands are grasped (or the arms if a very small infant) and he is pulled slowly towards the sitting position. The position of the head is observed in relation to the trunk and graded accordingly. In a small infant the head may initially be supported by one hand. Score 0: Complete lag; 1: Partial head control; 2: Able to maintain head in line with body; 3: Brings head anterior to body.

Ventral suspension: The infant is suspended in the prone position, with the examiner's hand under the infant's chest (one hand in a small infant, two in a large infant). The degree of extension of the back and the amount of flexion of the arms and legs is observed. Also noted are the relation of the head to the trunk. Grading is according to the diagrams.

*If score differs on the two sides, take the mean.

Newborn Maturity Rating and Classification

Physical Maturity

	0	1	2	3	4	5
Skin	Gelatinous red, trans-parent	Smooth pink, visible veins	Superficial peeling and/or rash, few veins	Cracking pale area, rare veins	Parchment, deep cracking, no vessels	Leathery, cracked, wrinkled
Lanugo	None	Abundant	Thinning	Bald areas	Mostly bald	
Plantar creases	No crease	Faint red marks	Anterior transverse crease only	Creases anterior two-thirds	Creases cover entire sole	
Breast	Barely perceptible	Flat areola, no bud	Stippled areola, 1–2 mm bud	Raised areola, 3–4 mm bud	Full areola, 5–10 mm bud	
Ear	Pinna flat, stays folded	Slightly curved pinna, soft with slow recoil	Well-curved pinna, soft but ready recoil	Formed and firm with instant recoil	Thick cartilage, ear stiff	
Genitals Male	Scrotum empty, no rugae		Testes descend-ing, few rugae	Testes down, good rugae	Testes pendulous, deep rugae	
Genitals Female	Prominent clitoris and labia minora		Majora and minora equally prominent	Majora large, minora small	Clitoris and minora completely covered	

Maturity rating

Score	Weeks
5	26
10	28
15	30
20	32
25	34
30	36
35	38
40	40
45	42
50	44

Neuromuscular Maturity

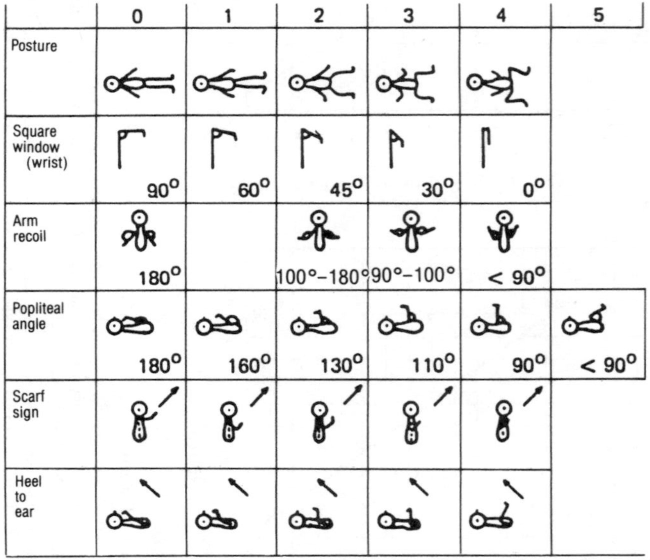

Fig. 3-15. Assessment of gestational age: Ballard exam. (From J. L. Ballard, K. K. Novak, and M. Driver. A simplified score for assessment of fetal maturation of newly born infants. *J. Pediatr.* 95 : 769, 1979. With permission.)

Once the infant's gestational age is estimated, the birth weight is then compared to standards for each gestational age. Figure 3-16 provides gestational age-specific birth weight values for infants born near sea level [50] and includes values falling between two standard deviations above and below the calculated mean values. Figure 3-17 identifies gestational age-specific birth weights for infants born one mile above sea level and values falling between the tenth and ninetieth percentiles. Infants whose birth weight exceeds the ninetieth percentile are called large for gestational age (LGA). Those who fall within the normal limits are appropriate for gestational age (AGA). A third group with birth weights less than the tenth percentile are small for gestational age (SGA). Many of the illnesses that afflict newborns are very evident when they are categorized according to statistically derived weight to gestational age relationships, as in Fig. 3-18. However, nothing substitutes for clinical judgment and the understanding of biologic variability.

These maturational assessments and the length of gestation as determined by the last normal menstrual period also may be used to categorize infants as having slow fetal maturation, average fetal maturation, or accelerated fetal maturation [2]. For example, chronic intrauterine stress secondary to chronic hypertensive disease of the mother may result in an infant with rapid fetal maturation. An infant of a mother with non-insulin-dependent diabetes mellitus sometimes has slow fetal maturation.

RECORDING THE PHYSICAL EXAMINATION
The physical examination begins with the chest and progresses to the abdomen, genitalia, skeleton, head structures, nervous system, and skin. It concludes with an evaluation of the infant's gestational age. Once this is completed, the weight is plotted against the gestational age to determine if the infant is appropriately grown.

As experience is gained with this examination, observing and evaluating multiple areas simultaneously will become second nature. The time it takes to complete the examination will be shortened to five to ten minutes. The examiner should not be discouraged by the feeling of initial ineptitude. Finally, when the history and physical examination are completed, the findings and impressions should be recorded in the infant's medical record. The following serves as an example:

39 week, AGA, female infant, normal.
or:
39 week, SGA, female infant.
Single umbilical artery.
Low-set ears.

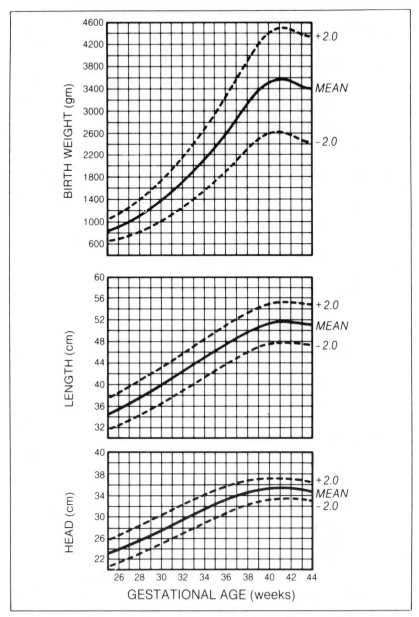

Fig. 3-16. Fetal growth measurements near sea level. (From R. Usher and F. McClean. Intrauterine growth of live-born Caucasian infants at sea level: Standards obtained from measurements in 7 dimensions of infants born between 25 and 44 weeks of gestation. *J. Pediatr.* 74 : 91, 1969. With permission.)

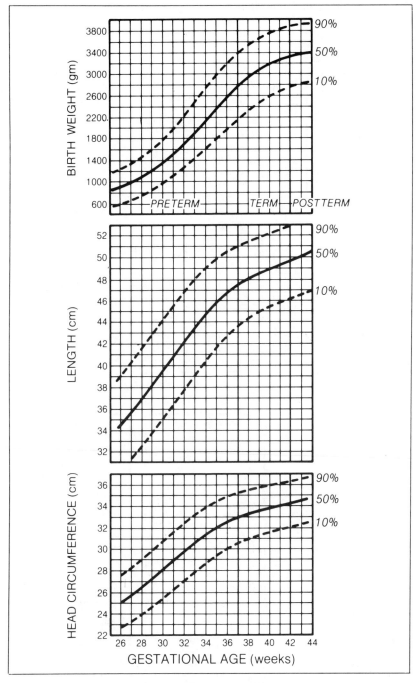

Fig. 3-17. Fetal growth measurements one mile above sea level. (From L. O. Lubchenco, C. Hansman, and E. Boyd. Intrauterine growth in length and head circumference as estimated from live births at gestational ages from 26–42 weeks. Reproduced by permission of *Pediatrics* 37 : 403, copyright 1966.)

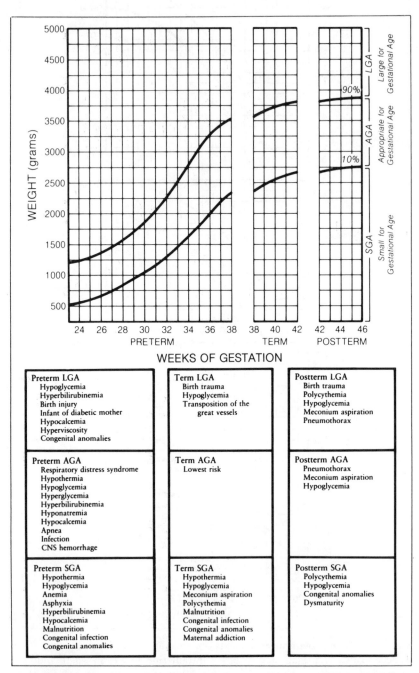

Fig. 3-18. Neonatal mortality and morbidity risk. (Adapted from L. O. Lubchenco, et al. Neonatal mortality rate: Relationship to birth weight and gestational age. *J. Pediatr.* 81 : 818, 1972. With permission.)

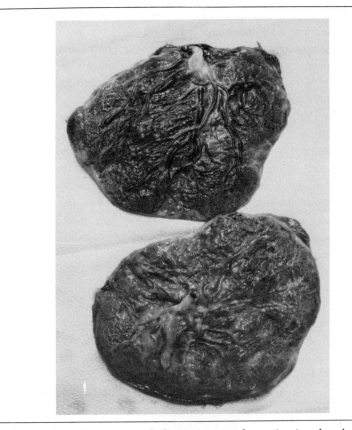

Fig. 3-19. Normal placenta with distinctive vasculature (top) and a placenta with chorioamnionitis. The cloudiness of the surface and loss of definition of the blood vessels on the placenta with chorioamnionitis should be noted.

Any area that has not been evaluated completely should be reexamined before the infant is discharged. Charting should be complete, concise, and written legibly.

EXAMINATION OF THE PLACENTA [6, 7]

The newborn examination is not complete without an evaluation of the placenta. The examination of the placenta in the delivery room includes an evaluation of the size, shape, color, and weight. Normally, the fetal surface is bright steel blue with blood vessels clearly visible through the amnion and chorioallantoic membranes. Fibrin deposits are yellowish-white plaques that normally lie adjacent to the blood vessels. The villi on the maternal surface are beefy red. Infarcts occur either in the main mass of the placenta or along the margin. They appear as dense or firm, white to yellow lesions of varying size. Clots secondary to marginal or retroplacental hemorrhages should be recorded.

The average weight of the placenta is approximately one fifth of the infant's birth weight if the cord, membranes, and clots are not removed, or one seventh of the infant's birth weight with the cord and membranes trimmed and clots removed.

Normally the umbilical cord measures 55 to 60 cm in length [33]. It typically inserts eccentrically into the placenta. Three vessels, two arteries and one vein, are present normally in the cord. If an additional vessellike structure is present, a surgical consultation should be obtained because the structure may be a patent urachus or a severed loop of bowel.

If infection is present, the placental surface is cloudy and the underlying vessels are less clearly visible (Fig. 3-19). Pus may be observed on the placental surface and foul odor may be present. Cultures plus histologic examination may provide important information relating to the etiology of an infection.

Other discolorations of the placenta may be present. For example, meconium excreted in utero will stain the fetal surface of the placenta and membranes green [31]. The presence of blood and hemosiderin will cause a red, brown, or yellowish stain. *Amnion nodosum,* brownish granular nodules of debris that have been rubbed into the membranes, are a sign of oligohydramnios.

In the case of hydrops fetalis, the placenta is large, heavy, and salmon-colored or pale.

REFERENCES
1. Aase, J. M., Wilson, A. C., and Smith, D. W. Small ears in Down's syndrome: A helpful diagnostic aid. *J. Pediatr.* 82 : 845, 1973.
2. American Academy of Pediatrics. *Standards and Recommendations for Hospital Care of Newborn Infants* (6th ed.). Evanston, IL: 1977.
3. American Academy of Pediatrics Joint Committee on Infant Hearing. Position statement 1982. *Pediatrics.* 70 : 496, 1982.
4. Avery, M. E., and Taeusch, H. W. Jr. *Schaffer's Diseases of the Newborn* (5th ed.). Philadelphia: Saunders, 1984.
5. Ballard, J. L., Novak, K. K., and Driver, M. A simplified score for assessment of fetal maturation of newly born infants. *J. Pediatr.* 95 : 769, 1979.
6. Benirschke, K., and Driscoll, S. G. *The Pathology of the Human Placenta.* New York: Springer-Verlag, 1974.
7. Benirschke, K. What pediatricians should know about the placenta. *Curr. Probl. Pediatr.* 2 : 3, 1971.
8. Brazelton, T. B. Neonatal behavioral assessment scale. *Clin. Develop. Med.* No. 50. Spastics International Medical Publications. Philadelphia: Lippincott, 1973.
9. Caputo, A. R., et al. Dilation in neonates: A protocol. *Pediatrics* 69 : 77, 1982.

10. Cohen, J. Skeletal problems of children. *Hosp. Prac.* 12 : 77, 1977.
11. Dine, M. S., et al. Relationship of head circumference to length in the first 400 days of life: A mnemonic. *Pediatrics* 67 : 506, 1981.
12. Dodge, P. R., and Porter, P. Demonstration of intracranial pathology by transillumination. *Arch. Neurol.* 5 : 594, 1961.
13. Dubowitz, L. M. S., and Dubowitz, V. *Gestational Age of the Newborn.* Menlo Park, CA: Addison-Wesley, 1977.
14. Eavey, R. D., et al. How to examine the ear of the neonate. *Clin. Pediatr. [Phila.]* 15 : 338, 1976.
15. El Haddad, M., and Corkery, J. J. The anus in the newborn. *Pediatrics* 76 : 927, 1985.
16. Faix, R. G. Fontanelle size in black and white term newborn infants. *J. Pediatr.* 100 : 304, 1982.
17. Feldman, K. W., and Smith, D. W. Fetal phallic growth and penile standards for newborn male infants. *J. Pediatr.* 86 : 395, 1975.
18. Fox, G. N., and Maier, M. K. Neonatal craniotabes. *Am. Fam. Physician* 30 : 149, 1984.
19. Haberkern, C. M., Smith, D. W., and Jones, K. L. The "breech head" and its relevance. *Am. J. Dis. Child.* 133 : 154, 1979.
20. Hensinger, R. N. Congenital dislocation of the hip. *Ciba Found. Symp.* 31 : 5, 1979.
21. Jacobs, A. H. Birthmarks: I. Vascular nevi. *Pediatr. Rev.* 1 : 21, 1979.
22. Jones, K. L., Hansen, J. W., and Smith, D. W. Palpebral fissure size in newborn infants. *J. Pediatr.* 92 : 787, 1978.
23. Kuhns, L. R., and Finnstrom, O. New standards of ossification of the newborn. *Radiology* 119 : 655, 1976.
24. Liebman, J. Diagnosis and management of heart murmurs in children. *Pediatr. Rev.* 3 : 321, 1982.
25. Lum, L. G., and Jones, D. M. The effect of cuff width in systolic blood pressure measurements in neonates. *J. Pediatr.* 91 : 963, 1977.
26. Marx, G. F., et al. Neonatal blood pressures. *Anaesthesist* 25 : 318, 1976.
27. Merlob, P., Metzker, A., and Reisner, S. H. Transient neonatal pustular melanosis. *Am. J. Dis. Child.* 136 : 521, 1982.
28. Miller, H. C., and Merritt, T. A. *Fetal Growth in Humans.* Chicago: Year Book, 1979.
29. Miller, J. R., and Giroux, J. Dermatologlyphics in pediatric practice. *J. Pediatr.* 69 : 302, 1966.
30. Miller, M. J., et al. Oral breathing in newborn infants. *J. Pediatr.* 107 : 465, 1985.
31. Miller, P. W., Coen, R. W., and Benirschke, K. Dating the time interval from meconium passage to birth. *Obstet. Gynecol.* 66 : 459, 1985.
32. Nadas, S. A. Role of the general pediatrician in pediatric cardiology. *Pediatr. Rev.* 3 : 103, 1981.
33. Naeye, R. L. Umbilical cord length: Clinical significance. *J. Pediatr.* 107 : 278, 1985.
34. Parmelee, A. H. *Management of the Newborn* (2nd ed.). Chicago: Year Book, 1959.
35. Peiper, A. *Cerebral Function in Infancy and Childhood.* New York: Consultants Bureau, 1963.

36. Perrin, E., Sutherland, J. E., and Baltazar, S. Inquiry into the nature of lentigine's neonatorum: Demonstration of a statistical relationship with squamous metaplasia of the amnion. *Am. J. Dis. Child.* 102 : 648, 1961.

37. Popich, G., and Smith, D. W. Fontanels: range of normal size. *J. Pediatr.* 80 : 749, 1972.

38. Rich, E. C., Marshall, R. E., and Volpe, J. J. The plantar reflex flexor in normal neonates. *N. Engl. J. Med.* 289 : 1043, 1973.

39. Scanlon, J. W., et al. *A System of Newborn Physical Examination.* Baltimore: University Park, 1979.

40. Shannon, D. A., et al. Hearing screening of high-risk newborns with brainstem auditory evoked potentials: A follow-up study. *Pediatrics* 73 : 22, 1984.

41. Siffert, R. S. Orthopedic checklist for neonates and infants. *Hosp. Prac.* 5 : 66, 1970.

42. Simmons, F. B., McFarland, W. H., and Jones, F. R. An automated hearing screening technique for newborns. *Acta Otolaryngol. (Stockh.)* 87 : 1, 1979.

43. Sivan, Y., Merlob, P., and Reisner, S. H. Sternum length, torso length, and internipple distance in newborn infants. *Pediatrics* 72 : 523, 1983.

44. Smith, D. W. *Recognizable Patterns of Human Malformation* (3rd ed.). Philadelphia: Saunders, 1982.

45. Smith, D. W. *Recognizable Patterns of Human Deformation.* Philadelphia: Saunders, 1981.

46. Smith, D. W., and Tondury, G. Origin of the calvaria and the sutures. *Am. J. Dis. Child.* 132 : 662, 1978.

47. Solomon, L. M., and Esterly, N. B. *Neonatal Dermatology.* Philadelphia: Saunders, 1973.

48. Stockard, J. E., Stockard, J. J., and Coen, R. W. Auditory brainstem response variability in infants. *Ear Hear.* 4 : 11, 1983.

49. Tan, K. L. The third fontanelle. *Acta Paediatr. Scand.* 60 : 329, 1971.

50. Usher, R., and McClean, F. Intrauterine growth of live-born Caucasian infants at sea level: Standards obtained from measurements in 7 dimensions of infants born between 25 and 44 weeks of gestation. *J. Pediatr.* 74 : 91, 1969.

51. Volpe, J. J. *Neurology of the Newborn.* Philadelphia: Saunders, 1981.

52. Weisman, L. E., et al. Clinical estimation of liver size in the normal neonate. *Clin. Pediatr. (Phila.)* 21 : 596, 1982.

4. The First 24 Hours: Common Problems

The preceding chapters have addressed the infant's adaptation to his new environment and the procedures for his initial care. In this chapter attention will be directed toward problems that commonly arise during the first 24 hours following birth. Many of these are not serious, but they are discussed because parents often question their significance. More complicated problems requiring more thorough investigation and special care will be mentioned but not reviewed in great detail.

HEAD

During the first day, cephalhematomas become more apparent and may increase in size over the next several days. However, the caput succedaneum and cranial molding, which are present at birth, begin to resolve. Scalp lacerations, including those caused by intrauterine monitor probes, and abrasions become erythematous and occasionally develop eschars as a normal inflammatory response to healing.

If the size of the anterior fontanelle exceeds normal limits, the differential diagnosis should include increased intracranial pressure, osteogenesis imperfecta, cleidocranial dysostosis, hypothyroidism, hypophosphatasia, and other less common disorders [49, 66]. The same differential diagnosis should be considered if the size of the posterior fontanelle is enlarged.

Widened cranial sutures result from defective bone formation or increased intracranial pressure. Ridging along the suture lines may be secondary to overlapped skull bones (molding) or their premature fusion (craniosynostosis) (Fig. 4-1).

EYES

If silver nitrate is used for ophthalmic prophylaxis, a brown or gray discoloration of the periorbital skin in a patchy or linear distribution usually is secondary to staining by the silver nitrate that spilled from the conjunctival area. It is often mistaken for a birthmark. The stain can be removed by firmly wiping it with a cotton ball moistened with tap water. It will resolve spontaneously over several days.

Abnormalities frequently found in the ocular region include congenital malformations, trauma, infections, corneal opacities, and retinal lesions. A list of congenital malformations is presented in Table 4-1.

Swelling, edema, discharge, or forceps marks involving the periorbital tissue should raise suspicion about a traumatic laceration of the cornea.

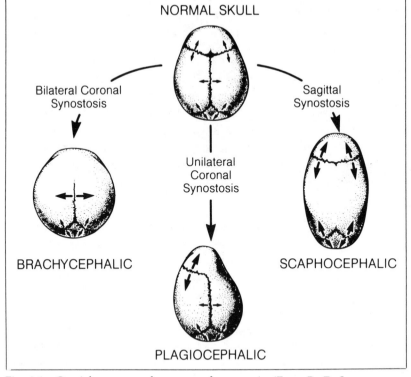

Fig. 4-1. Cranial sutures and patterns of synostosis. (From R. E. Stewart. Craniofacial malformations. *Pediatr. Clin. North Am.* 25 : 485, 1978. With permission.)

A laceration or abrasion can be visualized with an ophthalmoscope and will appear as a green linear streak or patch if stained with Fluoroscein.

Bulbar conjunctival hemorrhages are crescent-shaped red lesions located lateral or medial to the iris (margin of the cornea). These occur in association with difficult deliveries or acute obstruction to the superior vena cava secondary to a nuchal cord. They resolve spontaneously.

Chemical conjunctivitis frequently follows prophylactic treatment with silver nitrate. The conjunctivitis becomes evident and is most marked within the first 24 hours and resolves within three days. Any exudate from the eye that persists should be smeared, stained, and cultured to exclude bacterial conjunctivitis.

Complete or partial obliteration of the normal red reflex during ophthalmoscopy suggests a lesion of the cornea, the lens, the vitreous, or the retina. Cloudiness of the cornea is an early sign of congenital glaucoma [12, 56]. If congenital glaucoma exists, the eye is firm to palpation and

Table 4-1. Congenital malformations of the ocular region

---

1. Coloboma—a cleft in the eyelid or iris.
2. Epicanthal fold—a vertical fold of skin over the inner canthus.
3. Heterochromia—pigmentation differences between the two irises.
4. Mongoloid slant—positioning of the outer canthus in a plane above that of the inner canthus.
5. Antimongoloid slant—positioning of the outer canthus in a plane below that of the inner canthus.
6. Proptosis ("exophthalmus")—forward displacement of the eye.
7. Ptosis—drooping of the upper eyelid.
8. Strabismus—the deviation of one or both eyes from the point of focus.
9. Synophrys—fusion of the eyebrows in the midline.

Source: Adapted from J. W. Scanlon, et al. *A System of Newborn Physical Examination.* Reprinted with permission of Aspen Publishers, Inc., Rockville, MD, 1979.

the anterior chamber is narrowed. In the more severe state, the eye is enlarged and protuberant (buphthalmos). Although it is rare, glaucoma is an emergency and requires immediate identification and consultation with an ophthalmologist. *Cataracts* [68] are opacities of the normally transparent lens. Although the opacity may be seen with the unaided eye, it is usually best observed with an ophthalmoscope, dialing through 0 to +10 diopters. The opacity will be seen as a black spot that is distinct from the reddish backdrop of the retina. The etiology of the cataract may be genetic, infectious, or metabolic. Medical personnel who are planning a pregnancy or who are pregnant should not handle this infant until the diagnosis of congenital rubella is excluded.

Retinoblastoma [1] is rare at birth but should be strongly considered if there is a family history of this tumor. Strabismus and leukokoria (a white pupillary reflex) are the most common presenting signs of retinoblastoma in the newborn. Early diagnosis and treatment ensure the best prognosis.

The retina is not visualized routinely since it requires dilation of the pupils. The pupils should be dilated to identify (1) chorioretinitis associated with congenital infections, (2) optic atrophy accompanying neurologic abnormalities, and (3) retinal lesions associated with genetic diseases. Small retinal hemorrhages are present in 15 to 30 percent of normal newborns [45]. Papilledema rarely is found in the newborn infant because increases in intracranial pressures are decompressed by expansion of the nonfused cranial sutures rather than being transmitted to the optic nerve. A safe, effective mydriatic and cycloplegic agent [11] consists of a combined solution of Cyclogyl 0.5%, Mydriacyl 0.5%, and Neo-Synephrine 2.5%.

Spontaneous nystagmus [53] is also uncommon. However, it has been associated with poor visual performance and later abnormal neurologic development.

All corneal, lenticular, and retinal lesions should be evaluated by an ophthalmologist.

EARS

Traumatic lesions of the external ear, including simple bruises, abrasions, or more severe necrotic lesions, result from the use of forceps or from intrauterine positioning when the ear is pressed against the bony pelvis. Regardless of the etiology, these lesions should be kept clean and dry and should be inspected daily for signs of infection.

Preauricular tags and preauricular pits are observed frequently (Figs. 4-2, 4-3). The tags may be single or multiple and frequently occur without other pathology. Rarely, there may be multiple tags that occur on the cheeks and extend on a line toward the mouth (first embryonic arch syndrome). Ear pits commonly are found on the helix of the pinnae or just anterior to the point where the helix joins the scalp, but they may be found almost anywhere on the pinnae. They are only significant if they fill with debris and become infected, usually during childhood.

NOSE

Nasal "fractures" occur more frequently in firstborn infants. The fracture is actually a dislocation of the cartilaginous portion of the nose [32]. The nose is flattened or displaced without swelling or hemorrhage. Obstruction of the nasal passages with subsequent respiratory distress is common. Nasal dislocations require active treatment if they do not reduce

Fig. 4-2. Ear pit.

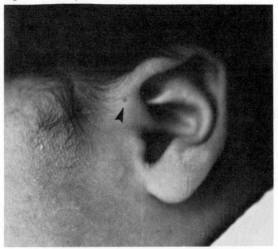

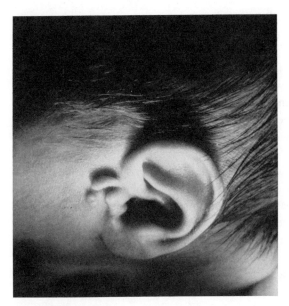

Fig. 4-3. Ear tags.

spontaneously in the first three days. Treatment consists of repositioning the cartilage in the septal groove by placing a cotton swab in each nostril, lifting the cartilage upward, and recentering it; or the cartilage may be grasped with thumb and forefinger and repositioned. Specialized care is needed only if the dislocation recurs.

Bilateral choanal atresia is diagnosed in the delivery room because it causes acute respiratory distress. Unilateral choanal atresia should be suspected in any newborn who remains persistently tachypneic or has breathing difficulties and in whom another explanation is not apparent. Nasal obstruction is excluded by passing a No. 8 French catheter through the external nares along the floor of the nose into the nasopharynx.

MOUTH

Congenital abnormalities of the mouth and jaw include cleft lip and palate, neonatal teeth, intraoral cysts, macroglossia, and micrognathia. *Cleft lip* is an obvious abnormality of the lateral portion of the upper lip (harelip). It ranges from a small notch in the lip to complete cleavage through the lip to the base of the nose. Palatal clefts occur in the midline. The cleft of the hard palate is recognized easily, whereas that involving the soft palate requires careful scrutiny. The finding of a bifid uvula [58] may portend a submucous cleft.

The occurrence in the general population of cleft lip or palate alone or together is 1 in 1000 to 1500 live births [6]. The risk to a second sibling is approximately 3 percent. The genetics of a cleft lip with or without cleft palate differs from that of isolated cleft palate. If a child has a cleft lip, the chances of it occurring in a sibling, either alone or in combination with the cleft palate, is increased. The sibling has no predisposition for an isolated cleft palate. On the other hand, the child with an isolated cleft lip may have a sibling with a cleft palate, but not a cleft lip.

Occasionally an infant is born with a tooth. Natal teeth are present at birth, while neonatal teeth erupt during the first month [14]. The majority of natal teeth are lower central incisors (Fig. 4-4). They may be supernumerary or part of the deciduous (primary) dentition. This can be determined by radiography of the anterior mandible. Natal teeth often are poorly formed and loosely attached to the gingival tissue. Teeth contribute to difficulty in breast-feeding and produce mucosal lacerations and abrasions of the tongue or lip. If a tooth has erupted and is loose, it should be removed because it may dislodge and be aspirated. If it is firmly attached or has not erupted completely, it is advisable to leave it alone. If there is doubt about what to do with a tooth, a pediatric dentist should be consulted.

A *ranula* [33], which is a thin-walled, bluish, translucent retention cyst of the sublingual salivary gland, may be located on the floor of the mouth beneath the tongue. It may increase in size and displace the tongue, ob-

Fig. 4-4. Natal teeth.

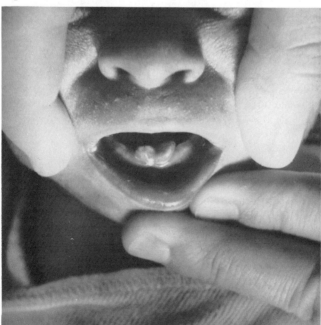

struct the airway, or complicate feedings. The cyst may be decompressed with needle aspiration. In most cases, definitive surgery should be done electively.

Lymphangiomas of the alveolar ridges appear as blue-domed, fluid-filled cysts. They resemble the eruption cyst in the central incisor region, but are not associated with an underlying tooth. They are located more posteriorly on either the maxilla or mandibular ridge. They resorb spontaneously.

Mandibular hypoplasia of a minimal degree is found in most normal newborns. More extreme micrognathia or mandibular hypoplasia occurs in association with glossoptosis and a high-arched palate (Pierre Robin syndrome).

Concave deformations [61] of the jaw secondary to intrauterine positioning are common. These depressions are produced by the shoulder on the affected side. Infants with mandibular deformations rest their heads preferentially to the affected side. By moving the head to the midline, the mandibular regions of both sides of the neck can be compared (Fig. 4-5).

Traumatic lesions of the oral cavity are noted occasionally. Petechial hemorrhages may be observed on the soft palate, as well as the classic *Bednar's aphthae*. The latter are abrasions that involve the mucous mem-

Fig. 4-5. Deformation of the mandible. It should be noted that the left side of the neck appears more full than the right. The right side of the mandible has been resting on the right shoulder in utero. Arrows indicate pressure points on the right side of the mandible.

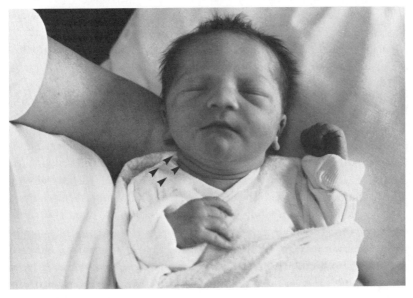

branes and soft palate just superior to the tonsils and the pterygoid processes. They result from suctioning or vigorous wiping of the oral cavity. The aphthous lesions heal within a week and treatment is unnecessary.

NECK

Congenital malformations of the neck include fistulas or cysts, lymphangiomas, congenital goiters, redundant skin (webbed neck), and fused vertebrae (Klippel-Feil syndrome). The most common congenital neck lesion is the *thyroglossal duct cyst* [3, 23]. Thyroglossal duct remnants are midline cysts or fistulas originating in the area of the larynx. Branchial cleft fistulas occur laterally along the anterior border of the sternocleidomastoid muscle. A unilateral multilocular cystic mass over the sternocleidomastoid muscle is a cavernous lymphangioma (cystic hygroma). The hygroma may be very large at birth or grow large enough to compress the airway and require surgical intervention.

Congenital goiters are of variable size. A large congenital goiter may prevent flexion of the fetal head and result in a face presentation, necessitating delivery by cesarean section. Some goiters are large enough to compress the trachea and produce respiratory difficulties. Congenital goiters may result from the ingestion of iodine or antithyroid medications during pregnancy, endemic deficiences of iodine, or metabolic defects. The infant may have either hyperactive, normally active, or hypoactive thyroid function.

Webbed neck, resulting from involution of ectactic lymph vessels, is characterized by redundant skin over the trapezius muscle. It often is associated with Turner's or Noonan's syndrome, and the trisomies 18 and 21.

The most common traumatic lesions of the neck are the sternocleidomastoid muscle hemorrhage (see Chapter 6) and injuries to the brachial plexus. Cervical cord transection, usually associated with breech delivery, is an uncommon traumatic lesion.

CHEST

Following admission to the nursery the infant may have tachypnea, nasal flaring, grunting, and retractions. Although these findings may exist as part of the normal adaptive process, their persistence and increasing severity usually herald an underlying pulmonary problem. Tachypnea is the single best indicator of respiratory disease. However, it also may reflect irritation of the central nervous system or the infant's attempt to compensate for an underlying metabolic acidosis. In the latter two situations, the blood PCO_2 will be less than 30 mm Hg, (respiratory alkalosis), whereas in primary respiratory disease, the PCO_2 usually is elevated above 40 to 45 mm Hg, (respiratory acidosis) [48].

In Chapter 3 it was stated that the chest normally moves in synchrony with the abdomen during breathing. If lung or airway resistance is increased, subcostal, intercostal, and sternal retractions are observed. *See-saw respirations,* which are characterized by a collapsing chest and a rising abdomen on inspiration, are associated with severe retractions.

Grunting occurs when there is lower airway obstruction or focal atelectasis of the lungs. Grunting increases the end-expiratory pressure, thereby increasing the lung volume and improving oxygenation. The grunting noise is moderately high pitched and is generated by a forced expiration against a partially closed glottis. Hypothermia or polycythemia also may be associated with grunting. In the term infant, grunting is an important clinical sign of pneumothorax.

Flaring of the nasal alae is an accessory maneuver to decrease upper airway resistance in the presence of compromised respiration.

Cyanosis occurs when greater than 5 gm of hemoglobin per dl of blood becomes unsaturated, approximating 75 percent hemoglobin saturation (Fig. 4-6). Cyanosis is a sign of either pulmonary disease, central nervous

Fig. 4-6. Oxygen dissociation curves of fetal and adult hemoglobins. Hemoglobin saturation at 75% is the level at which cyanosis appears. The corresponding PaO_2 can be estimated on the graph for both fetal (——) and adult (------) hemoglobin. (Adapted from M. Klaus and B. P. Meyer. Oxygen therapy for the newborn. *Pediatr. Clin. North Am.* 13 : 731, 1966.)

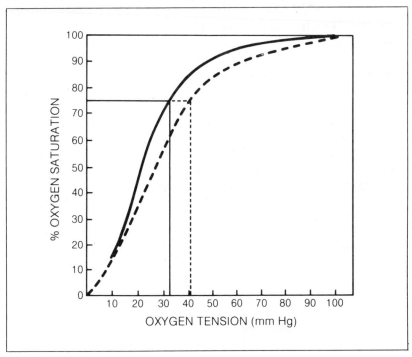

system pathology (central alveolar hypoventilation), heart disease (right to left shunt), hypothermia-induced vasoconstriction (acrocyanosis), or hematologic abnormalities such as polycythemia or methemoglobinemia.

Coughing occurs rarely in the newborn and is an abnormal sign. Sneezing is frequent, however, and is a mechanism for the normal baby to clear nasal passages.

Any signs or symptoms of respiratory distress may be evaluated serially with the Silverman score [59] (Table 4-2). A more critical evaluation also includes: (1) further elucidation of history, (2) a complete reexamination of the infant, (3) chest roentgenogram, and (4) determination of blood gases [47]. If pneumonia, with or without septicemia, is considered, a complete blood count and appropriate specimens for cultures also should be obtained before starting antibiotics.

The differential diagnosis of respiratory distress [35] is presented in Table 4-3. Many of these diseases present during the first 24 hours. They require immediate attention and possibly special support at the level III center.

HEART

Reassessment of the heart after the initial physical examination is unnecessary unless a murmur, arrhythmia, or respiratory distress persists or occurs. When these abnormalities exist, the history and clinical course since birth should be reviewed, with particular attention paid to the vital signs, skin color, feeding patterns, and fluid balance (weight, intake, and urine output). A detailed examination of the heart and lungs should be

Table 4-2. Silverman retraction score

Stage 0	Stage 1	Stage 2
Upper chest and abdomen rise synchronously	Lag or minimal sinking of upper chest as abdomen rises	"See-saw" sinking of upper chest with rising abdomen
No intercostal sinking on inspiration	Just visible sinking of intercostal spaces on inspiration	Marked sinking of intercostal spaces on inspiration
No xiphoid retraction	Just visible xiphoid retraction	Marked xiphoid retraction
No movement of chin	Chin descends; lips are closed	Chin descends, lips part
No expiratory grunt	Expiratory grunt heard with stethoscope only	Expiratory grunt heard with naked ear

Source: W. A. Silverman and D. H. Anderson. A controlled clinical trial of effects of water mist on obstructive respiratory signs, death rate and necropsy findings among premature infants. Reproduced by permission of *Pediatrics* 17 : 1, copyright 1956.

Table 4-3. Differential diagnosis of respiratory distress in term newborns

Pulmonary causes		Extrapulmonary causes			
Common	Uncommon	Metabolic	Heart	Brain	Blood
Transient tachypnea	Airway obstruction	Metabolic acidosis	Congenital heart disease	Hemorrhage	Acute hemorrhage
Meconium aspiration	Space occupying lesion (lobar emphysema, cystic adenomatoid malformation)	Hypoglycemia	Diabetic cardio-myopathy	Edema	Hypovolemia
Pneumonia		Hypothermia		Drugs	Hypervis-cosity
Pneumothorax	Pulmonary hypoplasia (oligohydramnios)				Twin-to-twin transfusion
Primary pulmonary hypertension	Chylothorax				

Source: Adapted from M. H. Klaus and A. A. Fanaroff. *Care of the High-Risk Neonate.* Philadelphia: Saunders, 1973. With permission.

repeated, with skin perfusion and the character of the pulse noted. Blood pressure in the upper and lower extremities should be obtained. A chest x-ray should be done to determine the heart size, the configuration of the heart and the great vessels, pulmonary blood flow, and the presence or absence of pulmonary pathology. Blood should be obtained for a complete blood count and check of blood gases. An electrocardiogram will document arrhythmias and abnormal atrial or ventricular preponderance. Sonography provides noninvasive, dynamic information regarding cardiac function. The interpretation of these test results will assist in establishing a differential diagnosis [41], (Table 4-4) and in determining whether the infant needs to be transferred to a regional center.

The signs and symptoms that are most referrable to cardiovascular disturbances include:

1. CARDIAC ARRHYTHMIAS.   These may be present in utero and persist into the newborn period. Approximately 1 percent of all live-born infants have an arrhythmia [63]; these arrhythmias will disappear by 3 months to 1 year of age. A tachyarrhythmia greater than 180 beats per minute is difficult to document by counting. Electrocardiographic documentation and analysis is mandatory. Figure 4-7 depicts examples of both sinus tachycardia and paroxysmal atrial tachycardia. Sinus tachycardia is associated with systemic illnesses, such as fever, anemia, sepsis, and congestive heart failure. Paroxysmal atrial tachy-

Fig. 4-7. Electrocardiogram. A. Sinus tachycardia. B. Paroxysmal atrial tachycardia. (From A. S. Nadas and D. C. Fyler. *Pediatric Cardiology* (3rd ed.). Philadelphia: Saunders, 1972. With permission.)

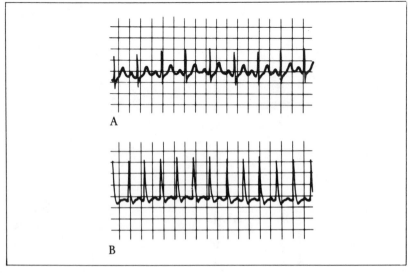

Table 4-4. Differential diagnosis of cardiac problems in term newborns

Cyanotic

Decreased pulmonary blood flow

RVH	Severe pulmonary stenosis; Pulmonary atresia (with or without VSD)
LVH	Tricuspid atresia; Pulmonary atresia with hypoplastic right ventricle
LVH, RVH, or CVH	Transposition with pulmonic stenosis; Truncus arteriosus with hypoplastic pulmonary arteries

Increased pulmonary blood flow

RVH	Aortic atresia; hypoplastic left heart syndrome; Total anomalous pulmonary venous return; Transposition of great arteries
LVH, RVH, or CVH	Transposition; Single ventricle; Tricuspid atresia with transposition

Acyanotic

Normal pulmonary blood flow

RVH	Coarctation; Mitral stenosis
LVH	Coarctation; Aortic stenosis; Endomyocardial disease (endocardial fibroelastosis, myocarditis); Mitral regurgitation

Increased pulmonary blood flow

RVH	Atrial septal defect; All left-to-right shunts with pulmonary hypertension (i.e., PDA, VSD, ASD)
LVH	Patent ductus arteriosus; Ventricular septal defect; Arteriovenous fistula

Key: RVH = right ventricular hypertrophy; LVH = left ventricular hypertrophy; CVH = combined ventricular hypertrophy; VSD = ventricular septal defect; PDA = patent ductus arteriosus; ASD = atrial septal defect.
Source: B. C. Morgan. Incidence, etiology, and classification of congenital heart disease. *Pediatr. Clin. North Am.* 25 : 721, 1978. With permission.

cardia (PAT) is the most common supraventricular tachyarrhythmia and often is intermittent. PAT may lead to congestive heart failure within 24 to 48 hours if not treated. Treatment with vagal stimulation, digitalis, or other medications should be done in consultation with a pediatric cardiologist.

Heart block with cardiac rates of 45 to 60 beats per minute is uncommon, but it is associated with a decreased cardiac output and shock. The etiology may be congenital, familial, or secondary to myocarditis or maternal systemic lupus erythematosus. Placement of a pacemaker is an emergency, life-saving procedure.

Sinus bradycardia (less than 60 beats per minute) also is a sign of central nervous system depression, often following perinatal asphyxia. It is rare in normal newborns.

2. CARDIAC MURMUR.   Murmurs that are persistent, maintain their intensity, or are associated with other abnormal findings have a high probability of being associated with organic heart disease. Functional (nonpathologic) heart murmurs and those associated with a patent ductus arteriosus (PDA) usually are heard during the initial examination and will decrease in intensity during the first 24 hours. Innocent murmurs will change in character when the position of the infant is altered, and they usually are not associated with major signs and symptoms.

3. HYPOTENSIVE STATES.   Low perfusional states in the newborn are either of myocardial or systemic origin. Those of cardiac origin are due to primary myocardial disease or structural abnormalities of the heart. In the early stages of heart failure, the infant's feeding tolerance is limited since feeding is a repetitive demand on cardiopulmonary reserve. The infant responds by nursing less continuously than normal. Some infants pant or hyperventilate between episodes of sucking. The newborn's heart responds to an increased demand by increasing its rate and to a lesser extent increasing its contractile force. More severe congestive heart failure results in decreased cardiac output or cardiogenic shock. In cardiogenic shock the heart enlarges, peripheral perfusion diminishes, cyanosis now appears, oxygen needs become apparent, and hepatomegaly may be detected. Pulmonary edema occurs if the left side of the heart fails. Peripheral edema almost never occurs until very late stages of heart failure.

A chest roentgenogram usually shows cardiomegaly, pulmonary congestion and edema, and, rarely, pulmonary effusion. The electrocardiogram shows evidence of chamber hypertrophy, ectopic beats if the coronary perfusion is decreased, and overall low voltage in myocardial disease.

Systemic causes of hypotension or shock [10] are shown in Table 4-5. The most common of these are hypovolemia and sepsis. Clinically, there is tachycardia, thready pulse, poor perfusion, low urine output, sometimes sweating, and hypoglycemia.

Systemic hypotension of noncardiac origin is treated with volume expanders such as plasma, whole blood, saline, or plasma substitutes such as Plasmanate. Cardiogenic shock or hypotension is uncommon and requires special pharmacologic therapy.

4. CYANOSIS [55, 70]. Cyanosis of cardiac origin often is difficult to differentiate from that of pulmonary origin. In both situations, oxygen should be administered to relieve the cyanosis. Pulmonary cyanosis may be differentiated from cardiac cyanosis by determining the PaO_2 from a preductal arterial sample (e.g., right radial artery specimen), and then determining the change in PaO_2 after administering 100 percent oxygen alone or in combination with positive end expiratory pressure (8–10 cm of water). Failure of the PaO_2 to rise significantly suggests, but does not prove, the existence of a right to left vascular shunt.

If the cyanosis is neither pulmonary nor cardiac in origin and the infant is surprisingly asymptomatic, congenital methemoglobinemia should be considered. The infant's skin and particularly his blood will darkle to a chocolate brown color even though the PaO_2 is normal. Methemoglobinemia is treated with intravenous methylene blue in a dose of 0.1 to 0.2 ml/kg.

Table 4-5. Etiology of shock in the newborn

I. Hypovolemia
    A. Antepartum blood loss: twin-to-twin transfusion, placenta abruption, placenta praevia, fetomaternal transfusion
    B. Postpartum blood loss: vitamin K deficiency, disseminated intravascular coagulopathy, hemorrhage, others
    C. Fluid and electrolyte loss

II. Cardiogenic
    A. Myocardial dysfunction: asphyxia, arrhythmias, myocardiopathies
    B. Mechanical restriction of cardiac function or venous return: tension pneumothorax, diaphragmatic hernia, tamponade, etc.
    C. Congenital heart defects
    D. Disturbance of transitional circulation: persistent pulmonary hypertension

III. Sepsis

Source: Adapted from L. A. Cabal and B. Siassi. Recognition and management of shock in the newborn. *Perinatol. Neonatol.* 3 : 35, 1979.

ELECTROCARDIOGRAPHY [24, 28]

An electrocardiogram (ECG) is used in the evaluation of suspected heart disease. The technique does not differ from that for the older patient except that smaller chest electrodes are necessary and additional precordial leads (V_{3R}, V_{4R}) are recorded. The electrocardiograph must be grounded both for electrical safety and the avoidance of 60-cycle artifact. Figure 4-8 depicts a normal newborn's ECG with an example of the three major components: the P wave-atrial depolarization, QRS complex-ventricular depolarization, and the T wave-ventricular repolarization. The PR, QRS, and QT intervals also are represented. Normal ECG values in newborn infants are provided in Appendix 10.

The presence of ventricular hypertrophy is a major feature of congenital heart disease. The ECG is helpful in determining cardiac enlargement. Table 4-6 provides ECG criteria for cardiac hypertrophy. Furthermore, the ECG is the only tool for distinguishing left axis deviation (less than 0 degrees), which is abnormal, from right axis deviation (90–180 degrees), which may be normal. Left axis deviation is most often associated with tricuspid atresia and endocardial cushion defects.

ABDOMEN

Following the initial transition period, the normal infant's abdomen should remain soft and nondistended. Emesis, distention, excess salivation, and feeding intolerance are signs of gastrointestinal disease. Usually these findings are noted first by the nursing staff. A differential diagnosis is developed by reviewing the history. The physical examination begins

Fig. 4-8. Normal newborn's electrocardiogram. (From T. Burch and T. Winsor. *A Primer of Electrocardiography* (4th ed.). Philadelphia: Lea & Febiger, 1971. With permission.)

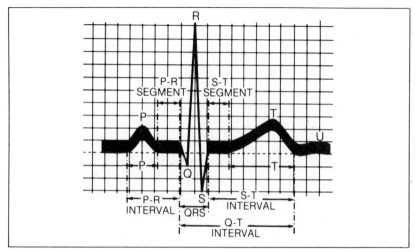

Table 4-6. ECG criteria of left and right ventricular hypertrophy

---

I. Left ventricular hypertrophy (in absence of left bundle branch block)
   A. Standard limb leads
      1. RII-III >45 mm
         RI-III >30mm
   B. Unipolar limb leads
      1. R in AVL or AVF >20mm
      2. Deep Q (>4mm) in AVL or AVF with tall symmetrical T waves
      3. Deep S in AVR
   C. Unipolar chest leads
      1. R in V_{5-6} >30mm
         R in V_{5-6} + S in V_{1-2} >50mm
      2. S in V_{1-2} >25mm
      3. "Strain" pattern in V_{5-6}
      4. Deep Q (>4mm) in V_{5-6} with tall symmetrical T waves
II. Right ventricular hypertrophy (in absence of right bundle branch block)
   A. Standard limb leads
      1. Right axis deviation >120 degrees
      2. Deep S in I-II-III
   B. Unipolar limb leads
      1. R in AVR >10mm
      2. Tall R in AVF
   C. Unipolar limb leads
      1. R' V_1 >15mm with deep S in V_{5-6}
      2. Tall, unslurred R in V_{1-2}
      3. qR in V_1
      4. "Strain" pattern in V_{1-2}
      5. Increased T in V_1
III. Combined ventricular hypertrophy
   A. The following in the presence of left ventricular hypertrophy:
      1. R in V_{1-2}
      2. Transitional zone shifted to the left
      3. Deep S1 or right axis deviation

Key: R, Q, S, T = ECG waves; I, II, III = standard ECG limb leads; AVR, AVL, AVF = unipolar limb leads; V_1–V_6 = unipolar chest leads; qR in V_1 = small q wave, large R wave in V_1 unipolar limb lead.
Source: A. S. Nadas and D. C. Fyler. *Pediatric Cardiology* (3rd ed.). Philadelphia: Saunders, 1972. With permission.

with inspection and then auscultation to determine if bowel sounds are present. Then each abdominal quadrant is palpated for masses. The infant may cry or guard if there is abdominal tenderness. Inspection of the rectum is indicated to exclude an imperforate anus and an accompanying rectoperineal fistula. An abdominal x-ray (KUB) should be obtained to determine if the distention is secondary to an ileus, obstruction, pneumoperitoneum, or ascites. In addition, further diagnostic studies should include a complete blood count and platelet count, serum electrolyte and glucose determinations, urinalysis, appropriate cultures, and coagulation studies if indicated.

Obstruction of the upper gastrointestinal tract is characterized by polyhydramnios, excessive salivation, and vomiting. This information suggests the presence of esophageal atresia, which can be excluded by passing a feeding tube into the stomach. The presence of the tube in the stomach may be verified by (1) auscultating a louder rush of air over the stomach than over the thorax as air is injected into the tube, (2) placing the end of the tube under water and applying gentle pressure on the abdomen and observing bubbles emerge, or (3) identifying the radiopaque tube in the stomach with roentgenography. If the tube does not pass, its position should be secured and the tube placed on gentle intermittent suction. Then a chest roentgenogram should be obtained, and it should be determined if the tube has coiled in a blind esophageal pouch (Fig. 4-9). Esophageal atresia often is associated with a tracheoesophageal fistula [7] (Fig. 4-10). If no fistula is present, the abdomen will be flat and scaphoid, and no air will be present on palpation, percussion, or a plain film of the abdomen. If the most common fistula from the trachea to the stomach exists, air will be apparent in the stomach both clinically and on roentgenography.

If the tube passes into the stomach and more than 30 ml of fluid is found, an upper gastrointestinal obstruction probably exists. If the fluid removed is bile-stained, the obstruction lies beyond the ampulla of Vater. Frequently, blood-stained fluid is vomited or noted in a gastric aspirate. More often than not, the blood was swallowed at birth. Fresh blood from the stomach should be tested to determine if it is of maternal or neonatal origin using the Apt test (see Appendix 20 for instructions on the Apt test).

The newborn infant normally defecates within the first 24 to 48 hours [13] (Table 4-7). If he does not, the abdomen gradually distends. The diagnosis of an imperforate or ectopic anus must be excluded. A benign cause of abdominal distention in an otherwise healthy infant is a meconium plug (Fig. 4-11). A *meconium plug* is a thick, opalescent mucoid cast of the rectum that is fused with and precedes meconium. Passage of the plug is facilitated by gentle digital examination, stimulation with a rectal thermometer, or a 5-ml saline enema.

The algorithm for the assessment and diagnosis of intestinal obstruction is shown in Fig. 4-12. In any case of abdominal distention [52], the infant should not be fed orally, and a No. 8 French gastric tube should be placed in the stomach and connected to low intermittent suction. A balanced electrolyte solution should be infused intravenously at a rate of at

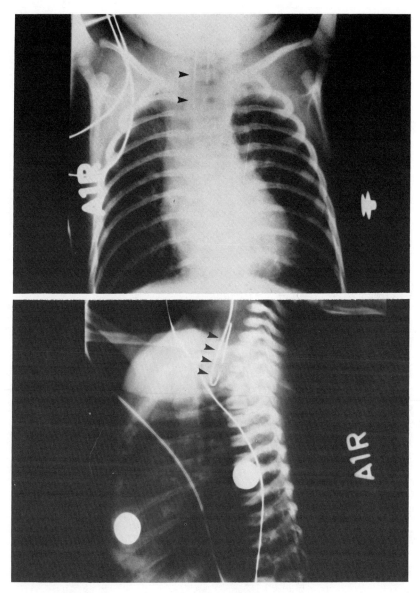

Fig. 4-9. Chest roentgenograms showing esophageal atresia. Arrows point to radiopaque catheter curled in atretic esophagus. (Courtesy of Dr. Ann Kosloske.)

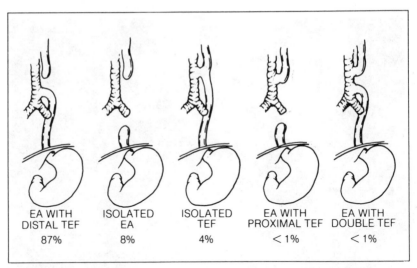

EA WITH DISTAL TEF	ISOLATED EA	ISOLATED TEF	EA WITH PROXIMAL TEF	EA WITH DOUBLE TEF
87%	8%	4%	< 1%	< 1%

Fig. 4-10. Esophageal atresia (EA) and tracheoesophageal fistula (TEF). (From J. D. Hardy (ed.). *Rhoads Textbook of Surgery* (5th ed.). Philadelphia: Lippincott, 1977. P. 1947. With permission.)

least 80 ml/kg per day. If the patient is pale, has a weak thready pulse, and has a capillary refill time that is prolonged, the circulating blood volume should be expanded with colloid (e.g., Plasmanate) at an initial rate of 10 to 20 ml/kg for 1 hour, followed by whatever volume is required to restore peripheral perfusion or the blood pressure. While stabilizing the infant, but before performing any contrast studies, consultation with a pediatric surgeon or neonatologist is suggested.

The stump of the umbilical cord should be dry by the end of the first 24 hours, and no signs of infection should be evident. Erythema of the periumbilical skin often is part of the normal healing process. The ery-

Table 4-7. Time of first defecation for 395 term infants

Age (hrs)	Number of infants	Cumulative %
In delivery room	66	16.7
1–8	169	59.5
9–16	125	91.1
17–24	29	98.5
24–48	6	100.0
>48	0	——

Source: D. A. Clark. Times of first void and first stool in 500 newborns. Reproduced by permission of *Pediatrics* 60 : 457, copyright 1977.

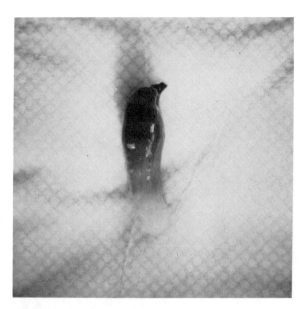

Fig. 4-11. Meconium plug.

thema does not spread and is not associated with a malodorous umbilical stump or systemic symptoms. The cord clamp should be removed when the stump is dry. A watery discharge from the umbilicus is a sign of a patent urachus. Hemorrhage from the margins of the umbilical cord is rare, but if it occurs it may be specifically related to factor XIII deficiency or any other coagulation disturbance, including the omission of vitamin K prophylaxis.

An umbilical hernia occurs where the left umbilical vein penetrated the abdominal wall during fetal development. Umbilical and inguinal hernias are detected by inspection and palpation.

Other congenital malformations that involve the abdominal wall include deficient abdominal musculature (Fig. 4-13), gastroschisis, omphalocele [34], and exstrophy of the bladder. *Gastroschisis* is a rent in the abdominal wall located to the right of the umbilicus. An *omphalocele* is a hernia that protrudes through the umbilicus. It is covered with peritoneum and is frequently associated with other anomalies of the gastrointestinal, genitourinary, or cardiovascular system. *Exstrophy* is a fissure involving the anterior abdominal wall and the anterior wall of the urinary bladder. It also is associated with an epispadias. Gastroschisis, omphaloceles, and exstrophy of the bladder are obvious at birth and require expedient intervention by a pediatric surgeon. Exposed viscera should be covered with a gauze moistened with warm saline while awaiting operative management.

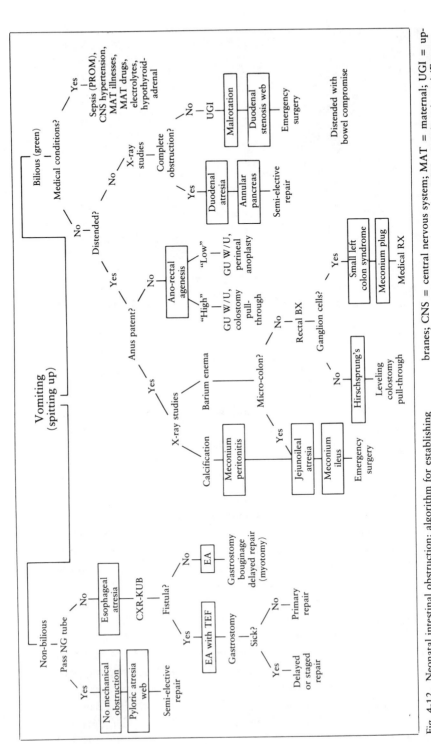

Fig. 4-12. Neonatal intestinal obstruction: algorithm for establishing the diagnosis. (Key: NG = nasogastric; CXR = chest x-ray; KUB = roentgenogram of abdomen (literally, kidney-ureter-bladder); EA = esophageal atresia; TEF = tracheoesophageal fistula; BX = biopsy; branes; CNS = central nervous system; MAT = maternal; UGI = upper gastrointestinal; W/U = workup; GU = genitourinary.) (From R. R. Ricketts. Workup of neonatal intestinal obstruction. *Am. Surg.* 50 : 517, 1984. With permission.)

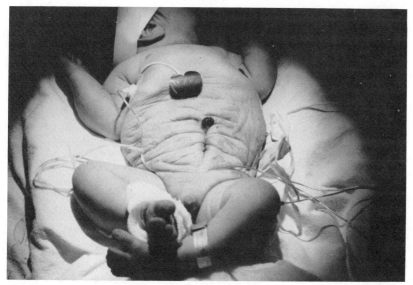

Fig. 4-13. Deficient abdominal musculature. Excessive skin folds should be noted.

GENITOURINARY TRACT

Problems of the urinary tract should be suspected if there is an abnormality in the volume of amniotic fluid. Oligohydramnios, if not secondary to chronic leakage, may be due to renal agenesis, renal abnormalities with nonfunctioning kidneys, or an obstruction of the fetal urinary tract. If a history of oligohydramnios was not documented on the delivery record, it still should be suspected if there is amnion nodosum of the placenta, the oligohydramnios tetrad (see Chapter 1), or abdominal masses of renal origin. Overall the infant's prognosis usually is poor because of accompanying respiratory failure secondary to pulmonary hypoplasia. Polyhydramnios is not a sign of urinary tract disease in newborn infants.

Most newborn infants urinate within the first 24 hours [13] (Table 4-8). The frequency of urination and force of the urinary stream should be recorded. In the early newborn period, uric acid crystals [64] often are observed on the diaper as "red brick dust" deposits at the point the urinary stream hits the diaper. A negative hematest or guaiac test for blood differentiates uric acid crystals from hematuria. The urine of the normal infant contains low concentrations of protein, a few white blood cells, and a few red blood cells (see Appendix 22).

The most common abdominal masses are of renal origin [25, 37]. These include multicystic dysplasia of the kidneys, hydronephrosis as a

Table 4-8. Time of first urination for 395 term infants

Age (hrs)	Number of infants	Cumulative %
In delivery room	51	12.9
1–8	151	51.1
9–16	158	91.1
17–24	35	100.0
>24	0	——

Source: D. A. Clark. Times of first void and first stool in 500 newborns. Reproduced by permission of *Pediatrics* 60 : 457, copyright 1977.

result of an obstructive uropathy (posterior urethral valves or uretero pelvic junction obstruction), and tumors (Wilms').

Neuroblastoma, although not of renal origin, often presents as a flank mass. Once the diagnosis of a solid tumor is made, further palpation is contraindicated because it potentially predisposes the tumor to metastatic spread.

GENITALIA

Problems involving the genitalia more often than not are apparent at birth. A testis that migrates in and out of the scrotum into the inguinal canal can be diagnosed by using the technique described in Chapter 3. An undescended (cryptorchid) testis [15] is a common genital abnormality that often is associated with an inguinal hernia. The scrotum that never has contained testes is very small. Bilateral cryptorchidism requires confirmation of the infant's sex before discharge from the nursery.

If the genitalia are ambiguous, the parents should be advised immediately that further tests are required to determine the sex of the infant since sexual development is not completed. Ambiguous genitalia require evaluation by a pediatric endocrinologist.

Virilism of the female, with scrotal rugation of labia and varying degrees of clitoral hypertrophy, most often is due to congenital adrenal hyperplasia [44]. Congenital adrenal hyperplasia with mild penile hypertrophy is more difficult to diagnose on inspection of the male. Hypoglycemia and electrolyte imbalance may occur with congenital adrenal hyperplasia, and the infant should be monitored closely.

A male with a small penis and associated hypoglycemia should be evaluated for hypopituitarism.

Structural anomalies involving the male's external urethra necessitate a diagnostic workup of the entire urinary tract at a future time [43]. The *hypospadias triad* is the most common anomaly and includes a hooded prepuce, shortened ventral raphe (chordee), and ventral position of the urethral meatus. It occurs in three forms: (1) First degree — the urethral meatus opens on the glans, inferior to the normal meatal position; (2) Second degree — the meatus opens on the ventral aspect of the penile shaft (Fig. 4-14); and (3) Third degree — the meatus opens at the base of the shaft on the perineum. Surgical correction of hypospadias requires the use of the foreskin. Circumcision should not be performed if hypospadias is diagnosed. *Epispadias,* dorsal placement of the urethral meatus, is rare and usually accompanies exstrophy of the bladder.

In the female, hydrometrocolpos occurs as a result of vaginal obstruction. It is recognized as a whitish mass protruding between the labia majora (Fig. 4-15). Occasionally it ruptures during examination. If rupture does not occur spontaneously, a pediatric surgeon or gynecologist should be consulted to release the obstruction. If not relieved, fluid and debris will accumulate, overdistending the vagina and uterus and obstructing the bladder.

CIRCUMCISION

Circumcision is the surgical removal of the foreskin of the penis. In the newborn period this procedure is performed electively or as part of a religious covenant. Parents frequently are confused about the issues of circum-

Fig. 4-14. Second-degree hypospadias.

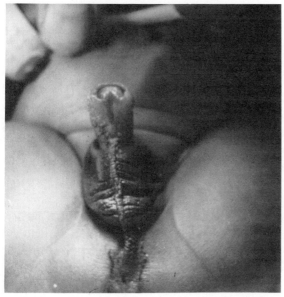

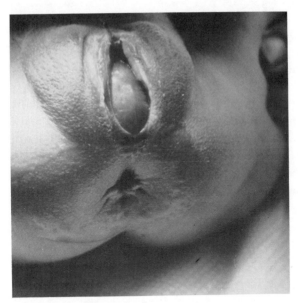

Fig. 4-15. Hydrometrocolpos.

cision and may seek advice in prenatal classes or following the birth of a son. This procedure should not be performed without informed consent.

The pros and cons of circumcision should be discussed with the parents in an unbiased fashion (see Appendix 25). The single most important determinant of whether a newborn male will be circumcised is the attitude of the family. The American Academy of Pediatrics [5] has issued a statement that "there is no absolute medical indication for routine circumcision in the newborn." However, when medical indications for circumcision (e.g., phimosis, recurrent balanitis, paraphimosis, and shortened frenulum) arise later in life, the number of complications increases. In addition, the procedure performed later in life carries a high risk because of the need for general anesthesia. There also is greater cost. Issues that may be discussed with the parents include: (1) cancer of the penis, prostate, and cervix; (2) hygiene; (3) venereal disease; (4) phimosis, paraphimosis, balanitis, meatal stenosis, hemorrhage, and infection; (5) sexual satisfaction; (6) psychological stress; (7) mortality; (8) aesthetics; and (9) cost (see Appendix 25).

If the parents decide in favor of circumcision they should not be dissuaded. However, the procedure should not be performed in the delivery room or before 24 hours after birth, nor should it be performed in the presence of bleeding or other neonatal complications. The two basic techniques for neonatal circumcision are described in Appendix 24.

SKELETON

Fractures and the presence of extra digits are the most common skeletal problems in the first 24 hours. Fractures of the clavicle and humerus are related to birth trauma. They are recognized by crepitus, swelling, restriction of movement, and crying when the baby is handled. Fractures of the humerus and clavicle usually are suspected by the obstetrician at delivery. The diagnosis is established with roentgenography (Fig. 4-16).

Supernumerary digits are found more often on the hands than on the feet and more often in black infants than in white infants. Those on the hands are of two types. In the first type the digit is attached by a fleshy pedicle to the lateral aspect of the proximal phalanx of the fifth digit. It looks like the tip of a finger, contains a rudimentary bone, and the fleshy stalk contains an artery and vein (Fig. 4-17). With permission of the parents, this rudimentary digit can be removed by simple ligation at its point of origin. The ligature must be tight enough to occlude both the arterial and venous circulations so that necrosis will ensue. It should not be cut off. The finger remnant will mummify and fall off in one to two days. The second type of digit contains skeletal elements relating closely to the fifth metacarpal. Amputation should be done by an orthopedic surgeon electively.

Fig. 4-16. Chest roentgenogram showing fractured left clavicle.

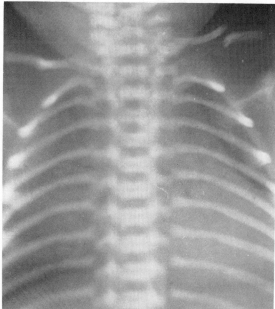

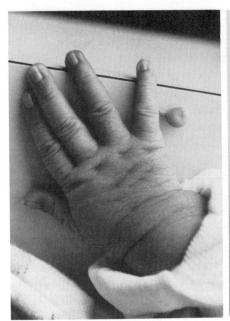

Fig. 4-17. Pedunculated supernumerary digits.

Partial or complete amputation of an extremity or digit may result from amniotic constriction bands [26] or thromboemboli from the placenta. Amniotic bands arise from the amnion, which ruptures at approximately 12 weeks' gestation (Fig. 4-18). Sometimes amniotic bands are seen attached to the affected extremity. They should be unwrapped to determine if the circulation to a viable but affected digit is compromised. Investigation of the placenta usually shows the ruptured, collapsed amnion at the base of the umbilical cord where it attaches to the placenta. A constriction band might arise from the ruptured amnion.

Skeletal dysplasias or dwarfism should be suspected if either the infant's length is short for gestational age, or if the limbs or trunk are disproportionately short.

Arthrogryposis [67] is a relatively uncommon disorder with multiple fixed flexion deformities of the joints. Joint contractures are recognized at birth. Detection of one such deformity may be a clue to similar but less severe deformities of other joints. These are identified by a very careful reexamination. The differential diagnosis of arthrogryposis is presented in Table 4-9.

Profound edema of the dorsum of the hands and feet of the female infant strongly suggests the diagnosis of Turner's syndrome. Marked lymphedema, particularly of the feet, is sometimes observed in the absence of

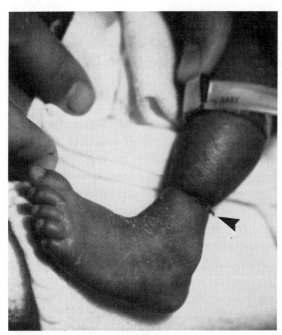

Fig. 4-18. Amniotic constriction band. Arrow points to strand of amnion that wrapped around leg. (Courtesy of Dr. Ken Lyons Jones.)

Table 4-9. Etiologies of arthrogryposis multiplex congenita

Site of major pathology	Disorder
Anterior horn cell	Werdnig-Hoffman disease
	Moebius syndrome
	Lumbosacral meningomyelocele
	Sacral agenesis
	Other
Peripheral nerve or root	Polyneuropathy
	Neurofibromatosis
Muscle	Congenital myotonic dystrophy
	Congenital muscular dystrophy
	Congenital fiber-type disproportion
	Other
Primary disorder of joint and/or connective tissue	Marfan's syndrome
	Intrauterine periarticular inflammation
	Other
Intrauterine mechanical restriction	Oligohydramnios, uterine abnormality

Source: J. J. Volpe. *Neurology of the Newborn*. Philadelphia: Saunders, 1981. With permission.

Turner's syndrome. The edema may wax and wane. The meaning and importance of this is not clear; it usually is not a reflection of other serious diseases.

NERVOUS SYSTEM

Following birth, the infant begins normal cycles of sleep and wakefulness. Although sleep is dominant, the nursery staff should be suspicious of any infant who is lethargic, does not awaken to feed, and does not have a sustained cry. The infant's lethargy or depression may be due to either extrinsic factors (e.g., maternal medications) (Table 4-10) or intrinsic anatomic, biochemical, or functional conditions. The anatomic conditions include central nervous system trauma, vascular accidents, malformations, and tumors. Biochemical abnormalities include asphyxia, hypoglycemia, and other metabolic disturbances. Subclinical or

Table 4-10. Maternal medications causing neonatal depression

Drugs	Effects
General anesthetics	
Nitrous oxide, methoxyflurane	Minor CNS depression
Halothane, enflurane, ketamine	More frequent CNS depression
Local anesthetics	
Bupivacaine	Occasional bradycardia
Lidocaine, mepivacaine	More frequent bradycardia
Benzodiazepines	
Diazepam	Lethargy, hypotonia, less heart rate variability
Chlordiazepoxide	Less frequent and less severe than diazepam
Narcotics	
Morphine, meperidine, alphaprodine	CNS and respiratory depression
Pentazocine, butorphanol, nalbuphine	Mild, infrequent depression
Barbiturates	CNS depression
Sympatholytic agents	
Propranolol	Bradycardia, hypoglycemia
Reserpine	Lethargy
Tocolytic agents	
Magnesium sulfate	Occasional respiratory depression
Ethanol	Occasional lethargy, intoxication, hypotonia

Key: CNS = central nervous system.
(Courtesy of Dr. Phil Anderson.)

akinetic seizures and hypotonia syndromes are examples of intrinsic functional abnormalities.

The infant's cry [21, 36] offers diagnostic clues to the presence of neurologic disease. The spectrum of behavior includes the absence of a cry in response to noxious stimuli, a weak or unsustained cry, or a high-pitched, irritating cry. An infant who has sustained severe brain injury often alternately sleeps and cries as his only behavior.

Jitteriness [54] (tetany) is a symptom that is never observed in a sleeping infant. It is characterized by low-amplitude, medium-frequency activity tremors of one or more extremities in an infant who is awake and looking about. It must be differentiated from seizure activity, which is characterized by generally low-frequency, high-amplitude clonic movements. Some jitteriness cannot be differentiated from seizures by observation alone. In these cases, jitteriness will cease when the extremity is grasped firmly and put at rest; seizures will not.

Neonatal seizures [8, 20] may occur at any time after delivery, although they tend to cluster in the first three days. Seizures currently are classified as subtle, generalized tonic, multifocal, focal clonic, and myoclonic. It often is difficult to recognize a neonatal seizure clinically. In the term newborn, clonic muscle activity tends to dominate over tonic activity. Subtle seizures are more difficult to recognize since they are expressed by deviation of the eyes, repetitive blinking, lip smacking, drooling or excess secretions, respiratory pauses, or "bicycling" movements. The causes, prognosis, and treatment of neonatal seizures are presented in Tables 4-11 and 4-12 and Appendix 27, respectively.

The normal infant's resting tone is predominately flexor. However, posture during the first 24 hours reflects his intrauterine or delivery position and his neuromuscular tone. For example, a *batrachian* or frog-leg position characterizes breech presentation and delivery. Persistent hyperextension of the head characterizes a face presentation and some breech presentations may be observed with a neck mass that tends to obstruct the airway, central nervous system irritation, or a vascular ring encircling the trachea.

The infant's state of alertness should be noted when evaluating tone. A decrease in muscle tone always accompanies sleep. However, persistent generalized hypotonia [18, 51] requires investigation since the etiology may be the consequence of a primary or secondary myopathy or of upper or lower motor neuron pathology (Table 4-13). Hypotonia or flaccidity of a single extremity usually signifies damage to a specific peripheral nerve.

Trauma to the brachial plexus before [19] or during delivery leads to unilateral Erb's or Klumpke's palsies [16]. *Erb's palsy* involves cervical

Table 4-11. Etiologies of neonatal seizures

Trauma and anoxia
  Subdural hematoma
  Intracortical hemorrhage
  Cerebral necrosis
  Cortical vein thrombosis
  Intraventricular hemorrhage
  Asphyxia
Congenital anomalies (cerebral dysgenesis) metabolic
  Hypocalcemia
  Hypoglycemia
  Electrolyte imbalance (e.g., hypernatremia, hyponatremia)
Infections
  Bacterial meningitis
  Cerebral abscess
  Herpes encephalitis
  Coxsackie meningoencephalitis
  Cytomegalovirus
  Toxoplasmosis
  Syphilis
Drug withdrawal
  Methadone
  Heroin
  Barbiturates
  Propoxyphene
Pyridoxine dependency amino acid disturbances
  Maple syrup urine disease
  Urea cycle abnormalities
  Nonketotic hyperglycemia
  Ketotic hyperglycemia
Kernicterus toxins
  Local anesthetics
  Isoniazid
Familial seizures
  Phakomatoses (tuberous sclerosis, incontinentia pigmenti)
  Genetic syndrome with mental retardation (e.g., Zellweger's
    Smith-Lemli-Opitz syndromes)
  Benign familial epilepsy

Source: I. Bergman, M. J. Painter, and P. J. Crumrine. Neonatal seizures. *Semin. Perinatol.* 6 : 54, 1982. With permission.

Table 4-12. Outcome of neonatal seizures

Etiology	% of total	Number	Mortality (%)	Normal (%)	Abnormal (%)	Recurrent seizures (%)
Total group of neonatal seizures	100.0	1667	24.7	47.0	38.3	17.0
Before 1970		1188	27.4	43.8	28.9	18.0
After 1970		479	18.0	55.1	26.9	15.0
Hypoxia + / −	31.5	180	25.0	39.4	35.6	22.0
Trauma + / −						
Hemorrhage						
Unknown	21.6	139		63.3	28.1	
Hypocalcemia	22.7 (0–40)	113		94.7	5.3	
Infection	7.0	52	34.6	30.2	34.6	
Subarachnoid hemorrhage	6.3	9	11.1	88.9	−	
Hypoglycemia	5.3	31	3.2	48.4	48.4	
Malformation	4.4	24	70.8	48.4	29.2	

Key: + / − = with and without.
Source: Adapted from I. Bergman, M. J. Painter, and P. J. Crumrine. Neonatal seizures. *Semin. Perinatol.* 6 : 54, 1982. With permission.

Table 4-13. Differential diagnosis of neonatal hypotonia

Cerebral hypotonia with acute encephalopathy
    Perinatal asphyxia
    Intracranial hemorrhage
    Sepsis and meningitis
    Intrauterine infection
    Inborn errors of metabolism
Cerebral hypotonia with chronic encephalopathies
    Intrauterine infection
    Primary cerebral malformations
    Maternal drugs and toxins
    Chromosomal disorders
    Genetic defects
        Familial dysautonomia
        Prader-Willi syndrome
        Cerebrohepatorenal syndrome
        Oculocerebrorenal syndrome
Motor neuron diseases
    Infantile spinal muscular atrophy
    Möbius' syndrome
    Cerebellar hypoplasia in spinal muscular atrophy
Cervical myelopathies
    Perinatal trauma
    Myelomeningocele
    Congenital atlantoaxial dislocation
Familial hypomyelinating neuropathy
Disorders of neuromuscular transmission
    Botulism
    Transitory neonatal myasthenia
    Congenital myasthenia
    Familial infantile myasthenia
Congenital myopathies with fiber type disproportion
    Myotubular myopathy
    Nemaline myopathy
    Central core disease

Source: Reprinted by permission from G. M. Fenichel. *Neonatal Neurology.* New York: Churchill Livingstone, 1980, P. 46.

spine nerves 5 and 6 and results in adduction of the shoulder, internal rotation of the elbow, pronation of the forearm, and a flexed wrist (the "waiter's tip" position). It rarely is associated with sensory loss. The lesion may be accompanied by a diaphragmatic palsy [2] since the phrenic nerve contains cervical nerves 3, 4, and 5. *Klumpke's palsy* is less common and involves spinal nerve segments C–8 and T–1. Although it usually is thought of as a palsy of only the wrist and hand, actually the entire upper extremity is involved. Clinically, there is motor weakness of the wrist, finger flexors, and intrinsic muscles of the hand. Sensory deficit of the palm may exist. This lesion may be associated with Horner's syndrome (ptosis, miosis, and segmental anhydrosis) if the cervical sympathetic chain is injured. The presence of either diaphragmatic involvement or Horner's syndrome indicates that the cervical nerve damage is in proximity to the spinal cord and that the prognosis for total recovery of function is guarded. If there are signs of bilateral brachial plexus injury, the spinal cord is definitely involved. Palsy of an upper extremity secondary to a brachial plexus injury may be treated by immobilizing the involved extremity by pinning the sleeve to the bodice of the infant's shirt. Physical therapy should begin within seven to 10 days and should include passive range of motion exercises to prevent contractures. In uncomplicated cases, 90 percent of the infants completely recover function by the end of the first year.

Facial nerve palsies secondary to a birth injury usually resolve spontaneously within the first month. Since the peripheral portion of the nerve is involved most commonly, the eyelid on the affected side remains open. The instillation of artificial tears is necessary to prevent corneal drying.

Transient myasthenia gravis in the newborn infant is a condition acquired by transplacental passage of circulating antibodies (7S) to acetylcholine receptor protein [46]. Profound respiratory and feeding difficulties occur within 72 hours of birth and persist for several days to three months depending on the rate of disappearance of the circulating antibody. Improvement of the infant's muscular activity after the administration of neostigmine methylsulfate (0.1 mg/kg intramuscularly) confirms the diagnosis. Continued administration may be needed to treat the infant until recovery is ensured. Congenital myasthenic syndromes are more complex. Since these cases occur so infrequently, it is suggested that a pediatric neurologist be consulted.

Neural tube defects are a composite of malformations of the central nervous system and overlying tissues. They include encephaloceles and meningoceles of the head and spine, myelomeningoceles, and spina bifida occulta [22, 42]. The malformations generally are obvious and require highly specialized care by a team of doctors, nurses, social workers, and counselors. Genetic counseling is extremely important since the occurrence of an affected infant increases the risk for future siblings. The recurrence risk for a second child is 5 to 6 percent, an increase 20 times over that for a family without an affected child. If there are two affected children, there is a 10 to 25 percent risk for each future pregnancy.

SKIN [62]

Bruises on the head may be (1) circumscribed on the vertex (skull cap distribution), (2) variably positioned over the scalp following vacuum extraction, or (3) generalized from the neck up when associated with venous congestion secondary to a tight nuchal cord or to compression of the superior vena cava. The latter occurs when there is a delay between delivery of the head and delivery of the thorax. Petechial hemorrhages often occur on the presenting part. Their location should be recorded. Inguinal petechiae are seen frequently and usually are of no consequence. Petechial hemorrhages are differentiated from capillary hemangiomas because petechial hemorrhages do not blanch with direct pressure. An increase in the size, number, or distribution of the petechiae suggests a more serious, evolving underlying problem that requires additional attention.

Harlequin sign is a fascinating phenomenon in which a longitudinal demarcation separates the red dependent half from the pale half of the infant's body. It is a transient phenomenon lasting only seconds to minutes. It is altered by changing the position of the infant. Usually, about the time someone is called to confirm the observation, the harlequin sign disappears.

Transient cutis marmorata, mottling or marbling of the skin, accompanies acrocyanosis and occurs when the infant is cold. It disappears with rewarming. Congenital cutis marmorata is persistent and rare.

An excessively warm, humid environment predisposes the infant to *miliaria,* an obstruction of the sweat glands. Miliaria appears in three varieties: (1) crystallina (superficial clear vesicles without inflammation), (2) pustularis (cloudy vesicles without inflammation), and (3) rubra (erythematous papules [heat rash]). Miliaria, although uncommon in the newborn, is frequently confused with toxic erythema and other pustuloses (see Chapter 6).

Icterus should not appear in the first 24 hours. Its presence should alert the nursery staff to an underlying hemolytic process or hepatitis.

Developmental heteroclites of the skin include squamous cell rests, supernumerary nipples, cutis aplasia, congenital nevi, hemangiomas, and pilonidal dimples. Squamous cell rests (Epstein's pearls) and cysts (Bohn's nodules) within the mouth have been described in Chapter 3.

Squamous cell inclusions are found on the male foreskin (Fig. 4-19) and should not be confused with pustules since there are no signs of inflammation. Parents will need reassurance that these do not require treatment.

Supernumerary nipples [40] appear as small, pink or brown papules that course from the midaxilla to the midclavicular axis and inferiorly toward the inguinal canal and middle thigh (the "milk-line"). Usually no

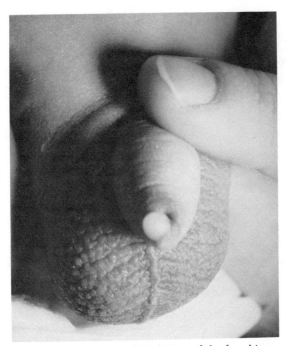

Fig. 4-19. Squamous cell inclusion of the foreskin.

more than one or two extra nipples appear below the true nipples (Fig. 4-20). The majority of supernumerary nipples do not contain glandular tissue and therefore do not hypertrophy or secrete "witch's milk" (neonatal colostrum) as do the normal breasts [38]. The supernumerary nipples persist throughout life and surgical removal is only for cosmetic reasons. Supernumerary breast tissue in the axilla is usually without a nipple and may swell and become tense in the neonatal period. If not removed during childhood, they will swell again during puberty.

By definition, nipples are widespread if the internipple distance exceeds 25 percent of the chest circumference [60]. Infants with XO Turner's syndrome commonly have this finding.

Aplasia cutis congenita [65] is a defect characterized by absence of the skin and occasionally the underlying tissue. Most commonly it appears as a hairless, round, 2- to 3-cm sharply demarcated lesion at the vertex of the scalp (Fig. 4-21). It may be inherited as a familial or genetic trait or may simply be due to mechanical disruptive forces. Congenital aplasia of the skin also occurs in other body areas. Aplasia may be the result of embolic microthrombi from the placenta and a fetus papyraceus [39] (Fig. 4-22). If the skin defect is found in the midline of the lumbosacral region, an occult spinal dysraphism should be expected [27, 50].

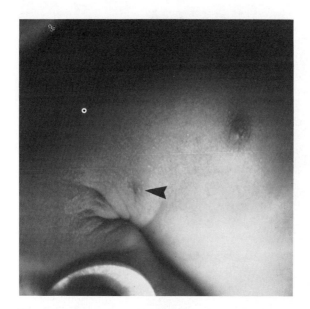

Fig. 4-20. Supernumerary nipple.

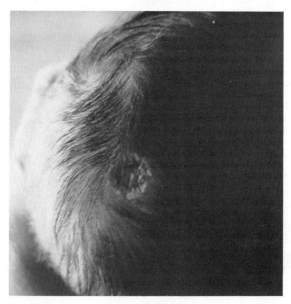

Fig. 4-21. Cutis aplasia of the scalp.

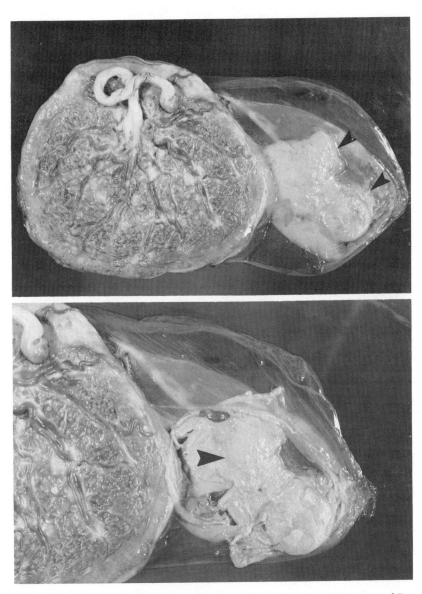

Fig. 4-22. Twin placenta showing fetus papyraceus (arrows). (Courtesy of Dr. Kurt Benirschke.)

Other birthmarks include vascular, melanocytic, and epidermal nevi [29, 30]. Vascular nevi are classified as either raised or flat. Both flat varieties, the *salmon patch* (or *flame nevus*) and the *port wine stain,* are present at birth. The salmon patch tends to resolve, whereas the port wine stain persists. When isolated as a superficial lesion, the port wine stain has only cosmetic significance. However, when it occurs in the distribution of the facial branch of the trigeminal nerve (cranial nerve V) the diagnosis of Sturge-Weber syndrome with intracranial vascular malformation should be considered.

Raised vascular nevi include *capillary* and *cavernous hemangiomas.* They rarely are present at birth. Their distribution is widespread. The most common superficial variety of capillary nevus is the *strawberry hemangioma.* None require therapy unless vital function is disturbed. Large cavernous hemangiomas, however, may be associated with sequestrations of platelets and may result in thrombocytopenia (Kasabach-Merritt syndrome).

True congenital pigmented (melanocytic or junctional) nevi are present at birth [4]. Congenital nevi are obvious because they are large (equal to or greater than 1 cm in size). It is important to document the location and size of smaller pigmented nevi for prognostic reasons. The congenital variety undergoes malignant degeneration in approximately 10 percent of cases, whereas malignant degeneration in the acquired form is very rare. "Café au lait" or light brown pigmented spots may be present at birth. The diagnosis of neurofibromatosis should be entertained if café au lait spots are found in the axillae, their size exceeds 1.5 cm, and their number exceeds six.

Epidermal nevi are hamartomas that are composed of epidermis and its appendages. These varieties of nevi are present in the newborn: (1) *Verrucous nevi* appear singly as fleshy or yellow-brown, rough, warty, oval, or linear plaques (Fig. 4-23). Cosmetic surgery should be performed after puberty when the lesion has achieved maximal size; and (2) *Sebaceous nevi* (of Jadassohn) are commonly found on the scalp or face as an isolated, waxy, orange or orange-brown plaque with a roughened hairless surface. They continue to grow and may undergo degeneration to basal cell carcinoma during puberty. Therefore, it is wise to have them removed before adolescence.

The linear sebaceous nevus is rare, but it is mentioned because it is associated with a syndrome complex of leptomeningeal hemangiomas, cystic adenoma of the liver, horseshoe kidney, patent ductus arteriosus, and conjunctival lipodermoids.

Dimples in the lumbosacral region usually are inconsequential and require no special care (Fig. 4-24). Other sinuses, skin tags, discolorations,

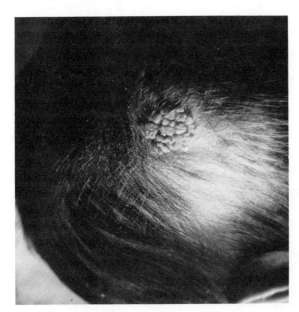

Fig. 4-23. Verrucous nevus of the scalp.

or tufts of hair along the midline of the back above the lumbosacral region suggest a significant underlying defect of the cranio-spinal axis. Body-computed tomography, magnetic resonance imaging, or ultrasonography of the involved area is useful in delineating the anatomic relationship of the superficial defect with the underlying dura and central nervous system. Excision is generally recommended.

Dry, scaling skin is noted particularly in the dysmature and postterm infant at birth. No special treatment is necessary. When the scaling is severe and occurs as large plaques, the term *ichthyosis* is applied. In patients with congenital ichthyosis [69], the abnormalities may persist or resolve. Without the test of time these are difficult to differentiate.

Striking among the scaling disorders is the harlequin fetus, an autosomal recessive lamellar icthyosis that presents with large dense scales and secondary deformities of both the skeleton and soft tissues. The restriction of respiration is incompatible with extrauterine existence for more than a few hours.

Equally striking but less severe is the *collodion baby*. In these cases, the infant is encased in a cellophanelike membrane that temporarily distorts the face and extremities. Peeling of the membrane begins shortly after birth and clears only after several months. Aside from preterm delivery, collodion babies have few problems in the neonatal period.

Monilial colonization may be acquired (1) in the presence or absence of ruptured placental membranes, (2) by passage through a contami-

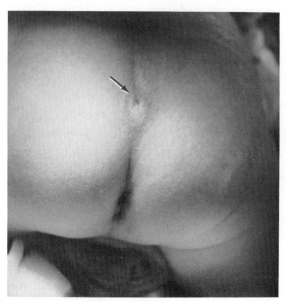

Fig. 4-24. Lumbosacral pit.

nated birth canal, and (3) by contact with contaminated hands. Intra-uterine infection results in lesions of the placenta and umbilical cord as well as the skin of the infant [17, 31]. The dermatitis is recognizable at birth as a generalized, discrete tiny reddish papular lesion on a confluent erythematous base (scarlatinoid rash). Involvement of the umbilical cord is characterized by a yellow-whiteish granuloma or plaque that can be readily distinguished from the normally white Wharton's jelly. Congenital moniliasis is treated with antimonilia or antifungal agents administered topically as well as orally. Monilial diaper dermatitis appears after the first 24 hours (see Chapter 6).

Purpuriclike subcutaneous nodules that are present at birth (the "blueberry muffin baby") [57] portend either metastatic neuroblastoma or dermoerythropoiesis [9] secondary to intrauterine viral disease (rubella or cytomegalovirus infection).

REFERENCES

1. Abramson, D. H. Retinoblastoma: Diagnosis and management. CA 32 : 130, 1982.
2. Aldrich, T. K., Herman, J. H., and Rochester, D. F. Bilateral diaphragmatic paralysis in the newborn infant. J. Pediatr. 97 : 988, 1980.
3. Allard, R. H. B. The thyroglossal cyst. Head Neck Surg. 5 : 134, 1982.
4. Alper, J., Holmes, L. B., and Mehm, M. C. Jr. Birthmarks with serious medical significance: Nevocellular nevi, sebaceous nevi, and multiple café au lait spots. J. Pediatr. 95 : 696, 1979.

5. American Academy of Pediatrics. Report of the ad hoc task force on circumcision. *Pediatrics* 56 : 610, 1975.
6. Anderson, C. E., Rotter, J. J., and Zoncina, J. Hereditary considerations in common disorders. *Pediatr. Clin. North Am.* 25 : 539, 1978.
7. Ashcraft, K. W., and Holder, T. M. Esophageal atresia and tracheoesophageal fistula malformations. *Surg. Clin. North Am.* 56 : 299, 1976.
8. Bergman, I., Painter, M. J., and Crumrine, P. J. Neonatal seizures. *Semin. Perinatol.* 6 : 54, 1982.
9. Brough, A. J., et al. Dermal erythropoiesis in neonatal infants. *Pediatrics* 40 : 627, 1967.
10. Cabal, L. A., and Siassi, B. Recognition and management of shock in the newborn. *Perinatol. Neonatol.* 3 : 35, 1979.
11. Caputo, A. R., et al. Dilation in neonates: A protocol. *Pediatrics* 69 : 77, 1982.
12. Chew, E., and Morin, J. D. Glaucoma in childhood. *Pediatr. Clin. North Am.* 30 : 1043, 1983.
13. Clark, D. A. Times of first void and first stool in 500 newborns. *Pediatrics* 60 : 457, 1977.
14. Cohen, R. L. Clinical perspectives on premature tooth eruption and cyst formation in neonates. *Pediatr. Dermatol.* 1 : 301, 1984.
15. Colodny, A. H. Undescended testes—is surgery necessary? *N. Engl. J. Med.* 314 : 510, 1986.
16. Davis, D. H., Onofrio, B. M., and MacCarty, C. S. Brachial plexus injuries. *Mayo Clin. Proc.* 53 : 799, 1978.
17. Delprado, W. J., Baird, P. J., and Russel, P. Placental candidiasis: Report of three cases with review of the literature. *Pathology* 14 : 190, 1982.
18. Dubowitz, V. *The Floppy Infant* (2nd ed.). Philadelphia: Lippincott, 1980.
19. Dunn, D. W., and Engle, W. A. Brachial plexus palsy: Intrauterine onset. *Pediatr. Neurol.* 1 : 367, 1985.
20. Fenichel, G. *Neonatal Neurology.* New York: Churchill Livingstone, 1980.
21. Foye, H. R. Jr. Crying in Infancy. In M. Ziai, T. A. Clarke, and T. A. Merritt (eds.), *Assessment of the Newborn.* Boston: Little, Brown, 1984.
22. Golden, G. S. Neural tube defects. *Pediatr. Rev.* 1 : 187, 1979.
23. Guimaraes, S. B., Uceda, J. E., and Lynn, H. B. Thyroglossal duct remnants in infants and children. *Mayo Clin. Proc.* 47 : 117, 1972.
24. Hastreiter, A. R., and Abella, J. B. The electrocardiogram in the newborn period. I. The normal infant. *J. Pediatr.* 78 : 146, 1971.
25. Henderson, K. C., and Torch, E. M. Differential diagnosis of abdominal masses in the newborn. *Pediatr. Clin. North Am.* 24 : 557, 1977.
26. Higginbottom, M. C., et al. The amniotic band disruption complex: Timing of amniotic rupture and variable spectra of consequent defects. *J. Pediatr.* 95 : 544, 1979.
27. Higginbottom, M. C., et al. Aplasia cutis congenita: A cutaneous marker of occult spinal dysraphism. *J. Pediatr.* 96 : 687, 1980.
28. Hohn, A. R., Rose, A. P., and Robertson, R. J. A primer of electrocardiography for pediatricians. *Curr. Probl. Pediatr.* 9 : 1, 1979.
29. Jacobs, A. H. Birthmarks. I. Vascular Nevi. *Pediatr. Rev.* 1 : 21, 1979.
30. Jacobs, A. H. Birthmarks. II. Melanocytic and epidermal nevi. *Pediatr. Rev.* 1 : 47, 1979.

31. Jahn, C. P., and Cherry, J. P. Congenital cutaneous candidiasis. *Pediatrics* 33 : 440, 1964.
32. Jazbi, B. Subluxation of nasal septum in newborns: Etiology, diagnosis, and treatment. *Otolaryngol. Clin. North Am.* 10 : 125, 1977.
33. Jorgenson, R. J., et al. Intraoral findings and anomalies in neonates. *Pediatrics* 69 : 577, 1982.
34. Kim, S. H. Omphalocele. *Surg. Clin. North Am.* 56 : 361, 1976.
35. Koffler, H., and McAdams, A. J. Natal onset of respiratory distress. *J. Pediatr.* 81 : 166, 1972.
36. Lester, B. M., and Boukydis, C. F. Z. *Infant Crying.* New York: Plenum, 1985.
37. Longino, L. A., and Martin, L. W. Abdominal masses in the newborn infant. *Pediatrics* 21 : 596, 1958.
38. Malden-Kay, D. J. "Witch's milk": Galactorrhea in the newborn. *Am. J. Dis. Child.* 140 : 252, 1986.
39. Mannino, F. L., Jones, K. L., and Benirschke, K. Congenital skin defects and fetus papyraceus. *J. Pediatr.* 91 : 559, 1977.
40. Mimouni, F., Merlob, P., and Reisner, S. H. Occurrence of supernumerary nipples in newborns. *Am. J. Dis. Child.* 137 : 952, 1983.
41. Morgan, B. C. Incidence, etiology, and classification of congenital heart disease. *Pediatr. Clin. North Am.* 25 : 721, 1978.
42. Mortimer, E. A. Jr. The puzzling epidemiology of neural tube defects. *Pediatrics* 65 : 636, 1980.
43. Page, L. A. Inheritance of uncomplicated hypospadias. *Pediatrics* 63 : 788, 1979.
44. Parks, J. S. Endocrine disorders of childhood. *Hosp. Pract.* 12 : 93, 1977.
45. Parmelee, A. H. *Management of the Newborn* (2nd ed.). Chicago: Year Book, 1959.
46. Pasternak, J. F., et al. Exchange transfusion in neonatal myasthenia. *J. Pediatr.* 99 : 644, 1981.
47. Peckham, G. J., et al. A clinical score for predicting the level of respiratory care in infants with respiratory distress syndrome. *Clin. Pediatr. (Phila.)* 18 : 716, 1979.
48. Polgar, G. Practical pulmonary physiology. *Pediatr. Clin. North Am.* 20 : 303, 1973.
49. Popich, G. A., and Smith, D. W. Fontanels: Range of normal size. *J. Pediatr.* 80 : 749, 1972.
50. Powell, K. R., et al. A prospective search for dermal abnormalities of the craniospinal axis. *J. Pediatr.* 87 : 744, 1975.
51. Rabe, E. F. The hypotonic infant. *J. Pediatr.* 64 : 422, 1964.
52. Ricketts, R. R. Workup of neonatal intestinal obstruction. *Am. Surg.* 50 : 517, 1984.
53. Rosenblith, J. F., and Anderson, R. B. Nystagmus in the newborn as related to later development. *Pediatr. Dig.* March 1978, p. 27.
54. Rosman, N. P., Donnelly, J. H., and Braun, M. A. The jittery newborn and infant: A review. *J.D.B.P.* 5 : 263, 1984.
55. Sahn, D. J., and Friedman, W. F. Difficulties in distinguishing cardiac from pulmonary disease in the neonate. *Pediatr. Clin. North Am.* 20 : 293, 1973.

56. Seidman, D. J., et al. Signs and symptoms in the presentation of primary infantile glaucoma. *Pediatrics* 77 : 399, 1986.
57. Shown, T. E., and Durfee, M. F. Blueberry muffin baby: Neonatal neuroblastoma with subcutaneous metastases. *J. Urol.* 104 : 193, 1970.
58. Shprintzen, R. J., et al. Morphologic significance of bifid uvula. *Pediatrics* 75 : 553, 1985.
59. Silverman, W. A., and Anderson, D. H. A controlled clinical trial of effects of death rate and necropsy findings among premature infants. *Pediatrics* 17 : 1, 1956.
60. Sivan, Y., Merlob, P., and Reisner, S. H. Sternum length, torso length, and internipple distance in newborn infants. *Pediatrics* 72 : 523, 1983.
61. Smith, D. W. *Recognizable Patterns of Human Deformations.* Philadelphia: Saunders, 1981.
62. Solomon, L. M., and Esterly, N. B. *Neonatal Dermatology.* Philadelphia: Saunders, 1973.
63. Southall, D. P., et al. Frequency and outcome of disorders of cardiac rhythm and conduction in a population of newborn infants. *Pediatrics* 68 : 58, 1981.
64. Stapelton, F. B. Renal uric acid clearance in human neonates. *J. Pediatr.* 103 : 290, 1983.
65. Stephan, M. J., et al. Origin of scalp vertex aplasia cutis. *J. Pediatr.* 101 : 850, 1982.
66. Tan, K. L. Wide sutures and large fontanels in the newborn. *Am. J. Dis. Child.* 130 : 386, 1976.
67. Volpe, J. J. *Neurology of the Newborn.* Philadelphia: Saunders, 1981.
68. Williams, H. Congenital cataracts. *Dev. Med. Child. Neurol.* 18 : 806, 1976.
69. Williams, M. L. The icthyoses—Pathogenesis and prenatal diagnosis: A review of recent advances. *Pediatr. Dermatol.* 1 : 1, 1983.
70. Yabek, S. M. Neonatal cyanosis. *Am. J. Dis. Child.* 138 : 880, 1984.

SUGGESTED READINGS

Fletcher, M. A., MacDonald, M. G., and Avery, G. B. *Atlas of Procedures in Neonatology.* Philadephia: Lippincott, 1983.
Swischuk, L. E. *Radiology of the Newborn and Young Infant* (2nd ed.). Baltimore: Williams & Wilkins, 1982.
Warkany, J. *Congenital Malformations.* Chicago: Year Book, 1982.

5. The First 24 Hours: Special Problems

Attention now is turned from common problems in the first 24 hours to an array of special conditions that frequently are encountered in a level I nursery. These variations on the theme of normal, if understood, will prevent unnecessary morbidity for the infant and lessen the anxiety for parents and staff.

COOMBS' TEST

The Coombs' test is an in vitro laboratory test that identifies antibodies on the surface of the red blood cell. During pregnancy, the mother's serum is tested for the presence of antibodies by incubating it with red blood cells having known surface antigens other than those in the ABO system. Following incubation, rabbit antihuman gamma globulin (Coombs' sera) is added. The antihuman gamma globulin complexes with the maternal antibodies that have attached to the red blood cells, causing the red blood cells to agglutinate. This is a positive indirect Coombs' test or antibody screening test. It is used during pregnancy to search for possible hemolytic diseases engendered by a blood group incompatibility between mother and fetus.

Following delivery, the infant's red blood cells are incubated with the mother's sera and the Coombs' sera. This is the direct Coombs' test. It may be used by itself to screen for the possibility of a hemolytic process, rather than typing the infant's blood group and performing a Coombs' test.

By far the most common blood group incompatibilities involve the ABO and Rh systems, in that order of frequency. In both situations the mother is sensitized to the fetal antigen as fetal red blood cells enter the maternal circulation during pregnancy. In response, the mother forms an IgG antibody that passes back into the fetal circulation. The antibodies form a complex with antigen on the surface of the fetal red blood cells. The affected cells then are destroyed in the reticuloendothelial system (liver and spleen). If the hemolysis is severe, an anemia develops acutely, subsequently leading to severe congestive heart failure and hydrops fetalis. If the process is less severe or more chronic, the infant's red blood cell production may equilibrate with the destructive processes, allowing the fetus to adapt successfully.

In general ABO incompatibilities are associated with low-grade hemolysis [22] but rarely with hydrops fetalis. The severity of the hemolytic process is unpredictable in subsequent pregnancies.

Rh incompatibilities result in more severe disease with each succeeding pregnancy. The current method for assessing the status of the fetus is amniocentesis if the maternal serum antibody titers are elevated. The amniotic fluid sample is tested for the severity of hemolysis to determine whether the fetus should undergo intrauterine transfusion, be delivered immediately, or continue to be evaluated while still in utero. All of these cases should be referred to a perinatal center since they are often complicated.

Following birth, a positive Coombs' test should alert the nursery staff that hyperbilirubinemia and anemia secondary to hemolysis may be encountered in the first 24 hours or develop into a problem later.

POSITIVE SEROLOGY

If the serologic test for syphilis is positive on a cord blood specimen, it is compulsory to determine whether active infection is present or whether there has been passive transfer of maternal antibody. Aside from the identification of spirochetes in the blood or tissues, there is no rapid and reliable test to confirm or exclude the diagnosis of congenital syphilis. Even the IgM specific treponemal antibody screening test is not as reliable as originally reported [23].

The potential solution to this dilemma centers around (1) the documentation of the adequacy of the mother's treatment, (2) the current status of her serologic titers, and (3) whether continued surveillance of the infant after discharge is assured.

If there is any doubt, it is prudent to treat the infant. Regardless of cerebrospinal fluid involvement, the infant will be protected fully with the following treatment: aqueous penicillin G (50,000 U/kg administered every 12 hours intramuscularly or intravenously for 10 days) or procaine penicillin G (50,000 U/kg intramuscularly once a day for 10 days).

JAUNDICE [26, 30, 31, 36, 42]

Jaundice is a frequent problem in both well and sick newborns. Bilirubin is formed primarily from the breakdown of hemoglobin (75%), but it also is derived from extrahemoglobin sources (25%) (Fig. 5-1). Once in the blood, the indirect fraction (fat-soluble, unconjugated fraction) bound to albumin is transported to the liver for conjugation with glucuronic acid. The resultant water-soluble diglucuronide is excreted into the biliary system and then into the bowel. The enterohepatic recirculation of bilirubin occurs when conjugated bilirubin in the bowel is unconjugated by the activity of β-glucuronidase, an enzyme in the intestinal brush border. Bilirubin levels in the fetus, as indicated by cord blood levels, rarely exceed 1 to 2 mg/dl because fetal bilirubin, which is unconjugated, freely crosses the placenta to the mother, where it is conjugated

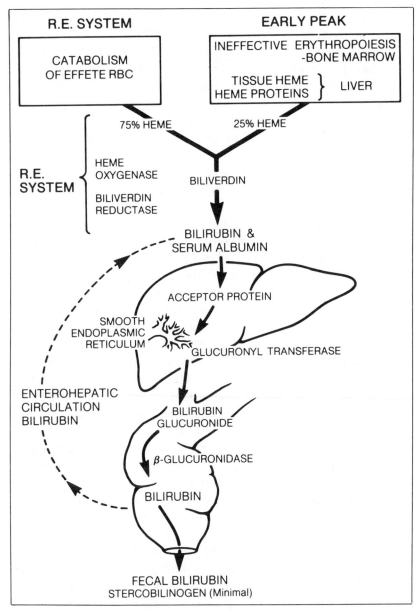

Fig. 5-1. Normal metabolism of bilirubin. (Key: R.E. = reticuloendothelial; RBC = red blood cell.) (From M. J. Maisels. Neonatal Jaundice. In G. B. Avery (ed.), *Neonatology, Pathophysiology, and Management of the Newborn* (3rd ed.). Philadelphia: Lippincott, 1987. With permission).

and excreted. Even in severe hemolytic conditions, the cord bilirubin concentration at birth seldom exceeds 6 mg/dl.

The normal term infant often becomes icteric after 24 hours. Jaundice in the first 24 hours or jaundice that rises progressively to a level greater than 12 mg/dl is abnormal and requires investigation. The basic clinical and laboratory data that are sought in the evaluation of hyperbilirubinemia include a review of the maternal and family history for evidence of jaundice, anemia, gallstones, or splenectomy. The infant is examined for bruising or entrapped hemorrhages, signs of infection, and hepatosplenomegaly, and his general well-being is evaluated. The laboratory evaluation includes determination of the serum bilirubin level, blood group typing of both mother and infant, an indirect Coombs' test on the mother and direct Coombs' test on the infant, a complete blood count, a platelet count, hematocrit, reticulocyte count, and a peripheral blood smear for the determination of red blood cell morphology and white blood cell differential. Serial bilirubin determinations are necessary every four to six hours in the icteric infant whose bilirubin is rising [46].

If the clinical jaundice is yellow-orange, it can be assessed serially by checking only the total serum bilirubin concentration. However, if the jaundice has a greenish hue, such as that observed with biliary obstruction in adults, the direct bilirubin fraction and total bilirubin concentration should be evaluated. Elevations in the direct reacting bilirubin fraction are seen in gram-negative bacterial infections as well as in hepatits and biliary obstruction (Table 5-1). These processes rarely are evident in the first week.

When jaundice is persistent and no specific etiology is discernible, blood and urine should be tested to exclude the diagnosis of galactosemia. Thyroid function tests should be obtained to exclude hypothyroidism. Breast feeding is associated with persistent low-grade jaundice. Guidelines for a more extensive workup of hyperbilirubinemia are presented in Fig. 5-2.

The primary aim of treatment of neonatal jaundice is the prevention of bilirubin encephalopathy, including kernicterus. Each case of hyperbilirubinemia must be evaluated carefully and managed individually [28]. For example, when a hemolytic process such as an Rh incompatibility is present, the infant should be evaluated for thrombocytopenia and hypoglycemia as well as anemia. If the hemolytic process is secondary to sepsis, however, antibiotics should be administered.

Reduction of the serum bilirubin, regardless of etiology, can be accomplished by the use of phototherapy [32, 52, 53] or exchange transfusion. Both treatments have risks. Exchange transfusion is invasive and requires both technical experience and the administration of blood products. Pho-

Table 5-1. Etiologies of neonatal conjugated hyperbilirubinemia

---

I. Impaired hepatocellular function
  A. Infection
    1. Congenital or neonatal (cytomegalovirus, rubella, herpes, etc.)
    2. ?Hepatitis A & B viruses
    3. Acquired bacterial infection
    4. ?Neonatal "giant-cell" hepatitis
  B. Hereditary diseases
    1. Galactosemia
    2. Hereditary fructose intolerance
    3. Tyrosinemia
    4. Cystic fibrosis
    5. Alpha$_1$-antitrypsin deficiency
    6. Familial intrahepatic cholestasis (Byler disease, arteriohepatic dysplasia)
    7. Infantile Gaucher's disease
    8. ?Dubin-Johnson and Rotor syndrome
  C. Other
    1. Massive hepatic necrosis
    2. Paucity of intrahepatic bile ducts
    3. Cholangitis
    4. Associated with intravenous nutrition
II. Extrahepatic obstruction
  A. Biliary atresia
  B. Bile-plug syndrome
  C. Choledochal cyst
  D. Bile ascites

Source: J. D. Johnson. Neonatal non-hemolytic jaundice. Reprinted by permission of the *New England Journal of Medicine,* (292 : 194, 1975).

totherapy, although of low risk, may cause eye damage, apnea by displacing the eye patches and obstructing the nares, increased incidence of insensible water loss, and difficulties with thermoregulation. Currently it is being recommended that phototherapy be initiated when the serum bilirubin concentration reaches a level of 3 to 5 mg/dl below what would normally be considered for an exchange transfusion. Thus, in the term newborn this concentration would be approximately 15 mg/dl.

Occasionally a healthy infant with a healed umbilicus will present late in the first week with idiopathic hyperbilirubinemia (a level greater than 20 mg/dl) [50]. The decision to treat this infant with phototherapy alone or in combination with exchange transfusion, which obviously will require a vascular cutdown, is difficult and should be discussed with a neonatologist at a regional level II or III center.

Serum bilirubin values should be assessed when an infant is treated with phototherapy. If the underlying etiology is a hemolytic process, seri-

116

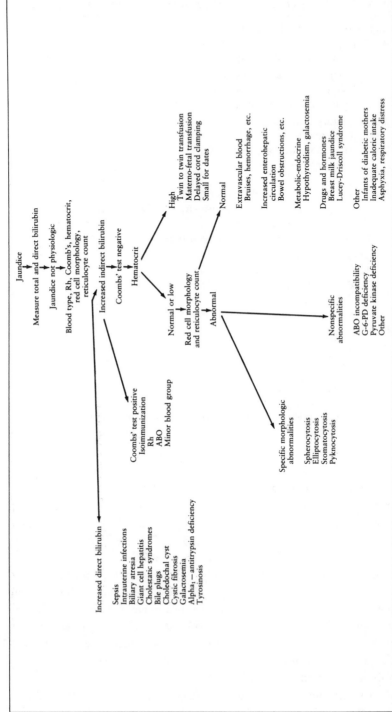

Fig. 5-2. Algorithm for workup of hyperbilirubinemia. (From M. J. Maisels. Neonatal Jaundice. In G. B. Avery (ed.), *Neonatology, Pathophysiology, and Management of the Newborn* (3rd ed.). Philadelphia: Lippincott, 1987. With permission.)

al hematocrits also must be followed. During phototherapy, bilirubin is expected to fall 2 to 4 mg/dl over a 24-hour period provided that the production of bilirubin is not continuing or accelerating and that the phototherapy lights are working properly. Extensive utilization of phototherapy has led to a dramatic decrease in the number of exchange transfusions performed and, as a result, in the number of practitioners who have experience with this procedure. An exchange transfusion is a complex procedure that may result in significant changes in the infant's blood chemistries and cardiac performance. Therefore, it should be performed with cardiorespiratory monitoring and by someone with experience. It also may be necessary to transfer the infant to a nearby level II or III unit for an exchange transfusion.

POLYCYTHEMIA [8, 37]

Polycythemia and associated hyperviscosity occur in approximately 5 percent of newborns. Some of the predisposing factors include maternal diabetes, placental insufficiency, maternal-fetal transfusion, twin-to-twin transfusion, and placental-fetal transfusion resulting from factors like delayed cord clamping or milking the cord blood into the infant at the time of delivery. Clinically, the infant may appear either normal, plethoric, pale, or cyanotic. The infant may be asymptomatic. If symptomatic, neurologic signs range from lethargy to irritability and seizures. Tachypnea, tachycardia, respiratory distress, hypoglycemia, and poor feeding are other associated findings. The chest roentgenogram shows increased pulmonary vascularity and cardiomegaly (Fig. 5-3). The diagnosis should be suspected when a hematocrit from a warmed heel sample at four to six hours after delivery exceeds 65 percent. Polycythemia, then, is confirmed when a central (venous) hematocrit exceeds 65 percent. Polycythemia should be treated with an isovolemic partial exchange transfusion, not simple phlebotomy. During the exchange transfusion, the infant's whole blood, drawn in 15- to 20-ml aliquots from a catheter in the umbilical vein, is replaced with an equal volume of either 5% albumin, fresh frozen plasma, or a commercially available human plasma protein fraction U.S.P. The latter may be preferable since it is prepackaged and requires no mixing, and there is no risk of hepatitis. The formula for the volume to be replaced is:

$$\text{Volume} = \frac{(\text{Observed hematocrit} - \text{Expected hematocrit}) \times \text{blood volume}}{\text{Observed hematocrit}}$$

The observed hematocrit is a central hematocrit obtained at four to six hours. The expected hematocrit is 55 percent. The blood volume is cal-

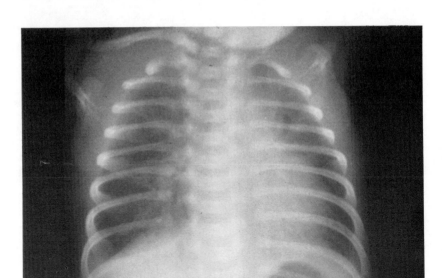

A

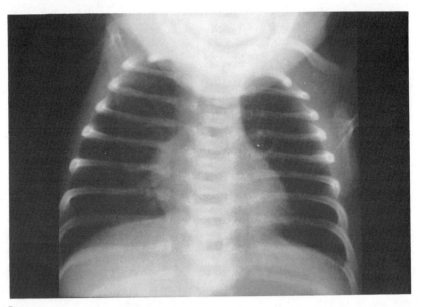

B

Fig. 5-3. Chest roentgenogram showing changes associated with symptomatic hyperviscosity. A. Preexchange film. Cardiomegaly and "wet" lung fields should be noted. B. Postexchange film. Normal size heart and clear (black) lung fields should be noted.

culated by multiplying the birth weight in kilograms by 80. For example, the volume for exchanging a 3-kg infant with a central hematocrit of 70 percent would calculate as follows:

$$\frac{(70 - 55) \times (3 \times 80)}{70} = \frac{15 \times 240}{70} = 51 \text{ ml}$$

Since the commercially available human plasma protein fraction is packaged in 50-ml aliquots, a 50-ml volume would be an acceptable volume for the exchange procedure. The peripheral hematocrit should be rechecked four hours after the exchange and certainly before discharge. Polycythemia and umbilical catheterizations predispose otherwise big, healthy infants to necrotizing enterocolitis. Thus, the polycythemic infant should be followed closely with repeated examinations of the stool for occult blood up to 48 hours. In some nurseries feedings are discontinued for 12 hours in infants who have had a partial exchange transfusion.

The prognosis appears to depend on the factors predisposing to polycythemia and whether the infant is symptomatic. Symptomatic polycythemic infants definitely should undergo partial exchange transfusion. Some believe that asymptomatic infants also should undergo partial exchange transfusion when the hematocrit value exceeds 65 percent. Others would delay the procedure until the hematocrit exceeds 70 percent.

HYPOGLYCEMIA [9, 17]

Near term, the fetal blood glucose concentration closely reflects the maternal value. Once delivery occurs and the maternal supply of glucose is abruptly discontinued, the infant's mean blood glucose level rapidly declines to a level of 50 mg/dl during the first hours after birth. Subsequently, the blood glucose rises and equilibrates to about 70 mg/dl by the third postnatal day. Blood glucose concentration results from complex interactions between the supply of glucose and its utilization. Blood glucose supplies are regulated and maintained by dietary intake, the synthesis of glucose from available precursors, and specific hormones (insulin, glucagon, catecholamines, and glucocorticoids) that control its storage into or release from tissues.

Hypoglycemia is a potential problem in every gestational age category except the term AGA infant. Fortunately, hypoglycemia is rare in a population of low-risk newborn infants. However, the homeostasis of glucose can become unbalanced in many different clinical situations.

Hypoglycemia is commonly found in conditions associated with acute distress, e.g., perinatal asphyxia, sepsis, hypothermia, surgical emergencies, cardiorespiratory failure, and conditions that delay or prevent enteral feeding. The hypoglycemia associated with these conditions readily responds to therapy and recurs infrequently once the underlying problem has been resolved.

A more severe form of hypoglycemia that tends to recur and often is symptomatic is that associated with chronic disorders. Any maternal (pregnancy-induced hypertension), placental (circumvallation), or fetal (multiple gestation, chromosomal abnormalities) disorder producing intrauterine growth retardation and decreased glucose stores predisposes the infant to severe and protracted hypoglycemia. Aggressive intravenous glucose therapy and continued surveillance are necessary.

A third form of hypoglycemia is that produced by neonatal hyperinsulinism secondary to pancreatic islet cell hyperplasia. Severe Rh erythroblastosis fetalis and maternal diabetes during pregnancy are the most common associated conditions; less common conditions include Beckwith-Wiedemann syndrome, nesidioblastosis, and islet cell adenomas. The blood glucose concentration must be monitored closely to keep the serum level stable within the normal range. The spectrum of therapy ranges from oral feedings alone to vigorous intravenous support.

Hypoglycemia also occurs in other miscellaneous conditions, such as congenital anomalies, endocrinopathies, congestive heart failure [6], and cardiac malformations that potentially compromise hepatic artery blood flow, such as hypoplastic left heart syndrome and coarctation of the aorta. Hypoglycemia may also occur if maternal tocolytic therapy was used [12].

Clinical signs of hypoglycemia range widely from the more specific findings of lethargy, apnea, and seizures, to those of a reactive nature such as irritability, jitteriness, tachycardia, and sweating. These signs and symptoms occur when the blood glucose falls below 30 mg/dl in the first 72 hours or below 40 mg/dl thereafter. Although the symptomatic level is defined, in fact reactive symptoms seem to accompany a rapidly falling blood glucose, irrespective of the absolute level.

The normal infant usually requires glucose screening on admission to the nursery and before the first feeding. If the glucose values remain normal, no further tests are required. The infant at risk, however, should be screened hourly until feedings are started. Subsequently, values should be obtained before and one to two hours after each feeding until the blood glucose concentration remains stable.

Simple hypoglycemia may be treated with either 5 or 10% glucose water or milk feeding if the infant has an intact suck-swallow mechanism, no abnormal central nervous system signs, and no suspected abnormalities of the gastrointestinal tract. Upon successful completion of the feeding, the blood sugar should be screened every one to two hours until a routine feeding pattern is established and the glucose concentration remains normal.

Intravenous therapy should be instituted if the infant cannot or will not feed or if the postprandial blood glucose values do not reach a normal level [27]. Intravenous therapy is indicated specifically in transient, symptomatic, and recurrent hypoglycemia. A continuous infusion of 10% glucose water at a rate of 8 to 10 mg/kg per minute (approximately 500 mg/kg per hour) usually will suffice. A bolus of hypertonic glucose (greater than 10%) should not be administered during hypoglycemia. However, in persistent profound hypoglycemia with apnea and seizures, an infusion of 0.5 to 1.0 gm/kg of 25% glucose water followed by a continuous infusion of 10% glucose at a rate of 8 to 10 mg/kg per minute should be administered. A sample calculation for a constant 8 mg/kg per minute rate of infusion for a 3-kg infant is given:

10% glucose water = 10 gm glucose/100 ml of solution
= 100 mg glucose/1 ml of solution

The calculation requires 8 mg/kg/min. Therefore $8 \times 3 = 24$ mg/min, or 1440 mg/hr. Since 10% glucose contains 100 mg/1 ml, the number of ml/hr will be 1440/100 ml or 14.4 ml/hr.

The 10% glucose should be administered with an intravenous infusion pump to deliver the glucose into a peripheral vein at a constant rate. Gravity-controlled infusions do not flow at consistent rates and, therefore, produce unacceptably wide fluctuations in the blood glucose.

Once the infusion begins, the blood glucose level should be determined each hour until the hypoglycemia has been corrected and the blood glucose is normal and stable. Once the oral feedings are established the intravenous glucose may be tapered by gradually reducing the rate of infusion (ml per hour), the concentration of glucose (from 10% to 5%), or both.

Hyperglycemia is defined as a blood glucose concentration in excess of 125 mg/dl. In the newborn, it is most commonly due to the inadvertent administration of intravenous glucose in quantities exceeding the demand. A nonketotic and transient form of diabetes occurs in the newborn and is associated with hyperglycemia and an insulin requirement.

Continued monitoring of the hyperglycemic and hypoglycemic infant is mandatory during both the initial phases of the problem and as intravenous therapy is withdrawn.

Occasionally problems arise that involve elevation or depression of the blood sugar for which there is no obvious explanation. Consultation with a neonatologist or pediatric endocrinologist and transfer to a special care facility for diagnostic and therapeutic purposes may be necessary.

INFANTS OF DIABETIC MOTHERS [51]

Infants of diabetic mothers (IDM) require special mention. As a result of hyperinsulinemia in the infant, the IDM's blood glucose concentration declines rapidly after delivery, reaching a nadir by one to two hours. The celerity of this response is directly related to the maternal glucose concentration at delivery. As a rule, the higher the glucose concentration is in the mother before delivery, the more rapid is the fall in the newborn's serum glucose after delivery. The management of hypoglycemia in the IDM is identical to that outlined in the section on hypoglycemia. The IDM may have additional problems including hypocalcemia, hyperbilirubinemia, polycythemia, hypomagnesemia, respiratory and cardiac problems, sepsis, and an increased incidence of congenital abnormalities.

CALCIUM [14, 49] AND MAGNESIUM DISTURBANCES

Lethargy and jitteriness are two states that may reflect disturbances in calcium and magnesium homeostasis.

CALCIUM

Hypocalcemia (less than 7 mg/dl) is rare in infants born after a normal pregnancy, labor, and delivery. Early onset hypocalcemia in the infant may be the first clue to maternal hyperparathyroidism. Late hypocalcemia is rarely seen because cow's milk and cow's milk formulas are no longer fed to newborns. Hypocalcemia is treated with administration of parenteral calcium gluconate (10% solution; 200–400 mg/kg per day) or oral calcium glubionate (Neo-Calglucon) at about 5 ml three times daily. Caution: The high osmolar load of this preparation may cause diarrhea.

MAGNESIUM [10, 16, 33]

Hypermagnesemia (more than 2.5 mg/dl) occurs in infants whose mothers are preeclamptic and were treated with intravenous magnesium sulfate during labor. It is unlikely that the infant will be lethargic or have bradycardia unless the magnesium level in the cord blood exceeds 6 mg/dl.

Hypomagnesemia (less than 1.5 mg/dl) may underlie a persistent hypocalcemia in an infant of a diabetic mother. Once identified, hypomagnesemia can be treated with 0.1 to 0.2 ml/kg of magnesium sulfate (50% solution) either intramuscularly or intravenously. When using the intramuscular preparation, it is suggested that the injection be limited to less than 0.5 ml at any one site.

SEPTICEMIA [43]

Bacterial septicemia occurs in one to four infants for every 1000 live births.

ACQUISITION OF INFECTION

Infections are acquired in utero via the transplacental route or through a rent in the fetal membranes. Hematogenous spread through the placenta is unusual but does occur in viral infections, tuberculosis, syphilis, and listeriosis. A direct relationship exists between the rupture of the membrane and contamination of the amniotic fluid [1, 15]. Bacteria have been recovered from the fetal environment in over 80 percent of cases in which the membranes were ruptured longer than 24 hours. When membrane rupture was accompanied by labor, the number of cases with bacterial isolates increases to 90 percent.

The infant also may acquire an infectious organism during passage through the birth canal. The most virulent of these include group B streptococcus, herpes simplex virus, pathogenic *Escherichia coli, Neisseria gonorrhoeae, Chlamydia trachomatis,* and *Listeria monocytogenes.* The spectrum of organisms that cause infection postnatally is remarkably wide and includes agents that usually are not pathogenic in older patients.

Infections acquired in the nursery emanate from contaminated supplies and equipment, and especially from persons who touch the infant with unclean hands. Hand washing is of paramount importance in preventing neonatal infections.

INFANT'S RESPONSE [13, 20, 34, 47]

Once the newborn infant is colonized, an organism may gain entry through the umbilicus, punctures and abrasions of the skin, or mucous membranes. Once it gains access to the bloodstream it then spreads to remote secondary foci, organs, tissues, and fluids.

Although newborn white blood cells respond to the organisms by chemotaxis, phagocytosis, and bactericidal activities, their overall function is impaired by maturational factors and by the infection itself. In addition to the cellular response, the normal infant activates complement and immunoglobulins in response to infection. The term infant acquires approximately 1 gm/dl of immunoglobulin G (IgG) through the placenta. The specificity of acquired IgG reflects the mother's immunologic responses to infectious agents. Since immunoglobulin M (IgM) does not cross the placenta, the infant's response to an intrauterine infection may be reflected by an elevated IgM level in the peripheral blood. Cord blood IgM levels may be spuriously elevated by maternal blood contaminating the specimen during collection at delivery.

DIAGNOSIS

The diagnosis of overwhelming septicemia is not difficult. However, recognition of sepsis in its earliest stages requires knowledge, skill, and especially experience. Septicemia should be suspected in the infant whose history includes prolonged rupture or leaking fetal membranes or who is malodorous, meconium-stained, or depressed at birth. An infant with thermal instability, poor feeding, lethargy, pallor, or a shock-like appearance also should be evaluated. Specific symptoms may reflect specific organ involvement. For example, tachypnea may be a sign of pneumonia, and seizures may be a sign of meningitis.

These signs and symptoms require a thorough examination and laboratory workup. There are areas that necessitate special scrutiny during the examination, including:

1. ANTERIOR FONTANELLE.   Fullness denotes increased intracranial pressure such as with meningitis. The anterior fontanelle is sunken with states of dehydration and hypotension. Nuchal rigidity is an unreliable sign and is practically never observed in neonatal meningitis [41].

2. TYMPANIC MEMBRANE.   Full visualization of the tympanic membrane with an otoscope is important to exclude otitis media when sepsis is suspected [7]. In the newborn, otitis media is acquired by the hematogenous route, rather than being secondary to an obstructed eustachian canal as in older infants.

3. UMBILICAL STUMP.   Particular attention should be paid to erythema, drainage, or a foul odor.

4. ABDOMEN.   The presence of abdominal distention should be noted. The infant with peritonitis will cry or guard the abdomen during palpation. The liver and spleen may be enlarged as a consequence of infections. Appendicitis [40] may occur in the newborn and is difficult to diagnose before appendiceal rupture and peritonitis are evident.

5. EXTREMITIES.   Osteomyelitis generally is uncommon, especially during the first 24 hours, but should be suspected if there is localized swelling when the affected extremity is moved. The characteristic finding of neonatal osteomyelitis is flaccid paralysis of the affected extremity. It is termed *pseudoparalysis* even though deep tendon reflexes in the affected extremity are not absent.

6. SKIN.   The proliferation of petechiae, the appearance of purpura, the greenish color of an elevated direct bilirubin, or other skin color

changes all may signify sepsis. Delayed capillary refill may be a sign of septic shock.

The nursing staff may note changes in vital signs such as temperature instability, tachypnea, tachycardia, and falling blood pressure. A nurse's or parent's comment that the "infant doesn't look or act right" may be the earliest omen of sepsis.

The placenta also may provide valuable evidence of information regarding infection acquired in utero. When it is odorous and the fetal membranes are cloudy, the membranes should be cultured. The umbilical cord and placenta should be examined microscopically for evidence of vasculitis or the presence of an etiologic agent. The placenta should be saved until the infant is stable or discharged.

Once the history has been reviewed and the examination completed, the laboratory workup for sepsis includes: [11]

1. A total blood cell, differential, and platelet count. A total white blood cell count of less than 5000 or greater than 30,000 is abnormal. In neonatal sepsis, absolute neutropenia less than 1500 is more predictive of infection than neutrophilia. (See Appendixes 17 and 18 for normal ranges of total white blood cells and neutrophils.) Platelet counts of less than 100,000 (thrombocytopenia) often accompany infection.

2. Bacterial cultures.

   A. Blood. Blood samples should be drawn aseptically from peripheral vessels for both aerobic and anaerobic cultures. Povidone-iodine (Betadine) is commonly used to prepare the skin site for venipuncture. Blood samples should not be obtained from the femoral vessels because of the potential for trauma and subsequent thrombosis of these vessels.

   B. Urine. Suprapubic aspiration of the bladder is the best method for obtaining an uncontaminated urine sample for cell count, Gram's stain, culture, and bacterial antigen detection. Suprapubic tap is performed by inserting a 22-gauge, 1½-in. needle into the bladder in the midline just above the pubis when the bladder is full (see Appendix 23). Since the infant may urinate during preparation and puncture of the suprapubic site, the urethral area should be thoroughly cleansed so that a clean voided specimen may be collected as an alternative. Suprapubic aspiration probably is not necessary when infants are investigated for sepsis immediately after birth, since the yield of positive cultures is extremely low at this time [18]. Insertion of a transurethral catheter is difficult, traumatic, and more likely to introduce infection than a suprapubic tap.

C. Others. Other sites to be cultured are the skin, nasopharynx, stool, and drainage from any lesion.

3. Lumbar puncture [19]. Lumbar puncture should be performed in infants whose mother was febrile during labor and delivery and in any infant who is foul-smelling at birth and displays central nervous system or other signs of sepsis. A lumbar puncture is performed with a 22-gauge 1 to 1½-in. needle containing a stylet. The lumbo-sacral area should be prepared with povidone-iodine (Betadine). Since the filum terminale of the newborn infant's spinal cord is at a lower level than that in the older child or adult, the site of the puncture should be at the level of the pelvic brim, approximately L-5 to S-1. Normal cerebrospinal fluid values are shown in Appendix 21.

   Although there is risk, in some cases in which the fetal membranes are ruptured for approximately 24 hours and the mother and infant pair are asymptomatic, a lumbar puncture may be deferred. In these cases, a peripheral total and differential white blood cell count, platelet count, blood culture, and prudent observation of the infant are essential. Early discharge is contraindicated in this situation unless the cultures are negative and the baby is doing well.

4. Appropriate roentgenograms.

5. Blood gases. These may document a metabolic acidosis, an early sign of sepsis. A metabolic acidosis may develop in the presence of either respiratory acidosis (elevated PCO_2) if the lung is involved or respiratory alkalosis (decreased PCO_2) if the central nervous system is affected.

6. Miscellaneous.

   A. An elevated IgM level of greater than 20 mg/dl obtained one to two days following birth reflects the infant's immune response to an acquired intrauterine infection. Generally an IgM response to infection acquired after birth will not become apparent for approximately one week following the onset of the infection.

   B. Examinations of the gastric aspirate, external ear cultures, serum C-reactive protein, erythrocyte sedimentation rate, and fibrinogen are of limited use.

7. Viral cultures. Cultures for herpes simplex, cytomegalovirus, coxsackie virus, echovirus, and other viruses may be indicated by clinical findings and are important for diagnostic purposes. Nasopharyngeal and stool samples have a better yield for viruses than blood or spinal fluid samples.

THERAPY

Antibiotic treatment should be started immediately after specimens are obtained for culture. Penicillin derivatives such as ampicillin or penicillin

G and an aminoglycoside derivative such as kanamycin or gentamicin should be continued until the culture results and antimicrobial sensitivity values are known. Appendix 26 contains current dose schedules for commonly prescribed antibiotics.

The duration of treatment depends on diagnostic findings, culture results, and the infant's response to therapy. If an infection is highly suspected and the infant improves with therapy but the cultures prove to be negative, antibiotics should be continued for approximately one week. If an infection is suspected but the infant is well and stable, the antibiotics may be discontinued after three to five days if the cultures are negative. With proven pneumonia, omphalitis, gastrointestinal infection, and septicemia, antibiotics should be continued for seven to fourteen days. Serious, deep-seated infections (e.g., meningitis or osteomyelitis) are treated with intravenous antibiotics for a minimum of three weeks after the last positive culture. A posttreatment observation period in the hospital is not necessary for infants who are asymptomatic and in whom cultures are negative after 48 to 72 hours. At discharge, specific instructions should be given to the parents to return with the infant to the physician for evaluation if lethargy, poor feeding, or any other suspicious signs appear. However, if cultures are positive or treatment is extended because of a positive diagnostic finding, such as an infiltrate on a chest x-ray, the infant should be observed for 48 hours following cessation of antibiotics. The reason for this is that infections have recrudesced at 48 hours when therapy has suppressed but not eradicated the offending organism.

SURGICAL EMERGENCIES [21, 25, 44, 45]
Those responsible for the medical care of infants should be familiar with the most common problems requiring surgery. Often the final outcome is determined by how quickly the diagnosis is made and the effectiveness of the initial supportive care in preventing infection and metabolic derangements. All conditions requiring major surgery should be referred to a tertiary care center. Many common conditions are presented in Table 5-2.

Some general principles of management bear mentioning. An orogastric or nasogastric tube should be inserted and attached to suction when a diagnosis of either diaphragmatic hernia (Fig. 5-4), esophageal atresia, or bowel obstruction is suspected or confirmed. Exposed viscera should be covered with a sterile, warm, saline wrapping. Acute respiratory distress secondary to a tension pneumothorax or congenital chylothorax requires either an immediate thoracentesis or thoracotomy and placement of a chest tube. Hydration must be maintained with intravenous fluids such as a 10% dextrose solution at a rate of 60 to 100 ml/kg

Table 5-2. Neonatal problems requiring surgery

Cardiopulmonary systems
  Congenital heart disease
  Choanal atresia
  Intrinsic or extrinsic neck mass
  Tracheoesophageal fistula
  Pneumothorax (tension)
  Congenital chylothorax
  Lobar emphysema
  Cystic adenomatoid malformation
Gastrointestinal system
  Diaphragmatic hernia
  Intestinal atresia
  Malrotation
  Mid-gut volvulus
  Gastroschisis
  Omphalocele
  Meconium ileus
  Hirschsprung's disease
  Imperforate anus
  Duplication
  Meckel's diverticulum
Genitourinary system
  Exstrophy of the bladder
  Urinary tract obstruction
  Renal tumors
Central nervous system
  Depressed skull fracture
  Meningomyelocele
  Encephalocele
  Hydrocephalus
Others
  Sacrococcygeal teratoma
  Neuroblastoma

per day. Electrolytes are added to the intravenous solution if the infant is urinating.

PRETERM INFANT [29]
By definition, an infant who is delivered before 37 completed weeks' gestation is preterm. The word *premature* implies biologic behavior rather than time and is incorrect nomenclature when describing an infant's gestational age.

Preterm infants frequently are delivered in hospitals with only a level I

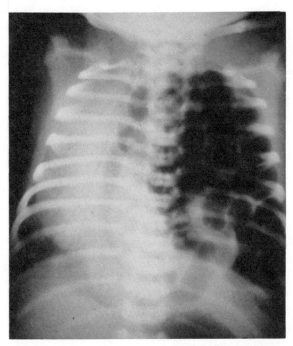

Fig. 5-4. Chest roentgenogram showing diaphragmatic hernia. Bowel in left pleural cavity and cardiac silhouette shifted to right should be noted.

nursery. In addition, preterm infants may be transferred to the level I nursery from level II and level III nurseries for convalescent care. Therefore, the level I nursery must be prepared to handle both routine and emergency situations involving preterm infants. Personnel in the level I nursery should easily identify the very low birth weight preterm infants who have respiratory distress and metabolic instability. These patients require transport to a critical care facility.

The key to the initial care of the sickly preterm infant is anticipation and preparedness. Resuscitation equipment must be appropriate and available. Smaller endotracheal tubes, ranging from 2.5 to 3.5 mm, sizes 0 and 1 laryngoscope blades, and a small mask should be available. A properly positioned umbilical artery or umbilical venous catheter or a peripheral intravenous setup should be available for administering medications and fluids. As previously emphasized, there is no indication for bicarbonate administration in the initial resuscitation of a newborn infant. Plasma expanders should be administered cautiously in the very small preterm infant because they may contribute to the occurrence and expansion of an intracranial hemorrhage if used overzealously. Attention to maintaining thermal stability throughout the period of resuscitation and stabilization is mandatory.

Metabolic disturbances, particularly hypoglycemia and hypocalcemia, must be identified and treated appropriately.

It is a challenge to identify preterm infants of 35 to 37 weeks' gestation who are not distressed and appear mature [39]. The telltale signs of their biologic immaturity are their sluggish feeding behavior and other behavioral aberrations and their need for thermal support. The obstetric history and clinical scoring techniques for evaluating an infant's gestational and maturational age should be applied. With experience, it will become apparent that all low birth weight infants (2500 gm or less) are not necessarily preterm and that all term infants do not necessarily weigh more than 2500 gm.

In general, the etiology of the preterm delivery is secondary to maternal diseases (preeclampsia or infection), placental problems (rupture of the fetal membranes or retroplacental hemorrhage), fetal abnormalities, inaccurate obstetric determination of gestational age, or finally, undetermined causes. In each case, a specific etiology for the preterm delivery should be sought because it clarifies the treatment plan for the newborn. It is of paramount importance to identify conditions that predispose the infant to sepsis. Examination of the placenta may provide clues for ascertaining an etiology of the preterm delivery.

Care of the "healthy" 35- to 37-week preterm (near-term) infant differs minimally from that described for the term infant but still offers special challenges. Vital signs should be checked every four hours rather than once a shift. Particular attention should be paid to temperature homeostasis. Incubator care should be initiated soon after birth and maintained or reinstituted if the core (rectal) temperature falls below 97.6°F or if the infant fails to grow despite adequate calorie intake. The incubator temperature is regulated according to standard guidelines shown in Appendix 7. The infant is weaned from the incubator when he maintains his body temperature without additional thermal support and continues his incremental growth at ambient temperatures. If the infant does not feed vigorously, sepsis should be excluded, but hypothermia alone may be the primary explanation. Most of the time a septic workup is negative. "Septiclike" behavior is typical for a cold infant in this age group.

It is the responsibility of level I nursery personnel to be attentive to the infant's fluid balance and alterations in body weight, the maintenance of normal blood glucose levels, and changes in serum bilirubin concentrations. Gavage feedings frequently are required and supplemental intravenous fluids are indicated until a consistent and satisfactory feeding pattern is established. Normal breast-feeding may be delayed because of the infant's sluggishness, but the mother should not be discouraged from breast-feeding. She should be instructed in the techniques of breast-pumping or manual expression to continue her milk flow until the infant nurses effectively. In the interim, expressed breast milk can be administered by intragastric tube feedings (gavage).

The near-term infant often is frustrating for the hospital staff because they expect the infant to feed and behave like a term infant. The parents often sense this frustration and, with their own frustration, become apprehensive. Once aware of this concern, the hospital staff can help the parents by explaining to them the peculiarities of the near-term infant. The parents should be supported and reassured that their infant's behavior is normal. Communication is important.

POSTTERM INFANTS [29, 48]
Approximately 10 percent of all pregnancies are postterm, exceeding 294 days or 42 weeks' gestation. Although the terms *postmature* and *postterm* frequently are used interchangeably, postterm is more precise because it is defined by age. *Dysmature* is another term used to describe the postterm infant, but this nomenclature also may be applied to the preterm and term infant who is scrawny and SGA and whose skin is desquamating and has poor turgor (Fig. 5-5A–C).

The etiology of the postterm delivery is poorly defined. If not "due to" miscalculated dates, postterm delivery may be associated with conditions that include anencephaly, sulfatase deficiency, and poor initiation of labor, especially in older mothers.

The postterm infant usually appears very alert. Approximately two out of three are overgrown. Thirty percent have evidence of significant placental insufficiency and subsequently have an increased morbidity manifested by intrauterine growth retardation, hypoglycemia, asphyxia, meconium aspiration, and the polycythemia-hyperviscosity syndrome.

MULTIPLE BIRTHS (TWINS) [2, 3, 4, 5]
The incidence of natural-occurring multiple births is estimated to be one in 80 pregnancies for twins, 80 squared (one in 64,000) for triplets, and 80 to the third power (one in 512,000) for quadruplets. Twins are the most frequent multiple births encountered in a level I nursery.

The incidence of monozygosity (identical twins) is similar throughout the world (3–3.5 per 1000 live births), while that for dizygosity (nonidentical or fraternal twins) varies with both ethnicity and geographic distribution. The chance of a woman having a second set of twins is 3 to 10 times greater than that of a woman who has never had twins.

Parents and relatives always ask if twins are identical [38]. Obviously, if they are different sexes they are not identical. Dichorionic same-sex twins are identical 20 percent of the time and fraternal 80 percent of the

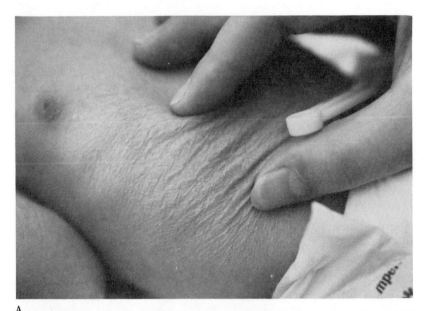

A

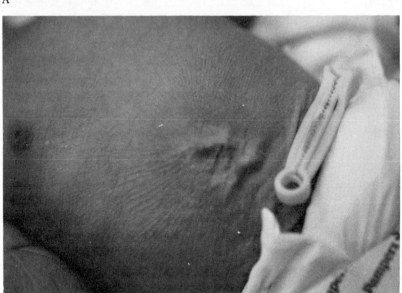

B

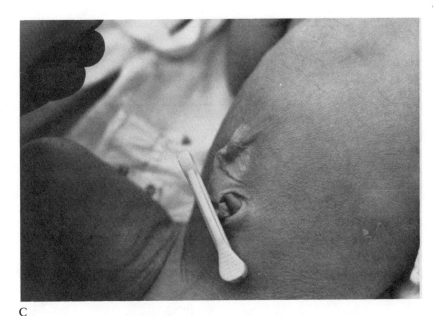

C

Fig. 5-5A, B, C. Tenting of the skin, indicating poor skin turgor, in a dysmature infant.

time. When there is a single chorion with two amniotic sacs, the twins are identical about two thirds of the time; a single amnion and chorion are always associated with identical twins (Fig. 5-6). If there is need for further determination of the zygosity of twins, sophisticated blood and HLA typing may be used.

There is an increased morbidity and mortality associated with twins. There is an increased chance of preterm delivery, cesarean sections, asphyxia, discordant growth, and twin-to-twin transfusion syndrome. Following delivery of the first twin there are changes in the intrauterine volume that consequently alter uteroplacental hemodynamics. Thus, it is the twin delivered second who is most apt to suffer asphyxia and require resuscitation. Other morbid conditions in twins also reflect their physical interrelationship and physiologic peculiarities in utero [24]. Cord entanglements and interlocking of fetal parts, either of which leads to a complicated delivery and asphyxia, are most likely to occur in monozygous twins with a monochorionic, monoamniotic placenta.

Twin-to-twin transfusion with disturbances in blood volume, hematocrit, and coagulation systems occurs only if the placenta is monochorionic, and then in only 15 percent of cases [37]. Although the vascular communication may be artery-to-artery or vein-to-vein, it is the arterio-venous com-

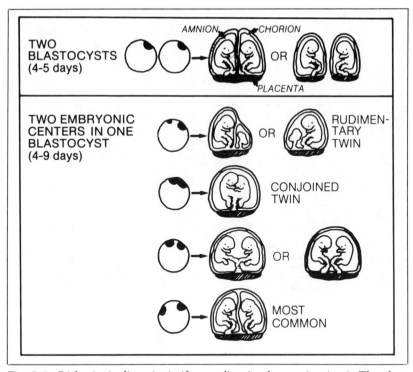

Fig. 5-6. Dichorionic-diamnionic (fraternal) twin placentation (top). The placentas may be either fused or separate. Monochorionic (identical) twin placentation is shown on bottom. Diamnionic-monochorionic is the most common. From D. W. Smith, C. Barlett, and L. M. Harrah: Monozygotic twinning and the Duhamel anomalad (imperforate anus to sirenomelia: A nonrandom association between two aberations in morphogenesis. In D. Bergsma and R. N. Schimke (eds.): *Cytogenetics, Environment and Malformation Syndromes.* New York: Alan R. Liss for The National Foundation—March of Dimes, BD : OAS 12(5) : 53–63, 1976, with permission of the copyright holder.

munication that usually results in the classical chronic twin-to-twin transfusion syndrome. In this syndrome, one twin is plethoric and hydropic while the other is pale and anemic. Clinically, the twin-to-twin transfusion diagnosis is confirmed by an elevated hematocrit in the recipient and a lower hematocrit in the donor, who is usually the smaller of the twins. The twin-to-twin transfusion also occurs acutely at the time of delivery and results in one pale and one plethoric twin. Initially the infants' hematocrit values are similar, but they may become discordant as the pale (hypovolemic) twin hemodilutes and the plethoric (hypervolemic) twin hemoconcentrates. An important diagnostic clue is the placenta, where the villous (maternal) surface is demarcated by pallor and plethora.

Another complication of monochorionic twins with a shared placental circulation is disseminated intravascular coagulation, which occurs in the living twin after the other twin dies in utero. As the dead twin macerates, tissue thromboplastins cross into the circulation of the surviving twin and produces the coagulopathy [35].

REFERENCES

1. Bada, H. S., Alojipan, L. C., and Andrews, B. F. Premature rupture of membranes and its effect on the newborn. *Pediatr. Clin. North Am.* 24 : 491, 1977.
2. Benirschke, K., and Driscoll, S. G. *The Pathology of the Human Placenta.* New York: Springer-Verlag, 1974.
3. Benirschke, K. Multiple births: Signal for scrutiny. *Hosp. Prac.* 1 : 25, 1966.
4. Benirschke, K., and Kim, C. K. Multiple pregnancy. *N. Engl. J. Med.* 288 : 1276, 1983.
5. Benirschke, K., and Kim, C. K. Multiple pregnancy. *N. Engl. J. Med.* 288 : 1329, 1983.
6. Benzing, G., et al. Simultaneous hypoglycemia and acute congestive heart failure. *Circulation* 40 : 209, 1969.
7. Berman, S. A., Balkany, T. J., and Simmons, M. A. Otitis media in infants less than 12 weeks of age: Differing bacteria among in-patients and out-patients. *J. Pediatr.* 93 : 453, 1978.
8. Black, V. D., and Lubchinco, L. O. Neonatal polycythemia and hyperviscosity. *Pediatr. Clin. North Am.* 29 : 1137, 1982.
9. Cornblath, M., and Schwartz, R. *Disorders of Carbohydrate Metabolism in Infancy* (2nd ed.) Philadelphia: Saunders, 1976.
10. Dincsoy, M. Y., et al. The role of postnatal age and magnesium on parathyroid hormones responses during "exchange" blood transfusion in the newborn period. *J. Pediatr.* 100 : 277, 1982.
11. Engle, W. A., Schreiner, R. L., and Baehner, R. L. Neonatal white blood cell disorders. *Semin. Perinatol.* 7 : 184, 1983.
12. Epstein, M. F., Nicholls, E., and Stubblefield, P. G. Neonatal hypoglycemia after beta-sympathomimetic tocolytic therapy. *J. Pediatr.* 94 : 449, 1979.
13. Galant, S. P. Development of host resistance in the fetus and newborn. *Perinatol. Neonatol.* Sept./Oct. 1980, p. 15.
14. Giacoia, G. P., and Wagner, N. R. Q-oTc interval and blood calcium levels in newborn infants. *Pediatrics* 61 : 877, 1978.
15. Gosselin, O. Contribution à L'Etude de L'Invasion des organismes Maternel et Foetal par les Microbes des voies Genitales Inferieures au Cours du Travail. Valliant-Carmareve, S. A. Liege, 1945. As mentioned in M. E. Avery, B. D. Fletcher, and R. G. Williams. *The Lung and Its Disorders in the Newborn Infant* (4th ed.). Philadelphia: Saunders, 1981.
16. Green, K. W., et al. The effects of maternally administered magnesium sulfate on the neonate. *Am. J. Obstet. Gynecol.* 146 : 29, 1983.
17. Gutberlet, R. L., and Cornblath, M. Neonatal hypoglycemia revisited, 1975. *Pediatrics* 58 : 10, 1976.
18. Hall, R. T., and Visser, V. E. Urine culture in the evaluation of suspected neonatal sepsis. *J. Pediatr.* 94 : 635, 1979.

19. Hall, R. T., and Visser, V. E. Lumbar puncture in the evaluation of suspected neonatal sepsis. *J. Pediatr.* 96 : 1063, 1980.
20. Handzel, Z. T., et al. Immune competence of newborn lymphocytes. *Pediatrics* 65 : 491, 1980.
21. Hendren, W. H. III, and Kim, S. H. Abdominal surgical emergencies of the newborn. *Surg. Clin. North Am.* 54 : 489, 1974.
22. Kanto, W. P. Jr., et al. ABO hemolytic disease: A comparative study of clinical severity and delayed anemia. *Pediatrics* 62 : 365, 1978.
23. Kaufman, R. E., Olansky, D. C., and Wiesner, P. J. The FTA-ABS (IgM) test for neonatal congenital syphilis: A critical review. *J. Am. Vener. Dis. Assoc.* 1 : 79. 1976.
24. Koffler, H., et al. Persistent cloaca with absent penis and anal atresia in one of identical twins. *J. Pediatr.* 93 : 821, 1978.
25. Kosloske, A. M. Birth defects causing neonatal surgical emergencies. *Continuing Ed. Fam. Phys.* 6 : 22, 1977.
26. Kramer, L. I. Advancement of dermal icterus in the jaundiced newborn. *Am. J. Dis. Child.* 118 : 454, 1969.
27. Lilien, D. L., Grajiver, L. A., and Pildes, R. S. Treatment of neonatal hypoglycemia with continuous intravenous glucose infusion. *J. Pediatr.* 91 : 779, 1977.
28. Lucey, J. F. Bilirubin and brain damage — a real mess. *Pediatrics* 69 : 381, 1982.
29. Lubchenco, L. O. *The High Risk Infant.* Philadelphia: Saunders, 1976.
30. Maisels, M. J. Jaundice in the newborn. *Pediatr. Rev.* 3 : 305, 1982.
31. Maisels, M. J., and Gifford, K. Neonatal jaundice in full term infants. *Am. J. Dis. Child.* 137 : 561, 1983.
32. McDonagh, A. F. Phototherapy: A new twist to bilirubin. *J. Pediatrics* 99 : 909, 1981.
33. McGuinness, G. A., et al. Effects of magnesium sulfate treatment on perinatal calcium metabolism. II. Neonatal responses. *Obstet. Gynecol.* 56 : 595, 1980.
34. Miller, M. E. Host defenses in the human neonate. *Pediatr. Clin. North Am.* 24 : 413, 1971.
35. Moore, C. M., McAdams, A. J., and Sutherland, J. Intrauterine disseminated intravascular coagulation: A syndrome of multiple pregnancy with a dead twin fetus. *J. Pediatr.* 74 : 523, 1969.
36. Odell, G. B. *Neonatal Hyperbilirubinemia.* New York: Grune & Stratton, 1980.
37. Oski, F. A., and Naiman, J. L. *Hematologic Problems in the Newborn.* Philadelphia: Saunders, 1982.
38. Paluszny, M. Queries that mothers of twins put to their doctors. *Clin. Pediatr. (Phila.)* 14 : 624, 1975.
39. Paneth, N., et al. Medical care and preterm infants of normal weight. *Pediatrics* 77 : 158, 1986.
40. Parsons, J. M., Miscall, B. G., and McSherry, C. K. Appendicitis in the newborn infant. *Surgery* 67 : 841, 1970.
41. Philip, A. G. S. *Neonatal Sepsis and Meningitis.* Boston: Hall, 1985.
42. Poland, R. L. Breast milk jaundice. *J. Pediatr.* 99 : 86, 1981.

43. Remington, J. S., and Klein, J. O. *Infectious Diseases of the Fetus and Newborn Infant* (2nd ed.). Philadelphia: Saunders, 1983.
44. Ricketts, R. R. Workup of neonatal intestinal obstruction. *Am. Surg.* 50 : 517, 1984.
45. Rowe, M. S., and Marchildon, M. B. Physiologic considerations in the newborn surgical patient. *Surg. Clin. North Am.* 56 : 245, 1976.
46. Schreiner, R. L., and Glick, M. R. Interlaboratory bilirubin variability. *Pediatrics* 69 : 277, 1982.
47. Siegel, I., and Gleicher, N. The development of the fetal immune system. *Mt. Sinai J. Med. (NY)* 47 : 474, 1980.
48. Steer, P. J. Postmaturity—Much ado about nothing? *Br. J. Obstet. Gynaecol.* 93 : 105, 1986.
49. Tsang, R. C., et al. Neonatal parathyroid function: Role of gestational age and postnatal age. *J. Pediatr.* 83 : 728, 1973.
50. Watchko, J. F., and Oski, F. A. Bilirubin 20 mg/dl = vigintiphobia. *Pediatrics* 71 : 660, 1983.
51. White, P. Diabetes mellitus in pregnancy. *Clin. Perinatol.* 1 : 331, 1974.
52. Wu, P. Y. K. Phototherapy update. *Perinatol. Neonatol.* Sept./Oct. 1981, p. 45.
53. Wu, P. Y. K. Phototherapy. *Perinatol. Neonatol.* March/April 1982.

6. Beyond the First 24 Hours

In the first 24 hours, many physiologic adjustments are made that ensure the infant's immediate survival. Now the infant's activities are directed toward growth and development. The transition period is over and changes in the infant's state become more closely linked to the cycle of sleeping and feeding with short periods of waking and crying. Periods of alertness are short but captivating to parents and caretakers.

Normal variations in infant behavior must be understood because subtle changes are the earliest signs of catastrophic illness. Unfortunately, many years of experience are required to gain confidence in being able to distinguish subtle clues of disease from the wide range of normal neonatal behavior. Any suspicious finding should never be dismissed as "normal" and then ignored. Continued observation and serial evaluations are the only techniques to ensure that the infant is, in fact, normal.

It is most important that physicians and nurses respect each other's experiences and observations. A nurse's comment that "the baby just doesn't look right" should raise the suspicion that a potential problem may be developing. The same holds true for parents' statements and concerns about their child.

As in the preceding chapters, this chapter reviews both normal and abnormal situations involving each body system.

GENERAL ASSESSMENT
Changes in the infant's condition become apparent if the vital signs are checked and recorded at least once during each nursing shift. The infant's state of well-being generally is reflected in feeding and sleeping. On the average, the normal infant sleeps approximately 3 to 3½ hours after each feeding. Shorter sleeping periods and fussiness may be the first sign of a feeding problem or major systemic illness such as sepsis. If the infant is continually fussy, the vital signs should be checked and the infant reexamined. If all findings are normal, the infant may be hungry and should be offered additional formula or allowed more time on the breast. Occasionally a pacifier is helpful if the infant's urge to suck is strong. If continued irritability and shortened sleep cycles persist, drug withdrawal should be considered.

In general, most infants lose weight during the first three days after birth. If the loss exceeds 7 percent, an explanation should be actively sought. Variations in weight measurement are minimized if the infant is weighed on the same scale at the same time each day. Feeding difficulties with poor weight gain or excessive weight loss, as well as alterations in behavior (persistent lethargy or fussiness) and changes in skin color (pallor or cyanosis), usually are the progenitors of serious illness. They should not be ignored.

Once feedings are established, the composition of the feces will change. Normal black meconium will be replaced by poorly formed copious greenish mucous (transitional) stools, and finally by yellow, seedy feces. Meconium should not be present after four days. Meconium stools may be differentiated from stools with melena or occult blood using a guaiac test.

HEAD

Bruises, abrasions, or puncture wounds resulting from the delivery or insertion of fetal monitoring devices should be dry and progressing toward complete healing. Scalp edema (caput succedaneum) should be resolved by the second 24 hours. Small cephalhematomas, which often are masked by a caput, now become more apparent as the caput resolves. The natural history of cephalhematomas is one of spontaneous resorption, the time required being related inversely to the size of the hemorrhage. Large hemorrhages gradually liquify and reabsorb. A small hematoma should not enlarge unless coagulation disturbances or infection result in continued bleeding. Scalp abscesses with generalized sepsis may occur following needle aspiration of cephalhematomas. Thus, it is recommended that cephalhematomas should never be aspirated.

Orange-peel skin overlying a scalp swelling may be due to subcutaneous fat necrosis secondary to trauma (Fig. 6-1). The lesion may heal without progressing or may point and drain. The lesion often is mistaken for a scalp abscess because the draining liquified fat resembles pus. Simple cleansing and topical antibiotics are the only treatment needed. Subcutaneous fat necrosis may occur at other sites of skin trauma.

Linear skull fractures may be present in as many as 25 percent of cephalhematomas [4]. Unless there are concomitant neurologic symptoms or clinical evidence of a depressed skull fracture, it is not necessary to obtain roentgenograms. Calcification may be palpable along the rim of the resorbing hemorrhage after several days. After several weeks, large cephalhematomas usually have a very marked circular ridge of ectopic calcification with an apparent central depression. The calcification is dense enough to be observed on a roentgenogram. An examiner who is unfamiliar with resorbing cephalhematomas may think that a depressed skull fracture is present. A depressed skull fracture [10] is distinguished easily from an old cephalhematoma by the fact that the hematoma was present

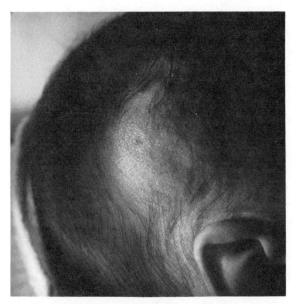

Fig. 6-1. Subcutaneous fat necrosis of scalp in early stages. Swelling and characteristic orange-peel skin should be noted.

shortly after birth, and the infant is otherwise healthy. Furthermore, depressed skull fractures are rare (1 per 4000 live births); cephalhematomas are not.

The presence of widespread sutures or a bulging anterior fontanelle requires immediate evaluation to exclude increased intracranial pressure. The infant's history should be reviewed for vomiting, irritability, lethargy, feeding intolerance, and changes in the vital signs, because trauma, drug effects, septicemia, and meningitis are included in the differential diagnosis. A physical examination will determine if there are signs of infection or previously unrecognized head trauma. The head circumference should be remeasured to determine if an increase has occurred since birth. Meningitis is excluded by performing a lumbar puncture. A cranial ultrasound exam, computed tomography, or a magnetic resonance imaging scan can be performed to discern anatomical evidence of pathology such as hemorrhage, hydrocephalus, hydranencephaly, or porencephaly. On occasion, the infant will not be sick, a cause for the bulging fontanelle will not be found, and the fullness will dissipate spontaneously. Since this can be appreciated only in retrospect and occurs infrequently, an aggressive evaluation is recommended, even if the infant appears healthy.

EYES

Swelling of the eyelids and any exudate produced by eye prophylaxis wane after 24 hours and are gone by 72 hours. Increasing periorbital inflammation with swelling, redness, and exudation is an important sign of bacterial conjunctivitis [7, 9]. Bacterial conjunctivitis commonly is caused by *Neisseria gonorrhoeae, Staphylococcus aureus,* and *Chlamydia trachomatis.* An etiologic agent should be sought in all cases by collecting the exudate for culture and performing a Gram's stain. Chlamydial infections may be verified by obtaining scrapings from the palpebral conjunctivae. The specimen may be stained with Giemsa agent to identify the typical intranuclear inclusion body, or tested with fluorescent antibody to identify chlamydial elementary bodies. As a very general guideline, conjunctivitis on the first day usually is of chemical origin; on days two to three it is secondary to gonococcal disease; on days three to five it is secondary to staphylococcal disease; and on days seven to ten it is secondary to chlamydial disease.

Excessive tearing and exudation from either or both eyes during the latter portion of the first week suggest tear duct obstruction [8]. Treatment consists of warm soaks, frequent massages of the tear duct sac, which is below the inner canthus, and the topical instillation of antibiotic ophthalmic ointments.

EARS

The infant's hearing may be checked just before discharge with either a clinical technique or available quantitative techniques [11, 12, 13] (see Chapter 3).

NOSE

Nasal congestion or stuffiness is recognized easily because the infant is fussy and refuses to feed, and the nasal noises are audible. Most commonly the congestion is unilateral and often is associated with a deformation of one side of the nose. If breast-feeding, the infant may have difficulty during nursing when the open nostril is compressed against the breast. The deformed nostril will not provide an adequate airway and the infant develops air hunger. The problem is solved by readjusting the infant's position or holding the breast away from the open nostril. Deformation of the nostril will resolve spontaneously over time.

Other causes of congestion include mucous membrane swelling from repetitive suctioning of the nose, congenital syphilis, acute viral infection, and, in the past, prenatal exposure to reserpine. Except for congenital syphilis, which requires penicillin therapy, there is little to do for the other conditions. Normal saline nose drops and bulb suctioning may be helpful if the secretions are thick and tenacious. If they are discolored or exudative, a specimen for culture, smear, and Gram's stain should be obtained and appropriate antibiotics administered.

Nosebleeds are rare but may occur in infants who fail to receive vitamin K prophylaxis.

MOUTH

Monilial plaques (thrush) resemble residual milk deposits on the tongue or buccal mucosa because they both appear as white patches. Scraping the lesion with a tongue blade removes the milk but not the yeast plaque. The following aphorism helps to differentiate the two: "Yeast is on the cheeks, milk is on the tongue." A definitive diagnosis of thrush is reached when candidal mycelia are identified on a wet mount laboratory preparation, using tissue scrapings mixed with 20% potassium hydroxide solution. Candida infections are treated with both the topical application of nystatin oral suspension applied directly to the mouth lesions and the oral administration of 1 ml of nystatin four times daily for a week.

NECK

Fibrotic shortening of the sternocleidomastoid muscle results from a hemorrhage within the muscle belly at the time of birth. The lesion is suspected when the infant persistently holds his head to one side. A circumscribed, small, 1- to 3-cm swelling may be felt within the midportion of the muscle on the contralateral side. The acquired torticollis should be stretched by gently turning and extending the head from side to side throughout its entire range of motion.

CHEST

Breast tissue of both male and female infants may hypertrophy during the first postnatal week and remain enlarged well into the first year [2, 6] (Fig. 6-2). Squeezing the prominent breast tissue should be avoided because it often leads to abscess formation.

Signs or symptoms referable to the chest are abnormal if they persist beyond the first hours following birth or recur during the remainder of the infant's hospitalization. The onset and persistence of tachypnea, retractions, cyanosis, or heart murmur usually signify major underlying disease. The infant should be examined carefully to evaluate cardiac and pulmonary functions and to determine if there are signs of infection. A complete blood count, chest roentgenogram, electrocardiogram, check of blood gases, and appropriate cultures should be obtained if physical findings warrant.

After the first 24 hours, heart murmurs accompanied by cyanosis or shock are harbingers of either sepsis or a ductus arteriosus-dependent car-

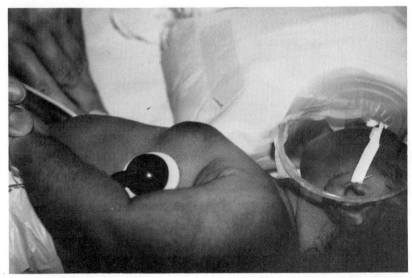

Fig. 6-2. Breast hypertrophy.

diac anomaly such as hypoplastic left heart, transposition of the great vessels without a septal defect, coarctation of the aorta, and pulmonary atresia. If a ductus arteriosus-dependent lesion is suspected, prostaglandin E-1
may be lifesaving. It is administered in a dose of 0.05 to 0.1 mg/kg. Consultation with and possible referral to a level III center is necessary to diagnose complex congenital heart disease and develop a treatment plan. Since
bacterial sepsis also mimics the clinical picture just described, it is prudent
to initiate antibiotics after cultures have been obtained.

ABDOMEN
The stump of the umbilical cord should dry and fall off by the end of the
second week [1, 14]. The presence of serosanguineous and sometimes
foul drainage is a sign of an infection or of an umbilical granuloma. The
latter is hypertrophic granulation tissue that is located at the base of the
stump. Granulomas are treated by cauterization with silver nitrate sticks.
A single treatment may suffice, but several treatments over three to four
weeks usually are required. Any delayed healing or fetid odor from the
umbilicus should raise the suspicion of underlying infection. Omphalitis
is of major concern because the infection may extend into the fascial
planes of the anterior abdominal wall. Fasciitis is characterized by pro-
gressive erythema and induration and requires aggressive treatment with
intravenous antibiotics and emergency surgical intervention. Staphylo-

cocci are the most common offending organisms, but gram-negative organisms also may be responsible. The treatment of this serious infection includes wide-spectrum antibiotic coverage, including penicillinase-resistant antimicrobials. Death usually ensues if the fasciitis is not identified early and treated aggressively.

Abdominal distention that appears between days two and four may be a sign of necrotizing enterocolitis, sepsis, or a bowel obstruction involving the jejunum, ileum, or colon. The nursing notes should be reviewed for information about the infant's behavior, feeding patterns, and the presence of emesis or diarrhea. Bowel obstructions are accompanied by abdominal distention and feeding problems. Systemic symptoms are not prominent unless the bowel circulation is compromised, such as with a volvulus or when infarction has occurred. Abdominal distention should be evaluated with a general physical examination and additional assessment as depicted in Fig. 4-12. Abdominal distention also should raise the question of the passage of meconium. If no meconium has been passed, a meconium plug may be present and can be removed with gentle rectal stimulation using a thermometer or a 3- to 5-ml saline enema.

Blood in the stool is always of concern. If the blood is bright red (hematochezia), it may be the result of rapid transit of swallowed blood, an infection, a rectal fissure, or tears in the perianal skin. The Apt test (see Appendix 20) differentiates fresh red blood of infant origin from maternal blood swallowed during delivery. If the infant is hemorrhaging, the vital signs and hematocrit should be followed closely. The nursing notes should be checked to determine if vitamin K was administered. The presence of a needle puncture mark on the anterior thigh of one leg is additional evidence that intramuscular vitamin K was administered.

Bleeding from the stomach is identified by passing a nasogastric tube. Bleeding from the perianal skin is identified by careful inspection of the area for tears and abrasions. Proctoscopy, using a clear glass test tube and the bright light of an otoscope, may demonstrate a rectal fissure. Special roentgenographic studies of the bowel usually are not helpful in establishing the site of hemorrhage but may be considered if additional signs of bowel pathology are present. Occult bleeding, detected by the guaiac test, may be associated with early necrotizing enterocolitis or other low-grade hemorrhages. Abdominal roentgenograms exclude necrotizing enterocolitis if pneumatosis intestinalis is absent.

In all cases of gastrointestinal hemorrhage the vital signs and peripheral hematocrit should be followed serially. Cultures may be necessary. Persistent bleeding and a drop in the hematocrit require consultation and possible transfer of the infant to a special care center.

GENITOURINARY SYSTEM

The major problems involving the genitourinary system should have been detected in the first 24 hours. The circumcised penis may be reddened, but it should not be swollen or discolored. If a protective dressing has been applied, it may be removed. Recurring urinary tract infections are the first indication of a congenital anomaly of the urinary tract.

SKELETON

It is not infrequent that a fractured clavicle [5] is noted for the first time during a discharge examination on day two or three. A fracture, if present, presents with superficial swelling and the loss of the normal distinct upper edge of the clavicle. Crepitus often is not present. The infant usually cries when the fractured site is palpated.

When an infant fails to move an extremity or cries loudly when it is moved passively, an underlying fracture or osteomyelitis may be present. The term *pseudoparalysis* applies to the guarding of a painful extremity. The classical signs of osteomyelitis, such as swelling and induration, usually are not present in the newborn during the acute phase. Osteomyelitis is an infection associated with or preceded by septicemia. It is diagnosed with cultures and is treated with appropriate antibiotics. Consultation with an orthopedic surgeon should be sought. Traumatic injury to the long bones should be diagnosed with appropriate roentgenograms.

NERVOUS SYSTEM

Most infants sleep for long intervals between feedings. Occasionally, an infant's transition to normal waking and sleeping patterns is delayed beyond the first 24 hours. Often there is no explanation. The nursing staff has no difficulty recognizing the infant who is irritable and jittery and who awakens after short intervals of sleep. These symptoms may be due to feeding problems, hypoglycemia, hypocalcemia, hypomagnesemia, infections, neonatal seizures, intracranial pathology, or drug withdrawal.

Drug withdrawal should be suspected in infants whose sleep patterns are disturbed and who remain jittery and develop symptoms of autonomic dysfunction, such as sweating, fever, diarrhea, tachypnea, and tachycardia [3]. Table 6-1 shows a clinical technique for quantitating these symptoms. An average score of 8 or above on three consecutive assessments indicates the need for therapy. Toxicologic studies of the infant's urine assist in verifying the diagnosis of drug exposure. When drug withdrawal is suspected or proven, child protective agencies must be notified to determine the suitability of the home environment.

SKIN

Dryness and peeling of the skin, occasionally to the point of cracking and weeping, becomes more pronounced after the initial 24 hours, particularly in infants whose protective coat of vernix was diminished or lost before birth, subjecting the infant to the macerating effects of amniotic fluid. These infants should be kept clean and warm. A hydrophilic ointment may be applied to the skin, but it is not necessary. Antibiotics also are unnecessary. Unless there are other complications, healing is spontaneous and usually complete within seven to 10 days. Sometimes horizontal postinflammatory stripes of pigmentation appear at the edges of large desquamating plaques and persist for many weeks.

Toxic erythema, or "flea-bite" dermatitis, is a papular erythematous eruption occurring in a nonspecific distribution (Fig. 6-3). Its etiology is unknown. Toxic erythema appears randomly in a nursery population. It frequently occurs in clusters of infants but rarely is observed in premature infants. Sometimes the papules progress to form pustular lesions whose contents show an abundance of eosinophils. Despite the presence of eosinophils, toxic erythema is not a preallergic or allergic condition. A flare reaction or dermatographia often appears where the skin is touched or handled, suggesting that the histamine content of the skin is increased in toxic erythema.

Contact dermatitis appears on the cheek and neck as intense erythema and superficial denudation, secondary to drooling of saliva and milk and chafing from soiled linens.

Fig. 6-3. Toxic erythema. Arrows point to papules and surrounding erythema.

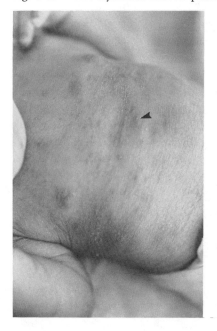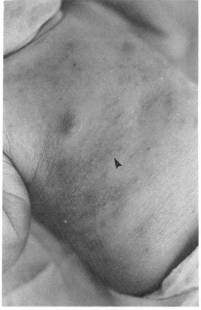

Table 6-1. Abstinence scoring technique for assessing withdrawal symptomatology

	Signs and symptoms	Score	A.M.	P.M.	Comments
Central nervous system disturbances	Excessive high-pitched cry	2			
	Continuous high-pitched cry	3			Daily weight
	Sleeps <1 hour after feeding	3			
	Sleeps <2 hours after feeding	2			
	Sleeps <3 hours after feeding	1			
	Hyperactive moro reflex	2			
	Markedly hyperactive moro reflex	3			
	Mild tremors disturbed	1			
	Moderate–severe tremors disturbed	2			
	Mild tremors undisturbed	3			
	Moderate–severe tremors undisturbed	4			
	Increased muscle tone	2			
	Excoriation (specify area: _____)	1			
	Myoclonic jerks	3			
	Generalized convulsions	5			

Sweating	1			
Fever <101 (99–100.8°F/37.2–38.2°C)	1			
Fever >101 (38.4°C and higher)	2			
Frequent yawning (3>3–4 times/interval)	1			
Mottling	1			
Nasal stuffiness	2			
Sneezing (>3–4 times/interval)	1			
Nasal flaring	2			
Respiratory rate >60/min.	1			
Respiratory rate >60/min. with retractions	2			
Excessive sucking	1			
Poor feeding	2			
Regurgitation	2			
Projectile vomiting	3			
Loose stools	2			
Watery stools	3			
Total score:				
Initials of scorer				

Metabolic/vasomotor/respiratory disturbances

Gastrointestinal disturbances

Source: L. P. Finnegan. Neonatal Abstinence. In Nelson, N. M. (ed.), *Current Therapy in Neonatal-Perinatal Medicine 1985–1986.* P. 265. Toronto: B.C. Decker, 1985. With permission.

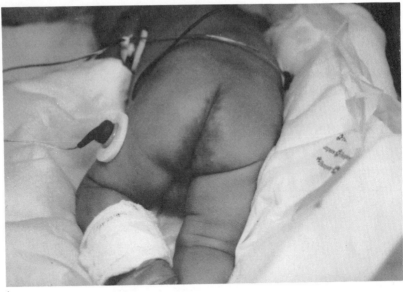

A

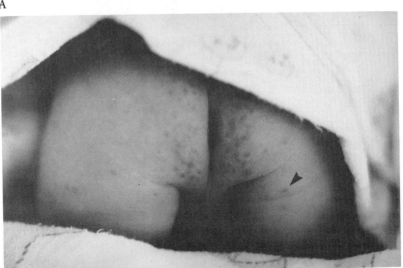

B

Fig. 6-4. Monilial dermatitis. A. Confluent intensely colored perianal rash. B. Satellite lesions should be noted (arrow). An intensely red color and the satellite lesions are characteristic of monilial cutaneous infections.

Punctate or confluent bright red papules involving the perineum and buttocks usually is secondary to a monilial infection (Fig. 6-4). Monilial diaper dermatitis is treated with topically applied nystatin ointment and nystatin oral suspension (1 ml by mouth four times daily for seven days).

Jaundice frequently becomes apparent after the first 24 hours. Bilirubin metabolism and problems are discussed more thoroughly in Chapter 5.

REFERENCES

1. Abramson, J. S., et al. Recurrent infections and delayed separation of the umbilical cord in an infant with abnormal phagocytic cell locomotion and oxidative response during particle phagocytosis. *J. Pediatr.* 99 : 817, 1981.
2. Berkowitz, C. D., and Inkelis, S. H. Bloody nipple discharge in infancy. *J. Pediatr.* 102 : 755, 1983.
3. Finnegan, L. P. Neonatal Abstinence. In N. M. Nelson (ed.), *Current Therapy in Neonatal-Perinatal Medicine 1985–1986.* St. Louis: Mosby, 1985.
4. Kendall, N., and Woloshin, H. Cephalhematoma associated with fracture of the skull. *J. Pediatr.* 41 : 125, 1952.
5. Levine, M. G., et al. Birth trauma: Incidence and predisposing factors. *Obstet. Gynecol.* 63 : 792, 1984.
6. McKiernan, J. F., and Hull, D. Breast development in the newborn. *Arch. Dis. Child.* 56 : 525, 1981.
7. Moore, R. A., and Schmitt, B. D. Conjunctivitis in children. *Clin. Pediatr. (Phila.)* 18 : 26, 1979.
8. Nelson, L. B., Calhoun, J. H., and Menduke, H. Medical management of congenital nasolacrimal duct obstruction. *Pediatrics* 76 : 172, 1985.
9. Rowe, D. S., et al. Purulent ocular discharge in neonates: Significance of *Chlamydia trachomatis. Pediatrics* 63 : 628, 1979.
10. Saunders, B. S., et al. Depressed skull fracture in the neonate. *J. Neurosurg.* 50 : 512, 1979.
11. Shannon, D. A., et al. Hearing screening of high-risk newborns with brainstem auditory evoked potentials: A follow-up study. *Pediatrics* 73 : 22, 1984.
12. Simmons, F. B., McFarland, W. H., and Jones, F. R. An automated hearing screening technique for newborns. *Acta Otolaryngol. (Stockh.)* 87 : 1, 1979.
13. Stockard, J. E., Stockard, J. J., and Coen, R. W. Auditory brainstem response variability in infants. *Ear Hear.* 4 : 11, 1983.
14. Wilson, C. B., et al. When is umbilical cord separation delayed? *J. Pediatr.* 107 : 292, 1985.

7. Nutrition

The gastrointestinal tract is sufficiently mature at term to meet the nutritional requirements of the newborn infant [8, 11] (Table 7-1). While the fetus passively depends on the transfer of nutrients from the mother, the newborn infant actively pursues his nutritional needs by crying, rooting, and sucking. Swallowing begins at approximately 16 to 17 weeks' gestation, but it is not coordinated with sucking until the thirty-second week. The suck-swallow mechanism is completely mature by 38 weeks. Intestinal peristalsis occurs in the fetus, but defecation does not occur in utero unless the fetus incurs marked distress. The gastrocolic reflex is present by term and results in colonic emptying when the stomach is filled. The digestive processes involved in carbohydrate, protein, and fat metabolism develop along a variable timetable and mature by 38 weeks (Table 7-2).

FIRST FEEDING

In the past, initial feedings were delayed for 12 to 24 hours after birth because of the concern that "birth shock" would predispose the infant to vomiting and aspiration. However, the healthy newborn tolerates feeding during the transition period (see Chapter 2), and early feedings may be necessary and beneficial. The mother who plans to breast-feed her infant can begin nursing in the delivery room if the infant is healthy and vigorous. Infants who are to be bottle-fed usually receive their first feeding within four to six hours after birth.

The object of the first feeding is to determine that the upper gastrointestinal tract is patent and that the suck-swallow mechanism is coordinated. Feedings may have to be delayed or prohibited if polyhydramnios is noted at delivery or if a cleft palate, respiratory distress, cyanosis, or abdominal distention are present. In many nurseries the first feeding consists of a 5% glucose solution because it is assumed that it will be consumed more eagerly than water, and, if aspirated, will be less injurious to the lungs than milk. Sterile water is a safer first feeding [13].

At the time of admission to the nursery, infants frequently gag and vomit either clear mucus or mucus mixed with blood. This behavior may be part of the normal transition (see Table 2-1), or it may be a sign of an esophageal atresia, gastrointestinal obstruction, or hemorrhage. In these latter cases a tube with a radiopaque line should be passed and its presence in the stomach should be determined by placing a stethoscope over the stomach and simultaneously injecting 2 or 3 ccs of air into the tube. If the tube is in the stomach, the injected air will be audible with the stethoscope. The placement of the tube may be confirmed with an A-P roentgenogram of the chest and abdomen.

Table 7-1. Development of the gastrointestinal tract in the human — maturation

Developmental markers		Weeks' gestation
Anatomic		
Esophagus	Superficial glands develop	20
	Squamous cells appear	28
Stomach	Gastric glands form	14
	Pylorus and fundus defined	14
Pancreas	Differentiation of endocrine and exocrine tissue	14
Liver	Lobules form	11
Small intestine	Crypt and villi develop	14
	Lymph nodes appear	14
Colon	Diameter increases	20
	Villi disappear	20
Functional		
Sucking and swallowing	Mouthing only	28
	Immature suck-swallow	33 to 36
Stomach	Gastric motility and secretion	20
Pancreas	Zymogen granules	20
Liver	Bile metabolism	11
	Bile secretion	22
Small intestine	Active transport of amino acids	14
		18
	Glucose transport	24
	Fatty acids absorption	
Enzymes	Alpha glucosidases	10
	Dipeptidases	10
	Lactase	10
	Enterokinase	26

Source: Adapted from E. Lebenthal, P. C. Lee, and L. A. Heitlinger. Impact of development of the gastrointestinal tract on infant feeding. *J. Pediatr.* 102 : 1, 1983. With permission.

FEEDING REQUIREMENTS

The number of calories needed to promote growth and meet other metabolic demands is approximately 120 cal/kg per day or 50 cal/lb per day. These calories are provided by approximately 180 ml/kg per day or 2½ oz/lb per day of 20 cal/oz formula. This volume of milk intake is usually not achieved until the end of the first week. Eventually, the infant's pattern will be to consume 3 oz every three hours or 4 oz every four hours.

The infant who is breast-fed receives 7 percent of the total calories [7, 12] from protein, 37 percent from carbohydrates, and 55 percent from fat. The caloric distribution in proprietary formulas overall is 9 percent, 42 percent, and 48 percent, respectively. Cow's milk is 22 percent, 29

Table 7-2. Development of the gastrointestinal tract in the human — digestion

Factors	First detectable (wk gestation)
Protein	
H+	At birth
Pepsin	16
Trypsinogen	20
Chymotrypsinogen	20
Procarboxypeptidase	20
Enterokinase	26
Peptidases (brush border and cytosol)	< 15
Amino acid transport	?
Macromolecular absorption	?
Fat	
Lingual lipase	30
Pancreatic lipase	20
Pancreatic colipase	?
Bile acids	22
Medium-chain triglyceride uptake	?
Long-chain triglyceride uptake	?
Carbohydrate	
Alpha amylases	
Pancreatic	22
Salivary	16
Lactase	10
Sucrase-isomaltase	10
Glucoamylase	10
Monosaccharide absorption	11 to 19

Source: Adapted from E. Lebenthal, P. C. Lee, and L. A. Heitlinger. Impact of development of the gastrointestinal tract on infant feeding. *J. Pediatr.* 102 : 1, 1983. With permission.

percent, and 50 percent, respectively. The composition of human breast milk is compared with other milk sources in Table 7-3.

BREAST-FEEDING [1, 3, 4, 10, 15]
Total nutritional support of the term infant from birth to six months can be achieved through breast-feeding. Success in breast-feeding requires an informed, motivated mother and family support. The decision to breast-feed an infant should be made before delivery so the expectant mother can prepare herself psychologically and physically for lactation. A major influencing factor is the family's belief that breast-feeding is best for their infant's nutrition.

The physiology of lactation during gestation and postpartum is represented in Fig. 7-1. Lactation involves three interrelated steps: mammogenesis (mammary growth), lactogenesis (initial milk secretion), and ga-

Table 7-3. Comparison of the content of human milk and selected formulas

Formula	Manufacturer	kcal/ml	Protein (%)	Fat (%)	CHO (%)	Protein source	Fat source	CHO source	Protein (gm)	Fat (gm)	CHO (gm)
								Nutrients per 100 ml			
Mature human milk	—	0.71	7	51	42	Whey/casein (80:20)	Butterfat	Lactose, glycoproteins	1.2	3.8	7.0
Cow's milk	—	0.70	20	51	29	Whey/casein (18:82)	Butterfat	Lactose	3.5	3.7	4.9
Goat's milk	—	0.67	14	53	28	—	Butterfat	Lactose	3.2	4.0	4.6
Evaporated milk	—	0.67	16	38	46	Whey/casein (18:82)	Butterfat	Lactose	2.9	3.3	8.8
Enfamil	Mead Johnson	0.67	9	50	41	Reduced mineral whey, nonfat milk	Soy, coconut	Lactose	1.5	3.8	6.9
Similac	Ross	0.68	9	48	43	Nonfat milk	Coconut, soy	Lactose	1.5	3.6	7.2
Similac with whey	Ross	0.68	9	48	43	Nonfat milk, whey	Soy, coconut	Lactose	1.5	3.6	7.2
SMA Infant Formula	Wyeth	0.67	9	48	43	Nonfat milk, demineralized whey solids	Coconut, soy, safflower, oleo	Lactose	1.5	3.6	7.2

Vitamins per 100 ml

Formula	Manufacturer	A (IU)	D (IU)	E (IU)	K (µg)	C (mg)	Folic acid (µg)	B₁ (µg)	B₂ (µg)	B₆ (µg)	B₁₂ (µg)	Niacin (mg)	Choline (mg)	Biotin (µg)	Panto-thenic acid (µg)
Mature human milk		190	2.2	0.20	1.5	4.3	0.5	16	36	10	0.03	1.47	—	—	200
Cow's milk		103	1.4	0.04	6.0	1.1	5.5	44	175	—	0.04	0.94	—	—	350
Goat's milk		208	2.4	—	1.2	1.5	0.6	40	184	70	0.19	—	—	—	340
Evaporated milk		185	4.0	0.01	—	0.5	5.5	28	190	37	—	0.10	—	—	350
Enfamil	Mead Johnson	210	42.0	2.10	5.8	5.5	10.6	53	110	42	0.16	0.85	10.6	1.58	320
Similac	Ross	200	40.0	2.00	5.5	5.5	10.0	65	100	40	0.15	0.70	—	1.00	300
Similac with whey	Ross	200	48.0	2.00	5.5	5.5	10.0	65	100	40	0.15	0.70	—	1.10	300
SMA Infant Formula	Wyeth	265	42.0	0.95	5.8	5.8	5.3	71	106	42	0.11	0.53	11.0	1.50	210

Table 7-3 (continued)

		Minerals per 100 ml												Estimated renal solute load
Formula	Manufacturer	Na (mEq)	K (mEq)	Cl (mg)	Ca (mg)	P (mg)	Mg (mg)	I (μg)	Mn (mg)	Cu (mg)	Z (mg)	Fe (mg)	Intestinal osmolality	
Mature human milk		0.5	1.3	39.6	34.0	14.0	4.0	3.0	1.10	0.04	0.4	0.50	300	—
Cow's milk		2.2	3.5	108.0	117.0	92.0	12.0	4.7	0.02	0.10	0.4	0.05	270	—
Goat's milk		1.4	4.5	—	129.0	106.0	—	—	—	—	—	0.01	—	—
Evaporated milk		2.6	3.9	—	126.0	102.5	—	—	—	—	—	0.05	300	—
Enfamil	Mead Johnson	0.9	1.8	42.0	46.0	32.0	5.3	10.6	0.01	0.06	0.5	0.11[a]	300	10
Similac	Ross	1.1	2.1	50.0	51.0	39.0	4.1	10.0	0.003	0.06	0.5	0.15[a]	290	105
Similac with whey	Ross	1.0	1.9	43.0	40.0	30.0	5.0	10.0	0.003	0.06	0.5	1.20	300	101
SMA Infant Formula	Wyeth	0.7	1.4	37.5	44.3	33.0	5.3	6.9	0.016	0.05	0.4	1.27[b]	300	91

[a]Enfamil with Iron and Similac with Iron have 1.2 mg Fe.
[b]SMA lo-iron has 0.15 mg Fe.
Key: CHO = carbohydrate.
Source: D. G. Kelts and E. G. Jones. *Manual of Pediatric Nutrition.* Boston: Little, Brown, 1984, P. 52. With permission.

lactopoiesis (milk production). Growth of the mammary ductules and lobules increases under the influence of estrogen, progesterone, and other hormones during pregnancy. Milk synthesis or lactogenesis occurs as prolactin levels rise throughout gestation [14].

Following birth, suckling by the infant stimulates the release of prolactin and oxytocin through neurohumoral pathways from the anterior and posterior pituitary. Prolactin stimulates the synthesis of milk, while oxytocin causes contraction of the myoepithelial cells and subsequently the release of milk from the alveolar cells (the "let-down reflex"). Suckling

Fig. 7-1. Physiology of lactation. A. Gestation. B. Postpartum. (From H. Vorherr. *The Breast. Morphology, Physiology and Lactation.* Orlando, FL: Academic, 1974. With permission.)

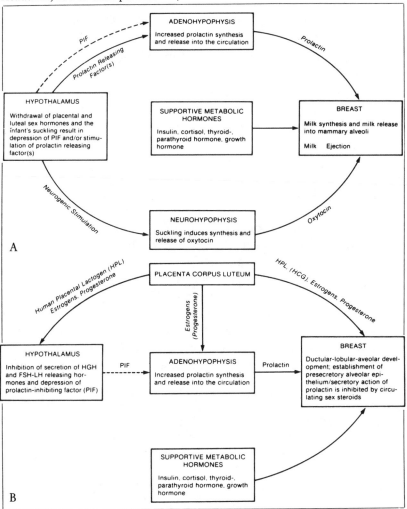

empties the breast ductules. The process of milk synthesis and release then recycles.

Colostrum is the initial breast milk. It is a yellow, thin fluid with a high content of protein, the fat-soluble vitamins A and E, and minerals. Vitamin K is lacking, and therefore supplementation with vitamin K at birth is necessary. Colostrum is rich in antibodies and contains factors that promote the growth of lactobacillus species in the infant's digestive tract.

Transitional milk appears between days seven and 14. It is composed of increased amounts of fat, lactose, and water-soluble vitamins, and a decreased concentration of protein, immunoglobulins, and fat-soluble vitamins.

Mature milk is present after the second week. It is secreted as foremilk and hindmilk. At the onset of suckling, *foremilk,* which is dilute and contains fewer calories, is released. As suckling continues, *hindmilk,* which is richer in fat and protein and thus has a higher caloric content is secreted.

Nursing should be comfortable, quiet, and unhurried for both the mother and the infant. The hungry infant has a very active rooting reflex that facilitates his search for the breast. The infant should be positioned and supported so that he may latch on to the areola and not the nipple. The mother may facilitate latching-on by compressing the areola and nipple so that the infant's mouth can fully encircle this area. If the infant latches on to the nipple alone, vigorous suckling may cause injury to the nipple and insufficient emptying of the breast.

Successful breast-feeding requires proper latching-on, sufficient time for the let-down reflex to occur, emptying of milk from the breast, and time for nonnutritive sucking. Most textbooks recommend that nursing be initiated with short feeding periods (3–5 minutes) and then extended in a stepwise fashion toward a goal of 10 to 20 minutes per breast within the first two weeks. However, limitation of feeding periods in the first few days may not afford the time necessary for the let-down reflex to occur. Furthermore, complete emptying of the breast may not occur, leading to breast engorgement and a cycle of lactation failure. Therefore, it is recommended that nursing schedules not be limited so rigidly but be based on the infant's hunger and the mother's lactation physiology.

At the conclusion of each nursing period, the infant's suction on the nipple may be released by the mother gently slipping her finger into the corner of the infant's mouth. Injury to the mother's nipple may occur if it is simply pulled from the infant's mouth.

Some of the problems that may occur during lactation include painful or cracked nipples, breast engorgement, blocked ducts, and mastitis. Injured nipples should be treated with air drying and the application of hydrous lanolin ointments, and nursing periods should begin on the unaffected breast. Complete emptying of the breast, either manually or by continued suckling, is mandatory in the treatment of engorgement and mastitis. Hot or cold packs may be comforting. Short-acting analgesics (e.g., aspirin) may also be indicated. Antibiotics should be used in the treatment of mastitis. It is unnecessary to interrupt breast-feeding when mastitis is present.

Following each nursing session, the nipple and areola should be cleansed with water and air dried. Breast pads without plastic liners may be placed in the brassiere to absorb the overflow of milk and to prevent abrasions of the areola and nipple.

The mother may find that a comfortable rocking chair with high armrests will help her support the infant while she is cuddling him to her breast. The father should be encouraged to assist the mother by bringing the baby to her for the late night feeding or early morning feeding. He also may be supportive by bathing and comforting the infant, changing diapers, and helping with household chores so that the mother may rest.

Contraindications to breast-feeding [6] include an incapacitating maternal or infant illness, an active infection that may be transmitted from the mother to the infant (e.g., tuberculosis), or exposure to drugs or toxins that may reach unacceptable levels in the breast milk [2]. Table 7-4 contains a list of drugs that are excreted into the breast milk and recommendations on maternal usage during lactation.

A breast pump is used to collect milk when suckling cannot occur because of mother-infant separation [9]. An effective pump will safely and comfortably completely evacuate the milk from the breast and also stimulate further milk production. Ease of cleaning and usage of the machine, cost, and portability are also features to review when considering the use or purchase of a breast pump. Initial usage should be supervised by someone with experience using the apparatus.

PROPRIETARY FORMULAS

Although there is a strong trend toward breast-feeding today, women who decide to bottle-feed their infants also should be supported. They should not be made to feel guilty or inadequate. In fact, if successful growth of the infant is the goal of any nutritional program, it may be accomplished by either breast- or bottle-feeding. The choice should rest with the parents.

Proprietary formulas differ from breast milk in their protein composition (lactalbumin to casein ratio) and the type of available carbohydrate. The protein in most proprietary formulas is derived from cow's milk protein. However, formulas have been synthesized from soy products to provide a source of protein for children who are intolerant of bovine protein.

Proprietary formulas are supplied as powders, liquid concentrates (see Appendix 31), and sterile ready-to-feed bottled formulas. Powders and concentrates are less expensive but require preparation at home. Instructions for preparation are usually furnished with the product. In some sit-

Table 7-4. Maternal drug usage during lactation: effects on newborn

No anticipated effects	Insufficient information	Avoid if possible
Acetominophen	Amantadine	Alcohol
Acetazolamide	Busulfan	Amphetamines
Amitriptyline (Elavil)	Chloroquine	Atropine
Ampicillin	Clonidine	Chloramphenicol
Antacids	Cromolyn	Cimetidine
Antihistamines	Diazoxide	Clindamycin
Aspirin	Doxepin	Cocaine
Caffeine	Ephedrine	Corticosteroids
Captopril	Ethchlorvynol	Cyclophosphamide
Carbamazepine (Tegretol)	(Placidyl)	Diazepam
Carbenicillin	Ethosuximide	Diethylstilbestrol
Cephalosporins	Fenoprofen	Diphenoxylate
Chloral hydrate	Indomethacin	(Lomotil)
Chlordiazepoxide (Librium)	Meprobamate	Ergotamine
Chlorothiazide	Metaproterenol	Heroin
Chlorpromazine	Nortriptyline	Hyoscyamine
Dicumarol (use with caution)	Novobiocin	Iodine
Digitalis preparations	Pentazocine (Talwin)	Isoniazid
Epinephrine	Perphenazine	LSD
Erythromycin	Phenylephrine	Marijuana
Ethacrynic acid	Phenylpropanolamine	Methimazole
Furosemide (Lasix)	Prazosin	Methotrexate
Gentamicin	Propantheline	Methyldopa
Griseofulvin	(Pro-Banthine)	Metronidazole
Haloperidol	Quinacrine	Oral contraceptives
Heparin	Terbutaline	Oxazepam
Hydralazine	Thioridazine (Mellaril)	Paregoric
Hydrochlorthiazide	Tolbutamide	Phencyclidine
Ibuprofen (Motrin)	Trifluoperazine	Phenylbutazone
Imipramine	(Stelazine)	Primidone
Insulin		Progesterone
Isoproterenol		Propoxyphene
Kanamycin		Propylthiouracil
Laxatives		Radiopharmaceuticals
Lincomycin		Reserpine
Lorazepam		Scopolamine
Meperidine		Sulfonamides
Methadone (with caution)		Tetracyclines
		Warfarin Sodium

Source: Adapted from R. J. Roberts. *Drug Therapy in Infants.* Philadelphia: Saunders, 1984.

uations evaporated milk formulas may be desirable because they are the least expensive. Evaporated milk formula is prepared by pouring a 13-oz can of evaporated milk and two tablespoons of corn syrup into a quart jar and then filling the jar to the top with boiled water (see Appendix 32).

Parents frequently question the need for sterilization of formula and bottles. Sterilization is unnecessary if the water used to reconstitute the formula is uncontaminated and if the bottles are thoroughly cleaned and free of residue. However, nipples should be sterilized by placing them in boiling water for approximately 10 to 15 minutes. Terminal sterilization is recommended when water purity is in question. The technique for terminal sterilization is presented in Appendix 33. Prepared formulas and expressed human milk require refrigeration for storage.

Infants who receive adequate quantities of breast milk or formula may not need vitamin or iron supplements during the first four to six months [5]. Some authorities suggest that the breast-fed baby be supplemented with vitamin D and iron. The use of evaporated milk formulas or unfortified cow's milk formula necessitates supplementation with vitamins C and D and iron. A fluoride supplement may be given if the local water contains less than 0.3 parts per million of fluoride. The fluoride may be started at any time in the first six months.

The infant who receives adequate calories but does not establish a satisfactory weight gain should be evaluated for malabsorption or a hypermetabolic state. The differential diagnosis of the latter includes hyperthyroidism, sepsis, narcotic withdrawal, and an elevated environmental temperature.

The subject of nutrition seems complicated because there have been so many volumes published with diverse advice and opinions. For the newborn term infant the subject could be simplified if every infant could be successfully breast-fed. The following poem illustrates how much latitude we as caretakers have in offering nutritional advice to our parents.

*Infant Feeding**

Soranus, he of ancient Rome,
He had a simple trick
To see if milk was fit for sale,
He merely dropped it on his nail
To see if it would stick;
Yet spite of this the babies grew
As any school boy'll tell to you.

*From J. Ruhrah. Infant feeding (Lines suggested by the papers on infant feeding). *J. Pediatr.* 50 : 638, 1967. With permission.

Good Metlinger in ages dark
Just called milk good or bad
No acid milk could vex his soul
He gave it good, he gave it whole
A method very sad;
Yet babies grew to man's estate
A fact quite curious to relate.

Time sped and science came along
To help the human race,
Percentages were brought to fame
By dear old Rotch, of honored name,
We miss his kindly face;
Percentages were fed to all
Yet babies grew both broad and tall.

The calorie now helped us know
The food that is required
Before the baby now could feed
We figured out his daily need
A factor much desired;
Again we see with great surprise
The babies grow in weight and size.

The vitamin helps clarify
Why infants fail to gain,
We feed the baby leafy food
Which for the guinea pig is good
A reason very plain;
And still we watch the human race
Go madly at its usual pace.

We have the baby weighed today
The nursing time is set,
At last we find we are so wise
We can begin to standardize
No baby now need fret;
In spite of this the baby grows
But why it does God only knows.

Away with all such childish stuff
Bring chemists to the fore,
The ion now is all the rage
We listen to the modern sage
With all his latest lore;
And if the baby fret or cry
We'll see just how the ions lie.

A hundred years will soon go by
Our places will be filled
By others who will theorize
And talk as long and look as wise
Until they too are stilled;
And I predict no one will know
What makes the baby gain and grow.

John Ruhrah (1872–1935)
Pediatric Profiles

REFERENCES

1. American Academy of Pediatrics. A gift of love. Breast feeding. 1984.
2. American Academy of Pediatrics. The transfer of drugs and other chemicals into human breast milk. *Pediatrics* 72 : 375, 1983.
3. American Academy of Pediatrics. The promotion of breast feeding. *Pediatrics* 69 : 654, 1982.
4. American Academy of Pediatrics. Nutrition and lactation. *Pediatrics* 68 : 435, 1981.
5. American Academy of Pediatrics. Vitamin and mineral supplement needs in normal children in the United States. *Pediatrics* 66 : 1015, 1980.
6. Berger, L. R. When should one discourage breast-feeding. *Pediatrics* 67 : 300, 1981.
7. Fomon, S. J. *Infant Nutrition* (2nd ed.). Philadelphia: Saunders, 1974.
8. Grand, R. J., Watkins, J. B., and Torti, F. M. Development of the human gastrointestinal tract. *Gastroenterology* 70 : 790, 1976.
9. Johnson, C. A. An evaluation of breast pumps currently available on the American market. *Clin. Pediatr. (Phila.)* 22 : 40, 1983.
10. Lawrence, R. A. *Breastfeeding: A Guide for the Medical Profession.* St. Louis: Mosby, 1980.
11. Lebenthal, E., Lee, P. C., and Heitlinger, L. A. Impact of development of the gastrointestinal tract on infant feeding. *J. Pediatr.* 102 : 1, 1983.
12. Lemons, J. A., Schreiner, R. L., and Gresham, E. L. Simple method for determining the caloric and fat content of milk. *Pediatrics* 66 : 626, 1980.
13. Olson, M. The benign effects on rabbit's lungs of the aspiration of water compared with 5% glucose or milk. *Pediatrics* 46 : 538, 1970.
14. Riddick, D. H. All about the human breast. *Contemp. Obstet. Gynecol.* 19 : 101, 1982.
15. Schneider, J. M. (ed.). Breast feeding bibliography. *Perinatal Press* 6 : 113, 1982.

8. Discharge

The primary emphasis in previous chapters has been on the management of the infant in the newborn nursery. Although his medical care in the nursery is extremely important, it is only a prelude to what he will receive in the following years. Therefore, in addition to providing general medical support, the role of the physician also should be to provide guidance in child-rearing.

ANTICIPATORY GUIDANCE [6, 20, 22, 23]
The education of parents as caretakers must not be ignored (Table 8-1), because the infant is totally dependent on his parents and because the concepts and abilities in rearing a child are neither innate nor an inalienable right. Some parents may have participated in prenatal courses. Additional instruction and information on basic child care and developmental milestones should be available for them on the postpartum unit.

While talking to the family, it is easy to lose rapport by mislabeling the sex of the infant or referring to the infant as "it." Rather than err, it is more appropriate to speak of "your baby" or "the infant." Unusual features or abnormalities of the infant must be discussed openly and assessed in the context of the family's features and medical history.

The parents' appreciation of their infant as an individual can be reinforced by discussions and demonstrations of their child's behavior [12]. This is simplified by condensing the six behavioral states presented in Table 3-2 into three basic behaviors: sleeping, waking, and crying.

The normal infant sleeps 18 to 20 hours per day. Sleep periods are interspersed with awakening and feedings every two to six hours. The development of consolidated sleep at night does not occur before four to six weeks.

The infant's physical and psychosocial capabilities become apparent in the alert state. The mother and father can appreciate their infant's remarkable abilities and competence by learning the maneuvers that demonstrate vision, hearing, touch, and the appreciation of faces, noises, and comfort states. While holding her alert infant in front of her, the mother should be instructed to look into his eyes, move him to one side, and observe his attention to her face. Hearing is demonstrated when she speaks to him in a high-pitched voice at conversational levels and he turns his head toward her. Touching is an important means of communication between the parent and infant; cuddling is the best example of a reciprocal tactile response. Suckling is not only part of the normal feeding process, it also is an important behavior by which infants comfort themselves.

Table 8-1. Preparing for parenthood

1. Select the doctor you want to care for your child before your expected delivery date and schedule at least one appointment with him to discuss any part of health care about which you have questions or concerns.

2. After delivery, make sure that someone teaches both mother and father the basic caregiving skills such as bathing, diapering, feeding, and dressing. Both parents should have experience holding, diapering, feeding, and dressing the baby while in the hospital.

3. If you have help coming to your home after your delivery (relative or friend), ask them to please help with the household tasks and let you adjust to caring for the new baby.

4. Talk to your baby while you are taking care of him. Use normal speech, not baby talk, and look at your baby's face while talking.

5. Spend time playing with and exploring your new baby. Make sure both parents get ample practice with the baby! Be sure to make time for this while your baby is rested, fed, and happy.

6. Try to develop standard caregiving routines and, within reason, stick with those routines. For example, it's a good idea to use the same place and the same procedures each time you diaper or bathe your baby.

7. Work very hard to hold and play with your child when he is quiet and happy instead of waiting for him to cry. Babies learn very quickly which behaviors gain them attention.

8. You will teach your infant something each time that you interact with him, so begin very early giving attention to those things that you want your baby to do.

9. Purchase an infant car seat before your baby is discharged from the hospital and use it on every trip you make in an automobile.

Source: E. R. Christopherson. Incorporating behavioral pediatrics into primary care. *Pediatr. Clin. North Am.* 29 : 261, 1982. With permission.

Crying [10, 14] communicates hunger, discomfort, or the desire for additional attention. Furthermore, crying may suppress disturbing stimuli, for after a period of fussy crying, the infant often sleeps more deeply. Parents learn to differentiate various crying states.

Recognizing these behaviors helps solidify the parents' relationship with their infant and helps them understand his uniqueness. This revelation strengthens the parents' feelings toward their child and makes the infant's basic day-to-day care a gratifying and rewarding experience.

Guidelines regarding routine office visits, immunization schedules, accident prevention, sibling jealousy, and other topics may be furnished to the parents in anticipation of their questions or as a focus for discussion. These instructions provide the parents with information that may keep them from becoming confused and frustrated when unsolicited advice is offered by family and friends.

Important instructions that should be discussed with the parents before discharge include:

1. SAFETY.   The infant should never be left unattended in a bath, on a dressing table, or on an elevated surface, such as a couch or bed.

2. UMBILICAL CORD CARE [26].   The umbilicus should be wiped with an alcohol swab to hasten drying. The mummified cord remnant should separate by the second week.

3. SKIN CARE.   The infant may be bathed with a sponge using warm water and a nonmedicated, noncosmetic soap. Tub or sink baths should not be used until the umbilicus is healed, which is usually by two weeks after birth. Powdering of the skin is unnecessary. However, if applied, the powder first should be dispensed into the hand and then rubbed directly on the baby's skin. The powder should not be showered on the infant because it may be inhaled [18]. Mineral oils, petroleum jellies, and lotions are not necessary and may cause contact or seborrheal dermatitis.

4. DIAPER RASH [2].   An erythematous dermatitis in the diaper region usually is caused by leaving a wet diaper on too long. The moisture compromises the skin's natural barriers. The presence of microbes, contact irritants, and frictional trauma increase the occurrence and intensity of the rash. Most diaper rashes are treated by frequent diaper changes, cleansing of the skin, and exposing the irritated areas to air. At each diaper change, a protective ointment, such as Desitin or zinc oxide paste, may be used. If the rash does not clear, the parents should consult a physician.

5. CARE OF THE PENIS.   If the penis is uncircumcised [1], the advice published by the American Academy of Pediatrics is to "leave it alone." Embryologically, the foreskin is fused to the glans and in most boys it will separate spontaneously over a period of weeks, months, or even years. Forceful retraction of the foreskin is unnecessary. Hygiene is accomplished with simple cleansing as part of the infant's daily bath. If the penis is circumcised, the genital area should be gently cleansed with soap and water with each diaper change for the first several days. An application of an ointment (medicated or nonmedicated) will prevent the circumcised glans from adhering to the diaper.

6. STAINS IN THE DIAPER [8, 21].   Normally the urine is clear and light-colored. Dark urine may be a sign of dehydration. Occasionally, par-

ents will note colored stains on the diaper. The most common is the "red brick dust" stain of urate crystals from the urine [24]. This is differentiated from blood by its appearance and confirmed with a negative guaiac or hematest study. It obviously is important to determine if blood in the diaper originated from the gastrointestinal or urinary tract. Often between seven and 14 days female infants have vaginal bleeding termed *vicarious menstruation*. It results from withdrawal of maternal hormones and is not a cause for concern.

7. INFANT TEMPERATURE.   Since fever (greater than 37.8°C) is a very important sign of infection, parents should know how to take their infant's temperature and how to read a thermometer. Hyperthermia [25], if not caused by infection, may be due to overdressing or over covering the infant, too warm a room, or placing the infant in direct sunlight passing through a window or too near another heat source. At home, the room temperature should be kept at a level comfortable for the parents, and the infant should be dressed accordingly.

    Antipyretics should never be given to a newborn infant for fever. Instead, the infant could be bathed in tepid water while notifying the physician. The parents should be reminded not to leave the infant unattended in the tub.

8. BOWEL HABITS (STOOLING FREQUENCY).   Bowel habits vary considerably from one infant to another. Many infants defecate after each feeding as a result of the gastrocolic reflex. Breast-fed infants have stringy, loose, yellow, sweet-smelling stools, whereas infants fed artificial formula have pasty, homogeneous, yellow-brown stools. Stools of infants fed some proprietary formulas also are sweet-smelling, whereas sour-smelling stools occur after cow's milk and evaporated milk feedings. Diarrhea is not defined by the number of stools but rather by the consistency of the stool. Constipation is hardened stools that are difficult to evacuate. They are observed most commonly in infants fed artificial formula. Simple constipation may be treated by increasing the concentration or changing the type of carbohydrate in the feeding. Obstipation may be due to an underlying disease, such as Hirschsprung's disease.

9. BREAST ENGORGEMENT [3, 17].   Neonatal breast engorgement occurs in both boys and girls, commonly increasing over the first week or 10 days and then subsiding during the first year. The engorged breast should not be manipulated because this predisposes it to serious infection.

10. DAILY ROUTINES. As far as possible, family routines should not be changed when the new infant arrives home. The infant will acclimate to ambient noises and daily routines. If possible, the infant should sleep in a room separate from the parents'. Visitors, although welcome, should not overburden the new mother or interfere with the complex adjustments of the infant and family in the first weeks of life. Handling and kissing of the infant by visitors should be discouraged.

11. SIBLINGS. Siblings should be prepared for the new infant long before his arrival. Sibling visits to the mother and new infant in the hospital help assure the young child that his mother is not gone forever and that the new infant really does exist. Once the mother and infant return home, it is helpful to encourage siblings to help with the infant's care. Special play time and attention should be set aside for the older child to reassure him of the parents' affection.

12. THUMB SUCKING. Sucking of fingers or pacifiers fulfills sucking needs and provides normal gratification. The parents should be reassured that this behavior is acceptable.

13. ANTERIOR FONTANELLE. Some parents are frightened by this "soft spot" and need reassurance that there is no risk in touching the anterior fontanelle when washing the infant's scalp.

14. TRAVELING WITH THE INFANT [7]. When traveling in a car, the infant should be properly supported in a car seat rather than carried on the lap or placed on the seat of the car (see Appendix 35). Insistence on the family having a car seat for the trip home from the hospital reinforces this. When walking with the infant, the parents may carry the infant in any position as long as his head and neck are supported.

15. SUDDEN INFANT DEATH SYNDROME ANXIETY. Some parents ask about sudden infant death syndrome (SIDS). Their questions suggest special knowledge or heightened anxiety. If the question arises, it is wise to pursue the subject in more depth so their anxieties can be allayed.

Raising a child is a rewarding experience. The father and other family members should be encouraged to participate in bathing, diaper changes, feeding, and playing with and consoling the infant.

ROUTINE VERSUS EARLY DISCHARGE [4, 27]
In the past, the mother and infant were kept in the hospital for nearly a week so that the infant could be observed for potential problems and the

mother could recuperate. Today, the only healthy infants who remain hospitalized for that long are those who await their mother's recovery from cesarean section. Nearly all infants are discharged in the first three days.

There has been a movement in American society toward very abbreviated hospital stays and home deliveries that has stimulated hospitals to develop alternative birth centers and early discharge programs. Although there is an element of risk in early discharge, a hospital delivery is still preferable to a home delivery. Hospitals are better prepared to handle unanticipated catastrophes occurring during the perinatal period.

Experience has shown that risks associated with early discharge can be minimized if the families are screened and agree to abide by certain criteria, such as the following:

1. The entire medical team should approve the delivery and early discharge in advance.
2. There are no high-risk factors in the pregnancy.
3. The prospective mother and father have attended and been certified in an approved education course in childbirth and caretaking procedures.
4. There is support at home for both mother and infant during the mother's recuperative period.
5. The parents understand that intrapartum or neonatal complications may extend the hospitalization in approximately 10 to 40 percent of deliveries.
6. Medical evaluation of the mother and infant should be done within 24 hours after discharge. Further evaluation may be needed at 48 and 72 hours and perhaps for even longer.

The family should not be permitted to take the infant home early if:

1. Extrauterine adaptation has not been successful within the first six hours.
2. There are abnormalities detected on the newborn physical exam.
3. The mother develops social or medical complications.
4. Successful feeding has not been established.

Even if these guidelines are followed, some infants may have to be rehospitalized because of feeding problems, hyperbilirubinemia, infection, or maladjustments within the family.

PROCEDURES FOR DISCHARGE

Before discharge, the infant should have a repeat physical examination. This examination is similar to that on admission and should emphasize any points omitted or abnormalities found during the previous examination.

A written summary should include the birth and discharge weights, head circumference measurements, and the mention of any abnormalities such as jaundice or malformations. The final note may read like the following:

This 3260-gm full-term, with weight appropriate for gestational age boy was born 48 hours ago to a 24-year-old gravida II, now para II woman whose blood type is 0, Rh positive, Coombs' test negative, serology nonreactive. Her last menstrual period was (date) and her expected date of confinement was (date). Delivery was sterile, spontaneous, controlled, and vertex, and a pudendal block was administered. Apgar scores at one and five minutes were 8 and 9. The infant has lost weight progressively and now weighs 3190 gm (only 2% below birth weight) and is being discharged today. The infant does not appear to be icteric and there have been no perinatal complications.

Birth statistics: weight 3260 gm, OFC 34.5 cm, length 50 cm.

Discharge statistics: Weight 3190 gm, OFC 34.5 cm, length 50 cm.

This information may be abbreviated in the following fashion:

This 3260 gm FT, AGA male was born 48 hours ago to a 24 y.o. GII-PI, now PII, O, Rh pos., VDRL/NR, woman whose LMP was (date) and EDC was (date). Pudendal block was used. Delivery was SSCVD and Apgars were $8^1/9^5$. The baby is now Br feeding and weight is 3190 gm (2% below birth weight)

Although succinct, the abbreviated paragraph contains a wealth of pertinent information.

SCREENING TESTS FOR METABOLIC DISEASES [15, 19]

Most states now require that newborn infants be screened for hyperphenylalaninemia (PHP), phenylketonuria (PKU), and congenital hypothyroidism (CH) (Table 8-2). Additional screening tests are available for sickle cell disease and other red blood cell abnormalities, galactosemia, homocystinuria, and maple syrup urine disease. Future neonatal screening may include congenital adrenal hyperplasia, precursors to atherosclerosis, and muscular dystrophy.

Guidelines for the screening tests are available from local and state public health departments. In general, the screening tests are performed on small quantities of blood collected on standardized filter paper cards. Some of the pitfalls that complicate the screening efforts include failure to obtain a proper specimen, cartage, and clerical and laboratory errors in processing the specimens. The specimens should be obtained at the time of discharge. A repeat sample for hyperphenylalaninemia and phen-

Table 8-2. Availability of metabolic screening tests by states

States	PKU	T$_4$	Galacto-semia	MSUD	Homo-cyst.	Tyro-sinemia	Sickle cell/abnormal hemoglobin
Alabama*	•	•					*
Alaska	•	•					
Arizona	•	•	•	•	•		• (all infants)
Arkansas	•	•					
California	•	•	•				*
Colorado	•	•	•	•	•		• (all infants)
Connecticut	•	•	•	•	•		
Delaware	•	•	•	•	•	•	
D.C.	•	•	•	•	•		
Florida	•	•	•	•			
Georgia	•	•	•	•	•	•	• (at risk)
Hawaii	•	•					
Idaho	•	•	•	•	•	•	
Illinois	•	•	•				
Indiana	•	•					
Iowa	•	•	•	•			
Kansas	•	•					
Kentucky	•	•	•				
Louisiana	•	•					
Maine	•	•	•	•	•		
Maryland	•	•	•	•	•	•	
Massachusetts	•	•	•	•	•		
Michigan	•	•	•				
Minnesota	•	•	•				
Mississippi	•	•					
Missouri	•	•					
Montana	•	•	•	•	•	•	
Nebraska	•	•					
Nevada	•	•	•	•	•	•	
New Hampshire	•	•	•	•	•		
New Jersey	•	•	•				
New Mexico	•	•	•	•	•		•
New York	•	•	•	•	•		• (all infants)
North Carolina	•	•					
North Dakota	•	•					
Ohio	•	•	•		•		
Oklahoma	•	•					
Oregon	•	•	•	•	•	•	
Pennsylvania	•	•					
Rhode Island	•	•	•	•	•		
South Carolina	•	•					
South Dakota	•	•					
Tennessee	•	•					

Table 8-2 (continued)

States	PKU	T$_4$	Galacto-semia	MSUD	Homo-cyst.	Tyro-sinemia	Sickle cell/abnormal hemoglobin
Texas	•	•	•				• (all infants)
Utah	•	•	•				
Vermont	•	•	•				
Virginia	•	•	•	•	•		
Washington	•	•					
West Virginia	•	•	•				
Wisconsin	•	•	•	•	•		
Wyoming	•	•	•	•	•		• (all infants)

*(on request)
Key: PKU = phenylketonuria; T$_4$ = thyroxine; MSUD = maple syrup urine disease.
Source: S. Klc. Screening status report. *Washington, D.C., Infant Screening Newsletter.*
April 1985. With permission.

ylketonuria screening should be obtained before the third week after birth in those children who are discharged within the first 24 hours or before insufficient milk intake for testing has occurred.

Before these screening programs were available, the clinician had to rely on a positive family history and a high level of suspicion before considering these disorders. The screening process now affords all infants an equal opportunity to be evaluated, provided that the tests are properly and effectively obtained, interpreted, and followed.

FETAL AND NEONATAL LOSS [5, 9, 11, 13, 16, 28]

The major thrust of this book has been towards new life and its impact on families, caretakers, and care systems. Equally important is the loss of a new life, either during pregnancy or in the neonatal period. When a fetal or neonatal death occurs, profound grief follows. The same grief process occurs when an infant is born with a serious congenital malformation or illness. Similar feelings may develop in a woman who has a stillborn or who gives up her newborn infant for adoption. Discussions with the parents regarding the process about to envelope them may temper their grief.

Shock or disbelief, mourning, and recovery comprise the major grief phase. In the initial phase, fear, anger, guilt, and sadness are the overwhelming feelings. Denial can be prevented and the grieving process facilitated if the parents see and hold their dead or dying infant. Sometimes the family will be so immobilized that they cannot cope with this experience. A photograph of the infant that is shared with the family at a later date often helps them cope with their grief.

The second phase of grief, the mourning phase, is a much more extended process. It is the period of adjustment to living without a loved one. Recovery, the third phase, is a time of resolution of the grief. The three phases often overlap, and backsliding may occur even months after the infant's death. In general, the phases are handled differently by the mother and the father.

A similar grief response may occur among hospital staff. They, too, need a support system.

A follow-up appointment with parents four to six weeks after the infant's death affords an opportunity to assess their adaptation, discuss any unresolved questions and feelings, and review the results of autopsy or other pre- or postmortem studies.

REFERENCES

1. American Academy of Pediatrics. Care of the Uncircumcised Penis. 1984.
2. American Academy of Pediatrics. Diaper Rash. 1986.
3. Berkowitz, C. D., and Inkelis, S. H. Bloody nipple discharge in infancy. *J. Pediatr.* 103 : 755, 1983.
4. Brann, A. W. Criteria for early infant discharge and follow-up evaluation. *Pediatrics* 65 : 651, 1980.
5. Christensen, A. Z. Coping with the crisis of a premature birth—One couple's story. *MCN: Am. J. Mat. Child. Nurs.* 2 : 33, 1977.
6. Christopherson, E. R. Incorporating behavorial pediatrics into primary care. *Pediatr. Clin. North Am.* 29 : 261, 1982.
7. Christopherson, E. R., and Sullivan, M. A. Increasing the protection of newborn infants in cars. *Pediatrics* 70 : 21, 1981.
8. Cone, J. E. Jr. Diagnosis and treatment: Some syndromes, diseases, and conditions associated with abnormal coloration of the urine or diaper. *Pediatrics* 41 : 654, 1968.
9. Elliott, B. A., and Hein, H. A. Neonatal death: Reflections for physicians. *Pediatrics* 62 : 96, 1978.
10. Foye, H. R. Jr. Crying in Infancy. In M. Ziai, T. A. Clarke, and T. A. Merritt. (eds.). *Assessment of the Newborn.* Boston: Little, Brown, 1984.
11. Harvey, K. Caring perceptively for the relinquishing mother. *MCN: Am. J. Mat. Child. Nurs.* 2 : 24, 1977.
12. Helfer, R. E., and Wilson, A. L. The parent-infant relationship. Promoting a positive beginning through perinatal coaching. *Pediatr. Clin. North Am.* 29 : 249, 1982.
13. Kowalski, K., and Osborn, M. R. Helping mothers of stillborn infants to grieve. *MCN: Am. J. Mat. Child. Nurs.* 2 : 29, 1977.
14. Lester, B. M., and Boukydis, C. F. Z. *Infant Crying.* New York: Plenum, 1985.
15. Levy, H. L., and Mitchell, M. L. The current status of newborn screening. *Hosp. Pract.* 17 : 89, 1982.
16. Lewis, E. Mourning by the family after a stillbirth or neonatal death. *Arch. Dis. Child.* 54 : 303, 1979.

17. McKiernan, J. F., and Hull, D. Breast development in the newborn. *Arch. Dis. Child.* 56 : 525, 1981.
18. Mofenson, H. C., et al. Baby Powder—A Hazard! *Pediatrics* 68 : 265, 1981.
19. Nyhan, W. L. Understanding inherited metabolic disease. *CIBA Found. Symp.* 32 : 1, 1980.
20. Rothenberg, M. B. Opportunities for psychological prophylaxis in the Neonatal Period. A checklist for the practicing pediatrician. *Clin. Pediatr. (Phila.)* 15 : 53, 1976.
21. Shirkey, H. C. (ed.). *Pediatric Therapy* (5th ed.). St. Louis: Mosby, 1975.
22. Sprunger, L. W., and Preece, E. W. Characteristics of prenatal interviews provided by pediatricians. *Clin. Pediatr. (Phila.)* 20 : 778, 1981.
23. Sprunger, L. W., and Preece, E. W. Use of pediatric prenatal visits by family physicians. *J. Fam. Pract.* 13 : 1007, 1981.
24. Stapleton, F. B. Renal uric acid clearance in human neonates. *J. Pediatr.* 103 : 290, 1983.
25. Voora, S., et al. Fever in full-term newborns in the first four days of life. *Pediatrics* 69 : 40, 1982.
26. Wilson, C. B., et al. When is umbilical cord separation delayed? *J. Pediatr.* 107 : 292, 1985.
27. Yanover, M. J., Jones, D., and Miller, M. D. Perinatal care of low-risk mothers and infants. Early discharge home care. *N. Engl. J. Med.* 294 : 702, 1976.
28. Young, R. K. Chronic sorrow: Parents' response to the birth of a child with a defect. *MCN: Am. J. Mat. Child. Nurs.* 2 : 38, 1977.

9. Organization and Management of the Nursery

A plan for the regionalization of perinatal care was published in 1976 [4] with guidelines for the organization of resources to provide optimum care for mothers and infants. In this system there are three levels of perinatal care. The level I perinatal center provides basic medical care for mothers with uncomplicated pregnancies and normal infants. The level II center provides care for normal mothers but also is equipped and staffed to handle selected high-risk pregnancies. The level III center has people and resources for care of the entire spectrum of low- and high-risk mothers and newborn infants. When fetal or neonatal risks are identified, pregnant mothers or newborn infants may be transferred to centers with greater resources. The majority of infants are delivered in level I hospitals.

The organization, management, goals, and integration of the level I nursery into the total system of perinatal care are discussed in this chapter. Since some level I nurseries are geographically distant from level III perinatal centers, and some high-risk situations cannot be anticipated, level I perinatal centers must be prepared to identify and stabilize all categories of high-risk infants for brief periods.

GOALS
The goals of the level I nursery are to promote health care by using measures that prevent disease and providing interrelated monitoring programs to detect warning signs and abnormalities so that intervention measures can be instituted and the effects of disease minimized. The design of the nursery and its provision of resources must support trained and knowledgeable personnel to meet these ends, whether the interventions are carried out in the hospital of birth or after transfer.

PHYSICAL FACILITIES [1]
The level I nursery includes areas for resuscitation, admission and observation, routine and extended newborn care, and procedures such as circumcision and lumbar puncture. Some level I perinatal centers are large enough to provide special rooms for each function, while smaller centers with limited space may have to provide for several functions in one or two rooms. In either case, there should be easy access to patients and supplies, and the nurseries should meet state and local regulations.

DELIVERY ROOM RESUSCITATION AREA
In each delivery room there should be space for the management and resuscitation of the newborn infant in the moments after birth. The area

should be well-lighted and equipped with an infant bed and radiant heat source, two air and oxygen outlets, an oxygen blender, electrical outlets, and suction apparatus. Additional resuscitation equipment must be close at hand and ready for use. The resuscitation wall board [2] accomplishes this purpose (Fig. 9-1). A 24-hour (digital) clock indicating minutes and seconds should be clearly visible.

ADMISSION AND OBSERVATION AREA

The admission and observation area is for the continued observation of the infant during the first 24 hours. This may be a separate room, but more often it is an area within the nursery where the infant lying in an incubator or under a radiant heater in an open bed can be observed until stable. Suction, oxygen, air outlets, at least six electrical outlets, a sink, and a trash container should be nearby.

NORMAL NEWBORN CARE AREA

The newborn nursery should be close to the postpartum unit. The bed or crib capacity must exceed the number of postpartum beds by 20 to 30 percent to accommodate multiple births, prolonged hospitalizations, and peaks in the postpartum census. For example, if the annual delivery rate

Fig. 9-1. Layout for resuscitation wall board. This should be hung in the delivery room near the resuscitation area for the newborn. (From J. M. Clark, Z. A. Brown, and A. L. Jung. Resuscitation equipment board for nurseries and delivery rooms. *J.A.M.A.* 236 : 2427, Issue 21, Nov. 22, 1976. Copyright 1976, American Medical Association. With permission.)

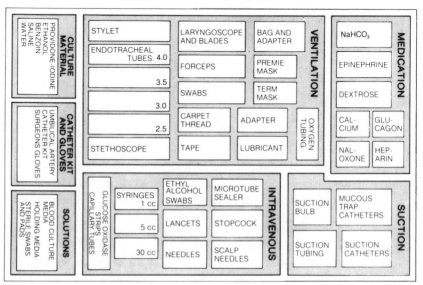

is 1500 and the average length of stay is two to three days, the number of bassinets required is 12 to 13. This figure is derived by dividing the average hospital stay into the number of days per year (365 divided by 2.5 equals 146), and dividing this result into the annual delivery rate of 1500 (1500 divided by 146 equals 10). An additional 20 to 30 percent results in the estimate of 12 to 13 beds.

Twenty sq ft or more of floor space is adequate for each bassinet and for access to the infant. When the number of bassinets in the room exceeds 10 to 12, a second nursery should be opened. When more than one room is used, a system of grouping or cohorting of infants according to admission and discharge dates can be instituted. For example, all infants born during a four-day period would be admitted to nursery A. During the next four days, admissions are to nursery B, while infants in nursery A are being discharged. When nursery A is emptied, it is cleaned and readied for new infant admissions. When nursery B is emptied the cycle is repeated. Either room can be isolated if need arises.

ENTRY AND SCRUB AREA

The entry and scrub area of each nursery needs racks and hooks or lockers for street clothing, cabinets or racks for clean gowns, a receptacle for used gowns, a hand-washing sink large enough to prevent splashing and equipped with knee, elbow, or foot controls, foot-operated soap dispensers, towel dispensers, scrub brush containers, nail-cleaning sticks, and instructions for hand washing before entering the nursery. Table 9-1 is a sample chart for a hand washing procedure that should be clearly visible near the sink.

Table 9-1. Instructions for hand washing before entering the nursery

A. Guidelines
 1. All personnel and family wishing to examine or handle an infant or infant care items are required to wash for 2 min.
 2. All personnel who enter the nursery from other areas of the hospital must wash before contacting an infant.
 3. All personnel must wash their hands between handling patients.
B. Procedure
 1. Remove all jewelry. Rings without stones may be worn.
 2. Wash hands, including areas between fingers, under nails, and knuckles. Wash wrists and forearms up to elbows. Rinse.
 3. Dry hands and forearms with paper towel.
 4. Turn off faucets with paper towels.
 5. Put on hospital gown.

EQUIPMENT

Within the nursery the following are required: (1) one sink with elbow, knee, or foot controls and a foot-operated covered waste can for every five to six bassinets; (2) one to two pairs of electrical outlets for every two bassinets; (3) one oxygen, compressed air, and a suction outlet for every five to six bassinets; (4) an appropriate electrical receptacle for a portable x-ray unit; (5) a foot-operated waste can for diaper disposal; (6) a foot-operated laundry hamper for soiled linens; (7) an area for storage of clean supplies and special equipment such as head hoods, oxygen analyzers, and a panic box with emergency resuscitation equipment; and (8) separate facilities for temporary storage or disposal of soiled bottles, syringes, and diapers.

DESIGN AND ENVIRONMENTAL CONTROL

The nursery must have wall and floor finishes that are attractive and easily cleaned. Color schemes using white or off-white are recommended because they enhance the observer's ability to detect cyanosis or jaundice. Illumination should produce a light intensity of approximately 100 foot candles at the bed level and enhance color appreciation without graying. Viewing windows provide visibility for friends and family to see the new infant.

The ambient environmental temperature in the nursery should be maintained between 24 and 26°C (75–79°F) for the infants' comfort. Relative humidity should be approximately 50 percent.

Special examining rooms are not necessary since infants may be examined in their bassinets. However, a room for circumcision and other procedures and demonstrations is recommended. If special examining areas or procedure rooms are used, they must be well-lighted and temperature-controlled. A clean or sterile measuring tape, tongue blade, otoscope, ophthalmoscope, blood pressure measuring device, and stethoscope should be readily accessible to the examiner.

Occasionally a term infant will require care in an incubator for easy observation or for thermal support. If thermostat control is employed, the incubator temperature should be set between 32.5 and 33°C (90.5 to 91.4°F). If skin servocontrol is used the set point should be 35 to 36°C (95 to 96.8°F).

Water in an incubator reservoir may be contaminated with waterborne bacteria. Growth of bacteria can be limited by (1) careful cleansing of incubators, including their water reservoirs, with an iodophor or quaternary ammonium disinfectant; (2) limiting the time a cleansed incubator may be used by an infant to four to five days; (3) filling and draining the incubator reservoir only with sterile water every 24 hours; or (4) by omitting incubator humidification altogether. In areas where ambient humidity is high, incubators may be operated safely without humidity. However, the relationship between incubator air temperature and the operative environmental temperature is altered when incubator humidity is the same as ambient humidity. In this case the incubator temperature of 32.5 to 33°C mentioned previously must be raised and the incubators operated at the upper end of the thermal range.

Space is needed in and around the nursery for clerical work. The nursery suite also must include a locker room for the nurses and a conference and demonstration room.

INFECTION CONTROL

Prevention of infection is a vital aspect of nursery management. The nursery and the equipment and supplies must be clean. Hospital personnel should be aware that they are the most likely agents for transmission of serious infection. Personal health and hygiene must be monitored and maintained. Meticulous hand washing [6] must be done and emphasized repeatedly to prevent contamination and spread of infectious agents from infant to infant or personnel to infant. The nursery will be less cluttered and easier to maintain if personnel consume all food outside the nursery.

Anyone, including the parents, who enters the nursery or directly contacts an infant and his environment must wash his hands according to nursery guidelines (see Table 9-1) and put on a cover gown. Although cover gowns are usually used, their efficacy in preventing infection is neither proven nor disproven [3, 7]. The use of gowns decreases unnecessary nursery traffic, however, and therefore the number of personnel to whom babies are exposed. Personnel must wash their hands after each patient contact, or whenever hands are contaminated, before touching an infant, an infant's clean equipment, or supplies. Each infant should have his own supplies and equipment (diapers, shirts, blankets, wash clothes, thermometer, and so forth) stored within his bassinet. Personnel also must wash their hands when completing work in areas of the nursery where diapers are weighed and various lab tests performed. If family members visit mother and infant either in a visitors' lounge or in her hospital room, the visitors must be instructed in the hospital's rules.

Specific infectious agents

Proven or suspected superficial and enteric infections such as an abscess or diarrhea require contact isolation (see Appendix 30) because their transmission is by secretions, exudates, or excrement. Personnel should wear gloves and a separate gown when caring for an infant with these conditions. Isolation is accomplished most efficiently by placing the infant either in an incubator, a separate nursery, or in the mother's room, or, if the infant's condition warrants, discharging the infant to home. The infant may be taken to his mother for breast-feeding if the status of both mother and infant permits.

Suspected or proven viral infections or TORCH (TOxoplasmosis, Rubella, Cytomegalovirus, Herpes) complex diseases are transmitted from oral-pharyngeal secretions, stool, skin lesions, urine, and blood. Patients with these infections must be strictly isolated from other infants (see Appendix 30). In addition, personnel must wear gloves, a separate gown, and a mask when handling these infants. If the mother desires, she may come to the nursery to nurse the infant. If the mother has genital herpes infection but the neonate is free of infection, the infant may feed in the mother's room, once the mother has washed her hands thoroughly and put on a gown. Personnel who are pregnant or planning a pregnancy should refrain from contact with infants having proven or suspected TORCH complex infections.

The infant born to a mother who has hepatitis B or is a carrier of HB_sAg (surface antigen positive) should be immunized. The infant need not be isolated (see Appendix 30). Treatment consists of (1) 0.5 ml hepatitis B immune globulin (HBIG) intramuscularly, and (2) 0.5 ml hepatitis B vaccine intramuscularly at a different site within 12 hours of birth. Two additional doses of hepatitis B vaccine are given·again at one and six months. These procedures prevent the acquisition of acute infection and the development of a chronic carrier state.

The infant whose mother has acquired immune deficiency syndrome (AIDS) or AIDS-related complex (ARC) should be strictly isolated from other infants. Breast-feeding should not be permitted. Guidelines for the care of these infants will change as additional information becomes available.

PERSONNEL
The director of the nursery should be a physician with interest in and current knowledge of the care of the newborn infant. The director, with the cooperation of the medical and nursing staffs, is responsible for developing policies to maintain high standards of medical and nursing care both in the nursery and in the delivery room. There must be a plan to ensure continuous availability of personnel skilled in both neonatal cardiopulmonary resuscitation and the recognition and treatment of other life-threatening emergencies. The implementation and assessment of the nursery policies and plans are the responsibility of both the director and the head nurse. The head nurse of the nurseries must be a registered nurse with training, experience, and understanding of perinatal and neo-

natal care. The head nurse is responsible for directing the nursing staff and for the development and implementation of policies (examples of nursing policies are included in Appendix 34). The head nurse is the primary liaison between nursing services, hospital administration, and the medical staff.

The nursery staff must be skilled in the care and feeding of the infants, the recognition of aberrations in infant behavior and adaptive physiology, and resuscitation techniques. The nursing staff must be familiar with the nursery policies and are responsible for their enforcement. The experienced nursery nurse subconsciously, but actively, surveys each infant in a nursery several times each minute and recognizes that infants undergoing transition and adaptation cannot be left unattended. The nurse should be aware of maternal-infant interactions and available to assist the family during visiting hours.

On each nursing shift, the nursery should be staffed with a minimum of one professional nurse for every eight babies. Rooming-in increases the need for nursing personnel to a ratio of one professional nurse for every four mothers and infants. The nurse responsible for a rooming-in facility must circulate when the babies are with their mothers to detect both maternal and infant problems.

EDUCATION
The level II or level III center must take an active role in maintaining the proficiency of the personnel at the level I unit with education and consultation programs. However, this does not preclude personnel in the level I nursery from taking responsibility for their own continuing education. The medical and nursing staff should have a minimum of one teaching conference each month. The topic of discussion may include a review of the previous month's morbidity and mortality or a subject relevant to the care of mothers and infants. It may be beneficial for personnel in the level I nursery to visit and work in the level III center and for level III personnel to visit and work in the level I unit so that each may experience and understand the other's problems.

Nursing Orientation and Training
Each center must have an orientation and training program for nursing personnel to enhance the quality of patient care and thereby ensure job satisfaction. New personnel should acquire their skills as quickly as possible under the direction of an education coordinator or head nurse. A well-planned program provides a more consistent, complete, and efficient training than a program based on on-the-job training that usually is inconsistent, incomplete, and undirected. A training program for nurses

in a level I hospital should include subject matter pertaining to both technical (Table 9-2) and factual information [5]. All the items in Table 9-2 are not encountered on a daily basis in a level I facility. However, a care plan should be formulated and available for each possible situation.

The hospital should provide the opportunity for personnel to attend regional educational perinatal programs. Audiovisual materials as well as textbooks should be available in the nursery conference room.

TRANSPORT

A practical system of regionalized perinatal care is based on a framework that offers high quality perinatal and neonatal diagnosis and treatment by appropriately utilizing available resources and precluding unnecessary duplication of effort and expense. Along with effective education, consultation, and communication, an efficient transport system is one of the essential factors in this network.

The decision to transfer a patient from the level I nursery is the responsibility of the primary physician. In most instances, the mechanics necessary to facilitate the transfer are the responsibility of the level II or level III center.

Even though the birth of many high-risk infants can be anticipated before the onset of labor [10], more than one third of high-risk infants are

Table 9-2. Technical skills to be taught during nursing orientation program

1. Admission procedures: bathing, weighing, hospital identification, maintaining thermal stability, prophylactic treatments, laboratory screening procedures, assessment of gestational age, and other factors causing morbidity.
2. Methods for obtaining vital signs, including blood pressure.
3. Formulation of nursing care plans and charting.
4. Techniques for control of infection, hand washing, and gowning.
5. Feeding procedures: lactation, bottle, gavage.
6. Umbilical cord care and diapering.
7. Special procedures: circumcision, sepsis workup, lumbar puncture, exchange transfusion, passage of NG catheter, stabilization for transport.
8. Administering medication.
9. Using monitoring equipment.
10. Performing chest physiotherapy and suctioning.
11. Care of tubes: chest, gastrostomy, jejunostomy, etc.
12. Care of "ostomies."
13. Resuscitation techniques.
14. Infection control.

Source: R. W. Coen. Training of personnel—Pediatrics. *Clin. Perinatol.* 3 : 459, 1976. With permission.

delivered by low-risk mothers. If the diagnosis is evident during the pregnancy, such as a mother with insulin-dependent diabetes mellitus, it would be foolhardy to expect the infant to not suffer any problems and to permit the mother to deliver without special resources. It is equally unwise to temporize and await the appearance of complications that cannot be handled. Wisdom dictates that delivery of this high-risk infant should occur at a center in which experience, pediatric subspecialists, and other resources are available to prevent or diagnose all problems and to support the infant and mother when complications arise.

The risk for some infants becomes apparent only shortly before delivery — for example, with premature labor or abnormal maternal bleeding. Transfer of mothers with such complications may be impossible. If so, communication with the referral center about stabilization of the infant in the delivery hospital and possible infant transport should begin.

In other situations, the risk for the infant may not be identified until birth or even later. Thus, skills and other resources for stabilization of the newborn infant must be available in the level I nursery during the interval before transport.

MATERNAL TRANSPORT [9, 11, 12]
Transporting a woman with a major complication of pregnancy to a perinatal center (1) ensures optimal utilization of resources for both the fetus and newborn, (2) decreases the exigencies of and the complications associated with neonatal transport, and (3) prevents separation of mother and infant at a critical time in their relationship. Despite the fact that some maternal transports will prove unnecessary and that care may take place away from a familiar community, the benefits of maternal transport are improved perinatal survival and a shortened, less-expensive hospital stay.

The need for maternal transport will depend on serial assessments of the pregnancy and future medical needs of the mother and infant. The diagnosis of a normal pregnancy is a retrospective one. Serious risk may be identified early in pregnancy (Table 9-3), sometimes later (Table 9-4), and at times only after the onset of labor (Table 9-5). The continuing challenge throughout pregnancy is to identify the infant with major problems before it is too late to match the mother and her fetus with the optimum resources.

The decision to transport a pregnant woman when a risk becomes apparent after the onset of labor depends on the indication for transport as well as local resources. Transporting a mother in early premature labor is possible. The decision depends on several factors, including the time required for transport, the elapsed labor time, the progress of cervical ef-

Table 9-3. Indications for early pregnancy
consultation, referral, or possible later maternal transport

1. Maternal disorders such as treated or untreated thyrotoxicosis, organic heart disease, renal disease, hematologic disease, or infectious disease, such as recurrent herpes.
2. Familial metabolic disease or abnormalities in previous infants.
3. Rh isoimmunization requiring intrauterine transfusion or early elective delivery.
4. Maternal insulin-dependent diabetes.
5. Other fetal diseases, abnormalities, or malformation identified through techniques such as ultrasonography or amniocentesis.
6. Multiple fetuses.
7. Previous premature onset of labor.
8. Previous infants with respiratory distress syndrome.
9. Hypertension or preeclampsia.
10. Placental abnormalities such as placenta previa or low-lying placenta identified by ultrasonography before the onset of overt disease.

facement and dilation, and whether fetal membranes have ruptured. On the other hand, fetal asphyxia in a term pregnancy may require immediate delivery and subsequent neonatal transport. Whenever maternal transport is judged impossible, consultation and plans for possible infant transport should begin.

INFANT TRANSPORT

Most neonatal transports occur within the first 24 hours following delivery because the infant's illness often is apparent at delivery or soon thereafter (Table 9-6). Less frequently, the illness becomes apparent only after a period of hours or days (Table 9-7).

Table 9-4. Indications for middle to later
pregnancy consultation, referral, or maternal transport

1. Polyhydramnios
2. Hydrops identified by ultrasonography
3. Severe maternal hypertension
4. Eclampsia or other maternal convulsive disease
5. Abnormal vaginal bleeding
6. Intrauterine growth retardation
7. Chronic fetal distress (detected by nonstress testing, oxytocin challenge, or other measures)

Table 9-5. Indications for consultation, communication,
and possible maternal transport after the onset of labor

1. Premature labor
2. Acute vaginal bleeding after the onset of labor
3. Fetal distress
4. Fetal malpositions
5. Failed (ineffective) labor

More often than not, the staff of the level I hospital already has been in communication with a level III unit by the time a high-risk infant is born. In fact, sometimes the transport process has already been initiated. In some instances, presentation of a sick infant in a level I hospital is unanticipated and requires stabilization efforts as discussed below.

In all instances, every request for transfer begins with a phone call from the referring health professional to the special care unit. The effectiveness and success of the communication depends on mutual respect and understanding and familiarity with the local and special care facilities. Specific requests and problem identification should be made during the phone communication. The call provides the opportunity to review the history, course, differential diagnosis, and diagnostic and therapeutic measures that can be performed at the birthing hospital. Sometimes problems may be solved over the phone and a transport prevented.

While arranging for the transport of a sick infant, the personnel at the level I unit must stabilize the infant's temperature, heart rate, blood pressure, ventilation and oxygenation, and fluid and electrolyte balance as efficiently and proficiently as possible. Meanwhile, a copy of the infant's and

Table 9-6. Indications for early transport of the infant

1. Respiratory disease lasting longer than 2 hr or respiratory disease of increasing severity*
2. Need for supplemental oxygen persisting longer than 2 hr
3. Birth weight less than 1,500 gm or gestation of 32 wk or less
4. Abnormalities requiring surgical or other special intervention (for example, myelocele, gastroschisis or omphalocele, diaphragmatic hernia, esophageal atresia)
5. Any infant requiring assisted ventilation and acute life support beyond 2 hr of age

*When there is a history of a previous low birth weight infant who has had respiratory distress syndrome and a later pregnancy produces an infant who has a low birth weight, there is a 90% chance that the infant will have respiratory distress [8].

Table 9-7. Indications for communication, consultation, and
transport of the infant after the first hours or days following delivery

1. Severe infection with evidence of shock or meningitis
2. Heart disease
3. Severe jaundice
4. Catastrophe such as intestinal perforation, ileus, intestinal obstruction, pneumothorax, or convulsions
5. Persistent metabolic derangements
6. Multiple congenital malformations

mother's medical records, roentgenograms, samples of maternal and cord blood, and the placenta should be prepared to accompany the infant.

The vehicle, the support equipment, and quality control of the transport system are the responsibility of the level III hospital in the regionalization program.

Once the neonatal transport team arrives, the referring physician should review the history and treatment plan with them and introduce the team to the infant's family. Together they can explain the infant's diagnosis, condition, prognosis, and anticipated problems to the family. This unified approach reassures the family that appropriate measures are being instituted. The transport team should provide the family with brochures about the special care unit as well as with names and phone numbers of those who will be caring for the infant. Before the infant leaves the referral hospital, the parents should see and touch him.

REFERENCES

1. American Academy of Pediatrics. *Standards and Recommendations for Hospital Care of Newborn Infants* (6th ed.). Evanston, IL: American Academy of Pediatrics, 1977.
2. Clark, J. M., Brown, Z. A., and Jung, A. L. Resuscitation equipment board for nurseries and delivery rooms. *J.A.M.A.* 236 : 2427, 1976.
3. Cloney, D. L., and Donowitz, L. G. Overgrown use for infection control in nurseries and neonatal intensive care units. *Am. J. Dis. Child.* 140 : 680, 1986.
4. Committee on Perinatal Health. *Towards Improving the Outcome of Pregnancy. Recommendations for the Regional Development of Maternal and Perinatal Health Services.* White Plains, NY: The National Foundation-March of Dimes, 1976.
5. Coen, R. W. Training of personnel—Pediatrics. *Clin. Perinatol.* 3 : 459, 1976.
6. Davies, P. A. Please wash your hands. *Arch. Dis. Child.* 57 : 647, 1982.
7. Donowitz, L. G. Failure of the overgown to prevent nosocomial infection in a pediatric intensive care unit. *Pediatrics* 77 : 35, 1986.

8. Graven, S. N., and Misenheimer, H. R. Respiratory distress syndrome and the high risk mother. *Am. J. Dis. Child.* 109 : 489, 1965.

9. Harris, T. R., Isaman, J., and Giles, H. R. Improved neonatal survival through maternal transport. *Obstet. Gynecol.* 52 : 294, 1978.

10. Hobel, C. J., Youkeles, L., and Forsythe, A. Prenatal and intrapartum high-risk screening II. Risk factors reassessed. *Am. J. Dis. Child.* 109 : 489, 1965.

11. Merenstein, G. B., et al. An analysis of air transport results in the sick newborn II. Antenatal and neonatal referrals. *Am. J. Obstet. Gynecol.* 128 : 520, 1977.

12. Miller, T. C., Densberger, M., and Krogman, J. Maternal transport and the perinatal denominator. *Am. J. Obstet. Gynecol.* 147 : 19, 1983.

Appendixes

Appendix 1
Normal Embryonic Development*

EMBRYONIC DEVELOPMENT

AGE days	LENGTH mm.	STAGE Streeter	GROSS APPEARANCE	C.N.S.	EYE	EAR	FACE
4		III	Blastocyst				
8	.1	IV	embryo trophoblast endometrium				
12	.2	V	ectoderm amnionic sac endoderm yolk sac				
19	1	IX	ant head fold body stalk heart	Enlargement of anterior neural plate			
24	2	X early somites	foregut allantois	Partial fusion neural folds	Optic evagination	Otic placode	Mandible Hyoid arches
30	4	XII 21-29 somites		Closure neural tube Rhombencephalon, mesen., prosen. Ganglia V VII VIII X	Optic cup	Otic invagination	Fusion, mand. arches
34	7	XIV		Cerebellar plate Cervical and mesencephalic flexures	Lens invagination	Otic vesicle	Olfactory placodes
38	11	XVI		Dorsal pontine flexure Basal lamina Cerebral evagination Neural hypophysis	Lens detached Pigmented retina	Endolymphic sac Ext. auditory meatus Tubotympanic recess	Nasal swellings
44	17	XVIII		Olfactory evagination Cerebral hemisphere	Lens fibers Migration of retinal cells Hyaloid vessels		Choana, Prim. palate
52	23	XX		Optic nerve to brain	Corneal body Mesoderm No lumen in optic stalk		
55	28	XXII			Eyelids	Spiral cochlear duct Tragus	

*From D. W. Smith. *Recognizable Patterns of Human Malformation* (3rd ed.). Philadelphia: Saunders, 1982. With permission.

The embryonic ages for Streeter's stages XII - XXIII have been altered in accordance with the human data from Iffy, L., et al.: Acta Anat. 66 : 178, 1967

EXTREMITIES	HEART	GUT, ABDOMEN	LUNG	UROGENITAL	OTHER
					Early blastocyst with inner cell mass and cavitation (58 cells) lying free within the uterine cavity.
					Implantation Trophoblast invasion Embryonic disc with endoblast and ectoblast
		Yolk sac			Early amnion sac Extraembryonic mesoblast, angioblast Chorionic gonadotropin
	Merging mesoblast anterior to prechordal plate	Stomatodeum Cloaca		Allantois	Primitive streak Hensen's node Notochord Prechordal plate Blood cells in yolk sac
	Single heart tube Propulsion	Foregut		Mesonephric ridge	Yolk sac larger than amnion sac
Arm bud	Ventric. outpouching Gelatinous reticulum	Rupture stomatodeum Evagination of thyroid, liver, and dorsal pancreas.	Lung bud	Mesonephric duct enters cloaca	Rathke's pouch Migration of myotomes from somites
Leg bud	Auric. outpouching Septum primum	Pharyngeal pouches yield parathyroids, lat. thyroid, thymus Stomach broadens	Bronchi	Ureteral evag. Urorect. sept. Germ cells Gonadal ridge Coelom, Epithelium	
Hand plate, Mesench. condens. Innervation	Fusion mid. A-V canal Muscular vent. sept.	Intestinal loop into yolk stalk Cecum Gallbladder Hepatic ducts Spleen	Main lobes	Paramesonephric duct / Gonad ingrowth of coelomic epith.	Adrenal cortex (from coelomic epithelium) invaded by sympathetic cells = medulla Jugular lymph sacs
Finger rays, Elbow	Aorta Pulmonary artery Valves Membrane ventricular septum	Duodenal lumen obliterated Cecum rotates right Appendix	Tracheal cartil.	Fusion urorect. sept. Open urogen. memb, anus Epith. cords in testicle	Early muscle
Clearing, central cartil.	Septum secundum			S-shaped vesicles in in nephron blastema connect with collecting tubules from calyces	Superficial vascular plexus low on cranium
Shell, Tubular bone				A few large glomeruli Short secretory tubules Tunica albuginea Testicle, interstitial cells	Superficial vascular plexus at vertex

Appendix 2
Normal Fetal Development*

FETAL DEVELOPMENT

AGE weeks	LENGTH cm C-R	LENGTH cm Tot.	WT. gm.	GROSS APPEARANCE	CNS	EYE, EAR	FACE, MOUTH	CARDIO-VASCULAR	LUNG
7½	2.8				Cerebral hemisphere / Infundibulum, Rathke's	Lens nearing final shape	Palatal swellings / Dental lamina, Epithel.	Pulmonary vein into left atrium	
8	3.7				Primitive cereb. cortex / Olfactory lobes / Dura and pia mater	Eyelid / Ear canals	Nares plugged / Rathke's pouch detach. / Sublingual gland	A-V bundle / Sinus venosus absorbed into right auricle	Pleuroperitoneal canals close / Bronchioles
10	6.0				Spinal cord histology / Cerebellum	Iris / Ciliary body / Eyelids fuse / Lacrimal glands / Spiral gland different	Lips, Nasal cartilage / Palate		Laryngeal cavity reopened
12	8.8				Cord-cervical & lumbar enlarged, Cauda equina	Retina layered / Eye axis forward / Scala tympani	Tonsillar crypts / Cheeks / Dental papilla	Accessory coats, blood vessels	Elastic fibers
16	14				Corpora quadrigemina / Cerebellum prominent / Myelination begins	Scala vestibuli / Cochlear duct	Palate complete / Enamel and dentine	Cardiac muscle condensed	Segmentation of bronchi complete
20						Inner ear ossified	Ossification of nose		Decrease in mesenchyme / Capillaries penetrate linings of tubules
24		32	800		Typical layers in cerebral cortex / Cauda equina at first sacral level		Nares reopen / Calcification of tooth primordia		Change from cuboidal to flattened epithelium / Alveoli
28		38.5	1100		Cerebral fissures and convolutions	Eyelids reopen / Retinal layers complete / Perceive light			Vascular components adequate for respiration
32		43.5	1600	Accumulation of fat		Auricular cartilage	Taste sense		Number of alveoli still incomplete
36		47.5	2600						
38		50	3200		Cauda equina at L-3 / Myelination within brain	Lacrimal duct canalized	Rudimentary frontal maxillary sinuses	Closure of: foramen ovale, ductus arteriosus, umbilical vessels, ductus venosus	
First postnatal year +					Continuing organization of axonal networks / Cerebrocortical function, motor coordination / Myelination continues until 2-3 years	Iris pigmented, 5 months / Mastoid air cells / Coordinate vision, 3-5 months / Maximal vision by 5 years	Salivary gland ducts become canalized / Teeth begin to erupt 5-7 months / Relatively rapid growth of mandible and nose	Relative hypertrophy left ventricle	Continue adding new alveoli

*From D. W. Smith. *Recognizable Patterns of Human Malformation* (3rd ed.). Philadelphia: Saunders, 1982. With permission.

GUT	UROGENITAL	SKELETAL MUSCLE	SKELETON	SKIN	BLOOD, THYMUS LYMPH	ENDOCRINE
Pancreas, dorsal and ventral fusion	Renal vesicles	Differentiation toward final shape	Cartilaginous models of bones / Chondrocranium / Tail regression	Mammary gland		Parathyroid assoc- iated with thyroid / Sympathetic neuro- blasts invade adrenal
Liver relatively large / Intestinal villi	Müllerian ducts fusing / Ovary distinguishable	Muscles well represented / Movement	Ossification center / Sternum	Basal layer	Bone marrow / Thymus halves unite / Lymphoblasts around the lymph sacs	Thyroid follicles
Gut withdrawal from cord / Pancreatic alveoli / Anal canal	Testosterone / Renal excretion / Bladder sac / Müllerian tube into urogenital sinus / Vaginal sacs, prostate	Perineal muscles	Joints	Hair follicles / Melanocytes	Enucleated R.B.C.'s / Thymus yields retic- ulum and corpuscles / Thoracic duct / Lymph nodes; axillary iliac	Adrenalin / Noradrenalin
Gut muscle layers / Pancreatic islets / Bile	Seminal vesicle / Regression, genital ducts		Tail degenerated / Notochord degenerated	Corium, 3 layers / Scalp, body hair / Sebaceous glands / Nails beginning	Blood principally from bone marrow / Thymus-medullary and lymphoid	Testicle-Leydig cells / Thyroid-colloid in follicle / Anterior pituitary acidophilic granules / Ovary-prim. follicles
Omentum fusing with transverse colon / Mesoduodenum, asc. & desc. colon attach to body wall. Meconium. Gastric, intest. glands	Typical kidney / Mesonephros involuting / Uterus and vagina / Primary follicles	In-utero move- ment can be detected	Distinct bones	Dermal ridges hands / Sweat glands / Keratinization		Anterior pituitary- basophilic granules
	No further collecting tubules			Venix caseosa / Nail plates / Mammary budding	Blood formation decreasing in liver	
						Testes-decrease in Leydig cells
						Testes descend
	Urine osmolarity continues to be relatively low			Eccrine sweat / Lanugo hair prominent / Nails to fingertips		
			Only a few secondary epiphyseal centers ossified in knee		Hemoglobin 17-18 gm / Leukocytosis	
			Ossification of 2nd epiph. centers-hamate, capitate, proximal humerus, femur / New ossif. 2nd epiph. centers till 10-12 yrs. / Ossif. of epiphyses till 16-18 yrs.	New hair, gradual loss of lanugo hair	Transient (6 wk) erythroid hypoplasia / Hemoglobin 11-12 gm / 7S gamma globulin produced by 6 wks. / Lymph nodes develop cortex, medulla	Transient estrinization / Adrenal-regression of fetal zone / Gonadotropin with feminization of ♀ 9-12 yr. (onset); masc. of ♂ 10-14 yr.(onset)

Appendix 3
Checklist of Significant Minor Anomalies in the Newborn

1. Ocular

_____ epicanthic folds in varying degrees
_____ lateral displacement of inner canthus
_____ down-slanting palpebral fissures
_____ true ocular hypertelorism
_____ up-slanting palpebral fissures
_____ brushfield spots

2. Auricular

_____ cutaneous tags or pits
_____ incomplete helix development
_____ lack of labulus
_____ prominent ears
_____ low-set ears
_____ slanted ears

3. Hands

_____ single transverse palmar crease
_____ bridged (modified transverse) palmar crease
_____ short and broad nails
_____ narrow hyperconvex nails
_____ hypoplasia of nail
_____ asymmetry of fingers
_____ short incurred fifth finger (clinodactyly)
_____ camptodactyly (flexion contracture)

4. Feet

_____ asymmetry of toes
_____ clinodactyly
_____ short metatarsal with dorsiflexion of hallus (hammer toe)
_____ syndactyly proximal second and third toes
_____ hypoplasia of nails
_____ deep crease between great toe and second toe
_____ wide gap between great toe and second toe

5. Skin and hair

_____ deep dimples or bony promentorils
_____ deep sacral dimple
_____ "punched out" scalp defects
_____ abnormal eyebrows
_____ low hairline
_____ hirsutism (not secondary to failure to thrive)
_____ multiple hair whorls

6. Miscellaneous
_____ aberrant frenula of mouth
_____ mild pectus excavatum
_____ short sternum
_____ scrotum extending distally on penis
_____ labile hypoplasia with prominent clitoris

Source: *Guidelines for Perinatal Care*. Evanston, IL/Washington, DC: American Academy of Pediatrics and American College of Obstetricians and Gynecologists, 1983. With permission.

Appendix 4
Major Findings of Trisomies at Birth

	21	18	13-15
Incidence	1.5/1000	0.3/1000	0.2/1.000
Gestational			
lfetal activity	—	+ +	—
Pre/Term/Post	—	$\frac{1}{3}$/$\frac{1}{3}$/$\frac{1}{3}$	—
Polyhydramnios	—	+ +	—
Small placenta	—	+ +	—
Low birth weight	—	+ +	—
Single umbilical artery	—	+ +	+ +
Neurologic			
Tone	Hypotonia + +	Hypertonia +	—
Seizure/apnea	—	—	+ +
Hearing	—	+ +	+ +
Craniofacial			
Facies	Flat + +	Narrow bifrontal +	Holoprosencephaly syndrome + +
Occiput	Flat + +	Prominent + +	—
Clefts	—	+	+ +
Ears	Small + +	Low + +	Shape + +
Eye fissure	Slanted + +	Short + +	—
Eye otherwise	Brushfield spots +	—	Microphthalmia +
Micrognathia	—	+ +	+

Skeletal			
Joint flexibility	Hyper + +	Hypo +	-
Pelvis	Hypoplasia + +	↓ abduction + +	Hypoplasia + +
Radial aplasia	-	±	+
Rocker bottom feet	-	+	-
Equinovarus	-	+	+
Hands			
Shape	Spade + +	Clenched + +	Clenched + +
Hypoplastic fifth	+ +	+ +	+
Simian crease	+ +	+ +	+ +
Hypoplastic nails	-	+ +	Toenails +
Dermatoglyphics	Ulnar loop +	Low arch + +	Low arch +
Cardiac defect	+	+ +	+ +
Abdominal defect	Duodenal atresia +	Omphalocele +	Omphalocele +
Genitals			
Cryptorchidism	-	+ +	+ +
Hypospadias	-	±	+
Hypoplastic labia	-	+	+
Prognosis (attrition)			
1 mo	CHD	30%	45%
2 mo		50%	
6 mo			70%
1 yr		90%	85%
Adult	Variable	99.9%	99.9%

Key: + + = major; + = minor; - = occasional; ↓ = decreased.
Source: Reprinted by permission of Elsevier Science Publishing Co., Inc. from A. G. S. Philip, *Neonatology* (2nd ed.), p. 77. Copyright 1980 by Medical Examination Publishing Company, Inc.

Appendix 5
Infant State-Related Behavior Chart

Behavior	Description of behavior	Infant state consideration	Implications for caregiving
Alerting	Widening and brightening of the eyes. Infants focus attention on stimuli, whether visual, auditory, or objects to be sucked.	From drowsy or active alert to quiet alert.	Infant state and timing are important. When trying to alert infants, one may try to: 1. Unwrap infants (arms out at least) 2. Place infants in upright position 3. Talk to infants, putting variation in your pitch and tempo 4. Show your face to infants 5. Elicit the rooting, sucking, or grasp reflexes. Being able to alert infants is important for caregivers, as alert infants offer increased feedback to adults
Visual response	Newborns have pupillary responses to differences in brightness. Infants can focus on objects or faces about 7–8 in. away. Newborns have preferences for more complex patterns, human faces, and moving objects.	Quiet alert.	Newborns' visual alertness provides opportunities for eye-to-eye contact with caregivers, an important source of beginning caregiver-infant interaction.

Auditory response	Reaction to a variety of sounds, especially in the human voice range. Infants can hear sounds and locate the general direction of the sound, if the source is constant and remains coming from the same direction.	Drowsy, quiet alert, active alert.	Enhances communication between infants and caregivers. The fact that crying infants can often be consoled by voice demonstrates the value this stimulus has to infants.
Habituation	The ability to lessen one's response to repeated stimuli. For instance, this is seen when the Moro response is repeatedly elicited. If a noise is continually repeated, infants will no longer respond to it in most cases.	Deep sleep, light sleep, also seen in drowsy.	Because of this ability families can carry out their normal activities without disturbing infants. Infants are not victims of their environments. Infants can shut out most stimuli, similar to adults not hearing a dripping faucet after a period of time. Infants who have more difficulty with this will probably not sleep well in active environments.
Cuddliness	Infant's response to being held. Infants nestle and work themselves into the contours of caregivers' bodies versus resist being held.	Primarily in awake states.	Cuddliness is usually rewarding behavior for the caregivers. It seems to convey a message of affection. If infants do not nestle and mold, it would be wise to discuss this tendency and show the caregivers how to position infants to maximize this response.
Consolability	Measured when infants have been crying for at least 15 seconds. The ability of infants to bring themselves or to be brought by others to a lower state.	From crying to active alert, quiet alert, drowsy, or sleep states.	Crying is the infant behavior that presents the greatest challenge to caregivers. Parents' success or failure in consoling their infants has a significant impact on their feelings of competence as parents.

Appendix 5 (continued).

Behavior	Description of behavior	Infant state consideration	Implications for caregiving
Self-consoling	Maneuvers used by infants to console themselves and move to a lower state: 1. Hand-to-mouth movement 2. Sucking on fingers, fist, or tongue 3. Paying attention to voices or faces around them 4. Changes in position	From crying to active alert, quiet alert, drowsy, or sleep states.	If caregivers are aware of these behaviors, they may allow infants the opportunity to gain control of themselves instead of immediately responding to their cues. This does not imply that newborns should be left to cry. Once newborns are crying and do not initiate self-consoling activities, they may need attention from caregivers.
Consoling by caregivers	After crying for longer than 15 seconds, the caregivers may try to: 1. Show face to infant 2. Talk to infant in a steady, soft voice 3. Hold both infant's arms close to body 4. Swaddle infant 5. Pick up infant 6. Rock infant 7. Give a pacifier or feed	From crying to active alert, quiet alert, drowsy, or sleep states.	Often parental initial reaction is to pick up infants or feed them when they cry. Parents could be taught to try other soothing maneuvers.

Motor behavior and activity	Spontaneous movements of extremities and body when stimulated versus when left alone. Smooth, rhythmical movements versus jerky ones.	Quiet alert, active alert.	Smooth, nonjerky movements with periods of inactivity seem most natural. Some parents see jerky movements and startles as responses to their caregiving and are frightened.
Irritability	How easily infants are upset by loud noises, handling by caregivers, temperature changes, removal of blankets or clothes, etc.	From deep sleep, light sleep, drowsy, quiet alert, or active alert to fussing or crying.	Irritable infants need more frequent consoling and more subdued external environments. Parents can be helped to cope with more irritable infants through the items listed under "Consoling by Caregivers."
Readability	The cues infants give through motor behavior and activity, looking, listening, and behavior patterns.	All states.	Parents need to learn that newborns' behaviors are part of their individual temperaments and not reflections on their parenting abilities or because their infants do not like them. By observing and understanding an infant's characteristic pattern, parents can respond more appropriately to their infant as an individual.
Smile	Ranging from a faint grimace to a full-fledged smile. Reflexive.	Drowsy, active alert, quiet alert, light sleep.	Initial smile in the neonatal period is the forerunner of the social smile at 3–4 weeks of age. Important for caregivers to respond to it.

Source: S. Blackburn. Infant state-related behavior chart. In "Early Parent-Infant Relationships," Series 1, Module 3. White Plains, NY: The National Foundation—March of Dimes, 1978, with permission of the copyright holder.

206

Appendix 6
Infant Sleep and Awake States

			Characteristics of state*			
State	Body activity	Eye movements	Facial movements	Breathing pattern	Level of response	Implications for caregiving
SLEEP						
Deep	Nearly still except for occasional startle or twitch.	None.	None except for occasional sucking movement at regular intervals.	Smooth and regular.	Threshold to stimuli is very high so that only very intense and disturbing stimuli will arouse infants.	Caregivers trying to feed infants in deep sleep will probably find the experience frustrating. Infants will be unresponsive, even if caregivers use disturbing stimuli (flicking feet) to arouse infants. Infants may only arouse briefly and then become unresponsive as they return to deep sleep. If caregivers wait until infants move to a higher, more responsive state, feeding or caregiving will be more pleasant.
Light	Some body movements.	Rapid eye movements	May smile and make	Irregular.	More responsive to internal and exter-	Light sleep makes up the highest proportion of newborn sleep and

State	Body activity	Eyes	Facial movements	Breathing	Response to stimulation	Implications for caregiving
(continued)		(REM), fluttering of eyes beneath closed eyelids.	brief fussy or crying sounds.		nal stimuli. When these stimuli occur, infants may remain in light sleep, return to deep sleep, or arouse to drowsy state.	usually precedes wakening. Due to brief fussy or crying sounds made during this state, caregivers who are not aware that these sounds occur normally may think it is time for feeding and may try to feed infants before they are ready to eat.
AWAKE Drowsy	Activity level variable, with mild startles interspersed from time to time. Movements usually smooth.	Eyes open and close occasionally, are heavy-lidded with dull glazed appearance.	May have some facial movements. Often there are none, and the face appears still.	Irregular.	Infants react to sensory stimuli although responses are delayed. State change after stimulation frequently noted.	From the drowsy state, infants may return to sleep or awaken further. To awaken infants, caregivers can provide something for infants to see, hear, or suck, as this may arouse them to a quiet alert state. Infants left alone without stimuli may return to a sleep state.
Quiet alert	Minimal.	Brightening and widening of eyes.	Faces have bright, shining, sparkling looks.	Regular.	Infants attend most to environment, focusing attention on any stimuli that are present.	Infants in this state provide much pleasure and positive feedback for caregivers. Providing something for infants to see, hear, or suck will often maintain a quiet alert state. In the first few hours after birth, most newborns commonly experience a period of intense alertness before going into a long sleeping period.

Appendix 6 (continued).

State	Characteristics of state*					Implications for caregiving
	Body activity	Eye movements	Facial movements	Breathing pattern	Level of response	
Active alert	Much body activity. May have periods of fussiness.	Eyes open with less brightening.	Much facial movement. Faces not as bright as quiet alert state.	Irregular.	Increasingly sensitive to disturbing stimuli (hunger, fatigue, noise, excessive handling).	Caregivers may intervene at this stage to console and to bring infants to a lower state.
Crying	Increased motor activity, with color changes.	Eyes may be tightly closed or open.	Grimaces.	More irregular.	Extremely responsive to unpleasant external or internal stimuli.	Crying is the infant's communication signal. It is a response to unpleasant stimuli from the environment or from within (fatigue, hunger, discomfort). Crying tells us the infants' limits have been reached. Sometimes infants can console themselves and return to lower states. At other times, they need help from caregivers.

*A *state* is a group of characteristics that regularly occur together: body activity, eye movements, facial movements, breathing pattern, and level of response to external stimuli (e.g., handling) and internal stimuli (e.g., hunger).
Source: S. Blackburn. Sleep and awake states of the newborn. In "Early Parent-Infant Relationships," Series 1, Module 3. White Plains, NY: The National Foundation—March of Dimes, 1978, with permission of the copyright holder.

Appendix 7
Neutral Thermal
Environmental Temperatures

Age and weight	Starting incubator temperature (°C)	Range of temperature (°C)
0–6 hr		
Over 2500 (and > 36 wk)	23.9	32.0–33.8
6–12 hr		
Over 2500 (and > 36 wk)	32.8	31.4–33.8
12–24 hr		
Over 2500 (and > 36 wk)	32.4	31.0–33.7
24–36 hr		
Over 2500 (and > 36 wk)	32.1	30.7–33.5
36–48 hr		
Over 2500 (and > 36 wk)	31.9	30.5–33.3
48–72 hr		
Over 2500 (and > 36 wk)	31.7	30.1–33.2
72–96 hr		
Over 2500 (and > 36 wk)	31.3	29.8–32.8
4–12 days		
Over 2500 (and > 36 wk)		
4–5 days	31.0	29.5–32.6
5–6 days	30.9	29.4–32.3
6–8 days	30.6	29.0–32.2
8–10 days	30.3	29.0–31.8
10–12 days	30.1	29.0–31.4

Source: *Guidelines for Perinatal Care.* Evanston, IL/Washington, DC: American Academy of Pediatrics and American College of Obstetricians and Gynecologists, 1983. With permission.

Appendix 8
Equivalent Centigrade and Fahrenheit Temperature Readings*

Fahrenheit degrees	Centigrade degrees
32.0	0
69.8	21
80.6	27
86.0	30
95.0	35
96.8	36
98.6	37
100.4	38
102.2	39
104.0	40
105.8	41
107.6	42
109.4	43
212.0	100

*Conversion of centigrade to Fahrenheit: multiply by 1.8 and add 32. Conversion of Fahrenheit to centigrade: subtract 32 and divide by 1.8.

Appendix 9
Weight Conversion Chart (Pounds/Ounces to Grams)

Pounds \ Ounces	0	1	2	3	4	5	6	7	8	9	10	11	12	13	14	15
0	0	28	57	85	113	142	170	198	227	255	284	312	340	369	397	425
1	454	482	510	539	567	595	624	652	680	709	737	765	794	822	851	879
2	907	936	964	992	1021	1049	1077	1106	1134	1162	1191	1219	1247	1276	1304	1332
3	1361	1389	1418	1446	1474	1503	1531	1559	1588	1616	1644	1673	1701	1729	1758	1786
4	1814	1843	1871	1899	1928	1956	1985	2013	2041	2070	2098	2126	2155	2183	2211	2240
5	2268	2296	2325	2353	2381	2410	2438	2466	2495	2523	2552	2580	2608	2637	2665	2693
6	2722	2750	2778	2807	2835	2863	2892	2920	2948	2977	3005	3033	3062	3090	3119	3147
7	3175	3204	3232	3260	3289	3317	3345	3374	3402	3430	3459	3487	3515	3544	3572	3600
8	3629	3657	3686	3714	3742	3771	3799	3827	3856	3884	3912	3941	3969	3997	4026	4054
9	4082	4111	4139	4167	4196	4224	4253	4281	4309	4338	4366	4394	4423	4451	4479	4508
10	4536	4564	4593	4621	4649	4678	4706	4734	4763	4791	4820	4848	4876	4905	4933	4961
11	4990	5018	5046	5075	5103	5131	5160	5188	5216	5245	5273	5301	5330	5358	5387	5415
12	5443	5472	5500	5528	5557	5585	5613	5642	5670	5698	5727	5755	5783	5812	5840	5868
13	5897	5925	5954	5982	6010	6039	6067	6095	6124	6152	6180	6209	6237	6265	6294	6322
14	6350	6379	6407	6435	6464	6492	6521	6549	6577	6606	6634	6662	6691	6719	6747	6776
15	6804	6832	6861	6889	6917	6946	6974	7002	7031	7059	7088	7116	7144	7173	7201	7229

Appendix 10
Normal Electrocardiographic Values in Newborn Infants*

Table 1. Heart rate, PR interval, P-wave duration, QRS
duration, and P-wave amplitude in lead II of mature newborn infants

Age	Minimum	5%	Mean	95%	Maximum	S.D.
	Heart rate					
0–24 hr	85	94	119	145	145	16.1
1– 7 days	100	100	133	175	175	22.3
8–30 days	115	115	163	190	190	19.9
	PR interval					
0–24 hr	0.07	0.07	0.10	0.12	0.13	0.012
1– 7 days	0.05	0.07	0.09	0.12	0.13	0.014
8–30 days	0.07	0.07	0.09	0.11	0.13	0.010
	P-wave duration					
0–24 hr	0.040	0.040	0.051	0.065	0.075	0.066
1– 7 days	0.035	0.038	0.046	0.061	0.065	0.066
8–30 days	0.040	0.040	0.048	0.057	0.065	0.064
	QRS duration					
0–24 hr	0.05	0.05	0.065	0.084	0.09	0.010
1– 7 days	0.04	0.04	0.056	0.079	0.08	0.010
8–30 days	0.04	0.04	0.057	0.073	0.08	0.009
	P-wave amplitude in II					
0–24 hr	0	0.8	1.5	2.3	2.6	0.50
1– 7 days	0.5	0.8	1.6	2.5	2.8	0.51
8–30 days	0.5	0.8	1.6	2.4	2.7	0.48

Table 2. Mean frontal, QRS, and T axes in mature newborn infants

Age	QRS axis (frontal plane)					T axis (frontal plane)				
	Minimum	5%	Mean	95%	Maximum	Minimum	5%	Mean	95%	Maximum
0–24 hr	60	60	135	180	180	–20	0	70	140	180
1– 7 days	60	80	125	160	180	–40	–40	25	80	100
8–30 days	0	60	110	160	180	–20	0	35	60	120

Table 3. Amplitudes of R and S waves in precordial leads

Age	R wave						S wave					
	Minimum	5%	Mean	95%	Maximum	S.D.	Minimum	5%	Mean	95%	Maximum	S.D.
Amplitudes in V_1												
0–24 hr	5.5	7.0	14.8	20.0	20.5	3.75	0	2.5	9.3	27.0	28.5	7.99
1– 7 days	5.5	9.0	18.2	27.4	29.5	5.44	1.5	4.6	10.4	18.8	25.5	4.70
8–30 days	2.5	4.2	11.4	19.8	26.5	4.97	0	2.5	5.0	12.8	18.5	3.73
Amplitudes in V_2												
0–24 hr	11.5	13.0	20.1	28.1	29.5	3.81	5.0	9.0	20.3	33.8	37.0	6.73
1– 7 days	8.5	11.7	19.9	31.1	32.5	5.89	5.0	9.3	20.2	34.1	37.0	7.26
8–30 days	5.5	6.8	17.5	29.0	32.5	6.48	1.0	4.2	14.0	25.7	29.0	6.24
Amplitudes in V_3												
0–24 hr	12.0	12.7	18.8	26.7	28.0	4.12	10.0	12.0	25.0	32.0	38.0	6.05
1– 7 days	4.0	8.8	18.1	30.0	40.0	6.55	0	2.6	17.1	33.0	38.0	8.37
8–30 days	0.0	8.3	18.8	33.8	36.0	7.50	2.0	4.2	12.4	20.0	26.0	5.47
Amplitudes in V_4												
0–24 hr	8.0	9.0	17.4	26.0	32.0	5.97	2	4.0	21.8	36.0	42.0	9.08
1– 7 days	4.0	4.9	18.8	33.1	36.0	7.24	0	3.4	13.2	27.7	30.0	8.11
8–30 days	4.0	3.3	15.9	33.3	36.0	7.82	0	3.1	6.8	16.3	18.0	5.05

Table 3 (continued).

Age	R wave Mini-mum	5%	Mean	95%	Maxi-mum	S.D.	S wave Mini-mum	5%	Mean	95%	Maxi-mum	S.D.
Amplitudes in V_5												
0–24 hr	0.0	4.0	10.2	18.0	24.0	5.44	0	0.0	11.9	24.0	31.5	6.87
1– 7 days	0.0	3.4	10.7	19.3	28.0	5.54	0	3.6	6.8	16.2	19.5	4.73
8–30 days	0.0	3.5	11.9	27.0	36.0	7.28	0	2.7	4.8	12.3	13.5	3.50
Amplitudes in V_6												
0–24 hr	0	2.3	3.3	7.0	7.5	2.10	0	1.6	4.5	10.3	14.0	2.78
1– 7 days	0	2.2	5.1	13.1	16.5	3.97	0	0.8	3.3	9.9	14.0	2.99
8–30 days	0	1.7	6.7	20.5	25.5	4.82	0	0.6	2.0	9.0	10.0	2.46
Amplitudes in AVR												
0–24 hr	–	–	–	–	–	–	–	–	–	–	–	–
1– 7 days	0	0.5	2.8	6.4	7.5	1.80	3.0	3.7	7.9	13.9	15.0	3.11
8–30 days	0	1.0	2.0	4.0	6.5	1.39	5.0	5.6	10.1	14.6	15.0	2.81
Amplitudes in AVL												
0–24 hr	–	–	–	–	–	–	–	–	–	–	–	–
1– 7 days	0	0.5	1.7	3.3	6.5	1.04	0	1.4	5.2	9.7	13.0	2.48
8–30 days	0	1.2	2.2	5.8	7.5	1.48	0	2.2	5.3	8.9	13.0	2.10
Amplitudes in AVF												
0–24 hr	–	–	–	–	–	–	–	–	–	–	–	–
1– 7 days	1.0	1.9	5.4	10.5	13.0	2.43	0	0.6	0.7	3.1	3.5	1.10
8–30 days	1.0	1.4	6.1	12.4	15.0	3.39	0	0.6	0.6	3.8	5.5	1.20

Table 4. Amplitude of T waves in precordial leads V_4 to V_6

Age	V_4				V_5				V_6			
	Mean	95%	Maximum	S.D.	Mean	95%	Maximum	S.D.	Mean	95%	Maximum	S.D.
0–24 hr	4.3	7.2	8.5	0.95	3.3	6.8	7.5	1.62	2.4	3.9	4.5	0.63
1– 7 days	4.4	7.7	8.5	1.39	4.9	7.3	7.5	1.44	2.9	4.2	4.5	0.67
8–30 days	5.3	8.1	8.5	1.49	5.3	7.5	10.5	1.50	3.5	5.3	7.5	1.01

*Source: A. R. Hastreiter and J. B. Abella. The Electrocardiogram in the newborn period. *J. Pediatr.* 78 : 146, 1971. With permission.

Appendix 11
Normal Capillary Blood Chemistry Values

Determination	Cord	1–2 hr	12–24 hr	24–48 hr	48–72 hr
Sodium, mEq/liter	147 (126–166)	143 (124–156)	145 (132–159)	148 (134–160)	149 (139–162)
Potassium, mEq/liter	7.8 (5.6–12)	6.4 (5.3–7.3)	6.3 (5.3–8.9)	6.0 (5.2–7.3)	5.9 (5.0–7.7)
Chloride, mEq/liter	103 (98–110)	100.7 (90–111)	103 (87–114)	102 (92–114)	103 (93–112)
Calcium, mg/dl	9.3 (8.2–11.1)	8.4 (7.3–9.2)	7.8 (6.9–9.4)	8.0 (6.1–9.9)	7.9 (5.9–9.7)
Phosphorus, mg/dl	5.6 (3.7–8.1)	6.1 (3.5–8.6)	5.7 (2.9–8.1)	5.9 (3.0–8.7)	5.8 (2.8–7.6)
Blood urea, mg/dl	29 (21–40)	27 (8–34)	33 (9–63)	32 (13–77)	31 (13–68)
Total protein, gm/dl	6.1 (4.8–7.3)	6.6 (5.6–8.5)	6.6 (5.8–8.2)	6.9 (5.9–8.2)	7.2 (6.0–8.5)
Blood sugar, mg/dl	73 (45–96)	63 (40–97)	63 (42–104)	56 (30–91)	59 (40–90)
Lactic acid, mg/dl	19.5 (11–30)	14.6 (11–24)	14.0 (10–23)	14.3 (9–22)	13.5 (7–21)
Lactate, mm/liter	2.0–3.0	2.0	—	—	—

Source: M. E. Avery and H. W. Taeusch, Jr. *Diseases of the Newborn* (5th ed.). Philadelphia: Saunders, 1984. With permission.
Note: First values given represent the mean; the values in parentheses represent the range.

Appendix 12
Additional Blood Chemistries
for Normal Term Infants

Determination	Value
Creatinine kinase	
Day 1	600 U (95% limits)
Days 2–10	440 U (95% limits)
Days 11–364	170 U (95% limits)
Magnesium	1.52–2.33 mEq/liter (2.1–2.2 mg/dl)
Manganese	2.4–9.6 µg/dl
Phosphorus	4.2–9.0 mg/dl
Gammaglutamyl transferase (GGT)	0–130 U/liter
Acid phosphatase	7.4–19.4 U/liter

Source: Adapted from S. Meites (ed.). *Pediatric Clinical Chemistry* (2nd ed.). Washington, DC: American Association for Clinical Chemistry, 1981.

Appendix 13
Serum Protein and Immunoglobulin Concentrations*

Table 1. Serum protein concentrations (gm/dl): Mean ± 1 SD and range

Age	Total proteins	Albumin	Alpha-1	Alpha-2	Beta	Gamma
Cord blood	6.22 ± 1.21 (4.78–8.04)	3.23 ± 0.82 (2.17–4.04)	0.41 ± 0.10 (0.25–0.66)	0.68 ± 0.14 (0.44–0.94)	0.74 ± 0.30 (0.42–1.56)	1.28 ± 0.23 (0.81–1.61)

Table 2. Immunoglobulin concentrations (mg/dl): Mean ± 1 SD and range

Age	IgG	IgA	IgM
Cord blood	1086 ± 290 (740–1374)	2 ± 2 (0–15)	14 ± 6 (0–22)

*Source: S. Meites (ed.). *Pediatric Clinical Chemistry* (2nd ed.). Washington, DC: American Association for Clinical Chemistry, 1981. Reprinted with permission from Clinical Chemistry.

Appendix 14
Concentrations of Thyroxine, Triiodothyronine, and Thyroid-Stimulating Hormone

Table 1. Thyroxine concentration
at various ages as measured by radioimmunoassay

Age	Thyroxine, μg/dl			
	No. pts.	Mean	SE	Range
Premature (cord blood)				
gestation age:	2683			
30 wk		9.4		5.7–15.6
35 wk		10.1		6.1–16.8
40 wk		10.9		6.6–18.1
45 wk		11.7		7.1–19.4
Full-term neonates				
(hr after birth):				
1	12	12.5		
18	13	13.5		
24	21	16		
68	18	14.5		
96	6	13		
120	6	12.5		

Table 2. Triiodothyronine concentration
at various ages as measured by radioimmunoassay

Age	T_3, ng/dl			
	No.	Mean	SE	Range
Full-term neonates	114	97.5	1.0	80–120
(cord blood):	29	48	3.0	11–90
	26	50.5	3.6	
Full-term neonates				
(time after birth):				
15 min	6	79	13	44–136
1 hr	12	293		
1.5 hr	6	191	16	136–231
24 hr	4	262	41	182–353
24 hr	15	419		
48 hr	4	191	37	127–287
69 hr	19	220		
72 hr	26	125	8	63–256

Table 3. Thyroid-stimulating hormone (thyrotropin)
concentration at various ages as measured by radioimmunoassay

Age	TSH, micro-int. U/ml			
	No.	Mean	SE	Range
Neonates (cord blood) gestation age:				
22–24 wk	22	9.6	0.93	2.4–20
38–40 wk	16	9.6	0.93	
Full-term	98	9.6		u–33
Full-term	20	5.5		2.1–10.7
Full-term neonates (time after birth):				
10 min	11	61	7.9	11–99
30 min	20	86	6.8	13–149
1 hr	16	68	4.8	43–92
1.5 hr	22	49	3.9	12–80
2 hr	7	48	9.4	14–80
3 hr	15	37	4.2	16–72
24 hr	7	17.1	3.0	8.6–33
48 hr	12	12.8	1.9	5.0–23.0

Source: S. Meites (ed.). *Pediatric Clinical Chemistry* (2nd ed.). Washington, DC: American Association for Clinical Chemistry, 1981. Reprinted with permission from Clinical Chemistry.

Appendix 15
Hematologic Values (Mean ± 1 SD) for Full-Term Infants

Age	Hemoglobin (Hb), gm/dl	Hematocrit (packed RBC vol), ml/dl	Erythrocytes (red cell count), $10^6/\mu l$	Mean corpuscular vol (MCV), μm^3/erythrocyte	Mean corpuscular hemoglobin (MCH), pg/erythrocyte	Mean corpuscular hemoglobin concentration (MCHC), gm/dl of erythrocytes
Cord blood	17.1 ± 1.8	52 ± 5	4.64 ± 0.5	113 ± 6	37 ± 2	33 ± 1
1 day	19.4 ± 2.1	58 ± 7	5.3 ± 0.5	110 ± 6	37 ± 2	33 ± 1
2–6 days	19.8 ± 2.4	66 ± 8	5.4 ± 0.7	122 ± 14	37 ± 4	30 ± 3
14–23 days	15.7 ± 1.5	52 ± 5	4.92 ± 0.6	106 ± 11	32 ± 3	30 ± 2
24–37 days	14.1 ± 1.9	45 ± 7	4.35 ± 0.6	104 ± 11	32 ± 3	31 ± 3

Source: S. Meites (ed.). *Pediatric Clinical Chemistry* (2nd ed.). Washington, DC: American Association for Clinical Chemistry, 1981. Reprinted with permission from Clinical Chemistry.

Appendix 16
Reticulocytes, Sedimentation Rate, and Blood Volume for Term Infants

	Value	Age
Reticulocyte count	3–7%	1–2 days
Sedimentation rate	1–10 mm/hr	1–7 days
Blood volume	70–100 ml/kg	

Appendix 17
White Blood Cell Values
in Term Infants During The First Week

Age (hr)	Total white cell count	Neutrophils	Lymphocytes	Monocytes	Eosinophils
0	10.0–26.0	5.0–13.0	3.5–8.5	0.7–1.5	0.2–2.0
12	13.5–31.0	9.0–18.0	3.0–7.0	1.0–2.0	0.2–2.0
72	5.0–14.5	2.0–7.0	2.0–5.0	0.5–1.0	0.2–1.0
144	6.0–14.5	2.0–6.0	3.0–6.0	0.5–1.2	0.2–0.8

Source: Adapted from F. Oski and J. L. Naiman. *Hematologic Problems in the Newborn* (3rd ed.). Philadelphia: Saunders, 1982. With permission.

Appendix 18
Reference Values for Neutrophilic Cells in the Newborn Infant*

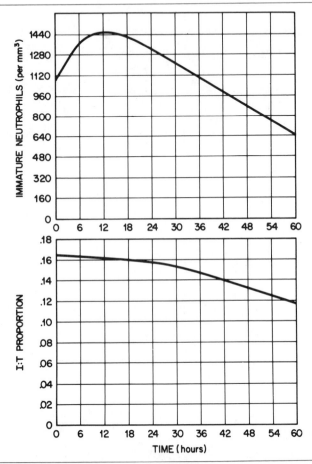

*Adapted from B. L. Manroe, A. G. Weinberg, C. R. Rosenfeld, et al. The neonatal blood count in health and disease. I. Reference values for neutrophilic cells. *J. Pediatr.* 95 : 89, 1979. With permission and courtesy of Dr. Charles R. Rosenfeld.

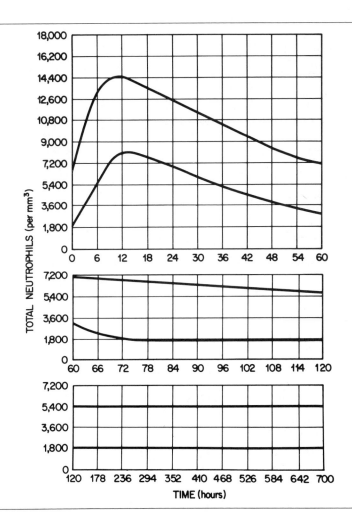

Appendix 19
Coagulation Factors in Term Newborns

Factors	
Fibrinogen (I)	246 +/− 55 mg/dl
Prothrombin (II)	45 +/− 15%
Proaccelerin (V)	98 +/− 40%
Proconvertin (VII) and Stuart (X)	56 +/− 16%
Antihemophilic factor (VIII)	105 +/− 34%
Christmas (IX)	28 +/− 8%
Plasma thromboplastin antecedent (XI)	29–70%
Hageman (XII)	25–70%
Fibrin stabilizing factor (XIII)	100%
Platelet count (per μl)	150,000–400,000
Plasminogen	43%
Fibrin split products	0
Antithrombin III	55%
Prothrombin time	13–20 sec
Activated partial thromboplastin time	55 +/− 10 sec

Source: F. Oski and J. L. Naiman. *Hematologic Problems in the Newborn* (3rd ed.). Philadelphia: Saunders, 1982. With permission.

Appendix 20
Technique for Apt Test for Fetal Hemoglobin Determination*

Mix freshly bloody specimen (stool, gastric aspirate, vomitus, and so forth) with an equal volume of tap water in order to lyse the red blood cells. Centrifuge or filter. The supernatant must be pink to complete the test. Add one part of 0.25 N (1%) NaOH to five parts of the supernatant.

If the pink color of the supernatant persists for longer than two minutes, fetal hemoglobin is present. If the pink color turns to yellow in two minutes or less, indicating denaturation of hemoglobin, adult hemoglobin is present.

---

*Adapted from L. Apt and W. S. Downey Jr. Melena neonatorum. The swallowed blood syndrome. *J. Pediatr.* 47 : 6, 1955.

Appendix 21
Normal Cerebrospinal Fluid Values in Term Infants

White blood cells	0–22/mm³	(mean = 22)	61% polymorphonuclear cells
Glucose	34–119 mg/dl	(mean = 52)	
Protein	20–170 mg/dl	(mean = 90)	
Opening pressure	80–110 cm H₂0		

Source: L. D. Sarff, L. H. Platt, and G. H. McCracken Jr. Cerebrospinal fluid evaluation in neonates: Comparison of high-risk infants with and without meningitis. *J. Pediatr.* 88 : 473, 1976. With permission.

Appendix 22
Urinalysis Values

Color: Initially dark and turbid, becoming pale (clear) and yellow.

Specific gravity: 1.012 (1–4 days after birth)
   1.002–1.006 (beyond 5 days)
   1.021 (maximum)

Urine dipstick:
   pH: 6–7 (1–3 days after birth)
   5 (beyond 14 days)

   Protein: Zero—Trace by dipstick. False positive created by presence of urate crystals during the first 7 days.

   Greater than 30 mg/dl of protein in urine is abnormal beyond the first 6 days.

   Glycosuria: Transiently present in 20% of term infants.

Microscopic evaluation:
   White blood cells/mm^3: 10 or less
   Red blood cells/mm^3: 2–3
   Casts may be present only during the first 7 days.

Appendix 23
Technique for Suprapubic Aspiration of the Bladder*

1. The infant should be restrained with the help of an assistant.
2. The assistant should prevent the infant from voiding by either pinching the proximal penile urethra or by compressing the female urethra anteriorly against the pubis during a rectal exam.
3. Aspiration is performed with a suitable needle and syringe, e.g. 21-gauge 3-cm needle attached to a 5- to 10-cc syringe.
4. The puncture site is 1.5 cm above the symphysis pubis in the midline. There is often a skin crease in this location.
5. The needle is inserted perpendicular to the table and advanced to a distance of 1 to 2 cm until a slight decrease in resistance is felt when the bladder is penetrated.
6. The volume of urine desired is aspirated, the needle is withdrawn, and gentle pressure is applied until bleeding stops.
7. If no urine is obtained, the area should not be probed nor the puncture repeated. It may be tried again later if necessary.

*Adapted from D. C. Stevens, R. L. Schreiner, and E. L. Gresham. Suprapubic bladder aspiration in the neonate. *Perinatol. Neonatol.* 5 : 47, 1981.

Appendix 24
Technique for Circumcision*

Once the genital area is prepped and draped, a straight hemostat is inserted into the preputial orifice and the ring is gently dilated. A blunt flexible probe is inserted between the glans and the inner epithelium of the prepuce. To free the entire glans from the adherent prepuce, it usually is necessary to make a dorsal slit in the prepuce. This is accomplished by clamping a straight hemostat on the prepuce in the midline. The external urethral meatus should be identified clearly before placing the midline hemostat. After waiting approximately one minute, the hemostat is removed and the dorsal incision is made in the portion of the prepuce that was clamped. The incision is made to within 0.5 cm of the coronal sulcus. The foreskin is pulled back and the blunt dissection continued until the entire glans is free of adhering tissue. Once this is accomplished the circumcision may be completed using either a Gomco clamp or a Plastibell.

If the Gomco clamp (Fig. A24-1) is used, it should be tightened for a minimum of five minutes before incising the foreskin. Once the clamp is removed, the penis should be wrapped with petroleum jelly gauze to protect it from adhering to a diaper.

Once a Plastibell (Fig. A24-2) is securely tightened in place, wait about five minutes and then incise the redundant foreskin. The Plastibell handle is separated from the cap, leaving the base of the foreskin fastened tightly to the cap. The opening in the cap permits urine to pass. Approximately five to 10 days later the cap and remaining foreskin fall off together.

Following the circumcision, it is necessary to instruct the parents to watch for signs of infection, problems in urination, and bleeding. Cleanliness is very important.

---

*Adapted from E. Wallerstein. *Circumcision: An American Health Fallacy.* New York: Springer, 1980. With permission.

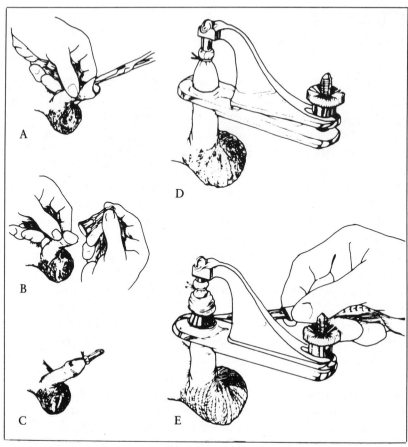

Fig. A24-1. Gomco clamp.

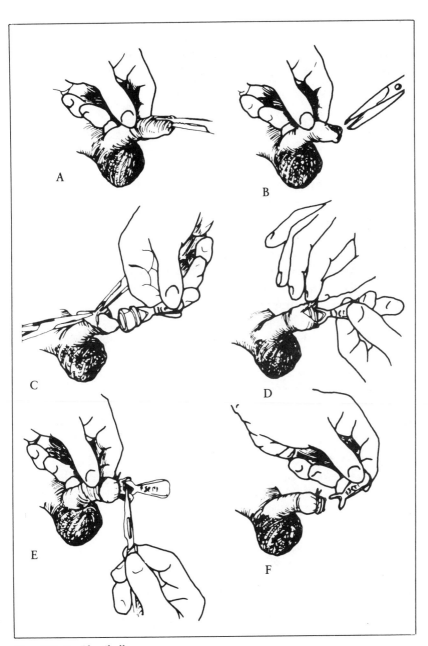

Fig. A24-2. Plastibell.

Appendix 25
Possible Benefits and Recognized
Risks of Neonatal Circumcision*

I. Benefits

    A. Controversial
        1. Decreases incidence of cancer of the prostate
        2. Decreases incidence of cancer of the cervix
        3. Increases sexual satisfaction
    B. Accepted
        1. Facilitates penile hygiene
        2. Prevents cancer of the penis
        3. Decreases the incidence of sexually transmitted diseases
        4. Prevents phimosis
        5. Prevents paraphimosis
        6. Prevents balanitis
        7. Avoids the pain and possible psychological effects of late circumcision
        8. Avoids the risk associated with anesthesia for late circumcision
        9. Avoids the cost of late circumcision

II. Risks

    A. Early complications
        1. Hemorrhage
        2. Infection (local or systemic)
        3. Surgical trauma
    B. Late complications
        1. Meatitis
        2. Meatal stenosis
    C. Death

*From E. Warner and E. Strashin. Benefits and risks of circumcision. Originally published in *Canadian Medical Association Journal* Vol. 125, November 1, 1981. With permission.

Appendix 26
Dosages for Antibiotics for Term Infants

Drug	Dosage	Serum drug level monitoring
Amikacin	7.5 mg/kg q12hr, IV or IM (need to increase interval to q18–24hr if $T^{1/2} > 8$ hr or decrease interval to q8hr if $T^{1/2} < 4$ hr)	E
Ampicillin		
Meningitis	50 mg/kg q8–12hr, IV (q6hr>1 wk of age)	R
Other indications	25 mg/kg q8–12hr, IV or IM (q6–8hr>1 wk of age)	
Carbenicillin	100 mg/kg IV initially, then 75 mg/kg q6–8hr (100 mg/kg IV q6hr>1 wk of age)	R
Cephalosporins		
Cephalothin	20 mg/kg q6–8hr IV or IM	
Cefazolin	20 mg/kg q8–12hr IV or IM	
Cefoperazone	50 mg/kg q12hr IV	
Cefotaxime	50 mg/kg q12hr IV (q8hr>1 wk of age)	
Moxalactam	100 mg/kg IV loading dose, then 50 mg/kg q12hr IV (q8hr>2 mos of age)	
Chloramphenicol	20 mg/kg PO or IV initially, then 5 mg/kg PO or IV q6hr (start maintenance dose 12 hr after loading dose). Maintenance dose requirements may vary from 2.5 up to 12.5 mg/kg PO or IV q6hr	E
Clindamycin	10 mg/kg IV q8hr	
Erythromycin	20 mg/kg q12hr PO	
Gentamicin	2.5 mg/kg q12hr IV or IM (need to increase interval to q18–24hr if $T^{1/2} > 8$ hr or decrease interval to q8hr if $T^{1/2} < 4$ hr)	E

Appendix 26 (continued).

Drug	Dosage	Serum drug level monitoring
Isoniazid	10 mg/kg PO qd	R
Kanamycin	7.5 mg/kg q12hr IV or IM (need to increase interval to q18–24hr if $T\frac{1}{2} > 8$ hr or decrease interval to q8hr if $T\frac{1}{2} < 4$ hr)	E
Methicillin		
Meningitis	50 mg/kg q8hr IV	R
Other indications	25 mg/kg q8–12hr IV or IM (q6–8hr > 1 wk of age)	
Metronidazole	15 mg/kg IV loading dose, then 7.5 mg/kg IV q12hr	R (meningitis)
Nafcillin		
Meningitis	50 mg/kg q8hr IV	R
Other indications	20 mg/kg q8hr IV or IM	
Netilmicin	2–3 mg/kg IV q12hr	
Oxacillin	25 mg/kg q12hr IV or IM (q6–8hr > 1 wk of age)	

Penicillins		
Penicillin G		
Meningitis	75,000 U/kg q8hr IV (q6hr>1 wk of age)	R
Sepsis	25,000–50,000 U/kg q12hr IV or IM (q8hr>1 wk of age)	
Benzathine	50,000 U/kg one dose	
Procaine	50,000 U/kg q24hr	
Piperacillin	50 mg/kg IV q4–6hr	R
Rifampin	10 mg/kg PO q12hr	
Ticarcillin	100 mg/kg IV initially, then 75 mg/kg q6–8hr (100 mg/kg q6hr>1 wk of age)	R
Tobramycin	2.5 mg/kg q12hr IV or IM (need to increase interval to q18–24hr if $T^{1/2}>8$ hr or decrease interval to q8hr if $T^{1/2}<4$ hr)	E

Trimethoprim-Sulfamethoxazole	loading dose:
	  trimethoprim 3 mg/kg IV
	  sulfamethoxazole 10 mg/kg IV
	
	maintenance dose
	  trimethoprim 1 mg/kg IV q12hr
	  sulfamethoxazole 3 mg/kg IV q12hr
		R

Vancomycin	15 mg/kg q12hr IV (q8hr>1 wk of age)	

Key: E = essential; R = recommended.
Source: R. J. Roberts. *Drug Therapy in Infants: Pharmacologic Principles and Clinical Experience.* Philadelphia: Saunders, 1984. With permission.

Appendix 27
Dosages for Anticonvulsants for Term Infants

Drug	Recommended dose
Phenobarbitol	Loading: 20 mg/kg (IV) Maintenance: 3–5 mg/kg/day in 2 divided doses (IV, IM, PO)
Phenytoin	Loading: 20 mg/kg (IV) over 30–60 min Maintenance: 4–8 mg/kg (IV) q8–12hr

Source: Adapted from R. J. Roberts. *Drug Therapy in Infants: Pharmacologic Principles and Clinical Experience.* Philadelphia: Saunders, 1984.

Appendix 28
Dosages for Cardiovascular Agents for Term Infants

Drug	Dosage
Digoxin	Loading: 30–40 µg/kg (IV or PO), administered in three equally or unequally divided doses (½, ¼, ¼) q8hr. Maintenance: 5 µg/kg (PO) q12hr.
Dobutamine	2–15 µg/kg/min (IV).
Dopamine	2.5–15 µg/kg/min (IV) (effects on renal and peripheral resistance are dose-dependent).
Hydralazine	0.1–0.5 mg/kg (IV, IM, or PO) q3–6hr as required for blood pressure control. Maximum dose: 2 mg/kg q6hr.
Isoproterenol	0.1–0.5 µg/kg/min (IV).
Tolazoline	Bolus: 2 mg/kg (IV). Follow with 1–2 mg/kg/hr. Caution: Maintain systemic blood pressure.

Source: Adapted from R. J. Roberts. *Drug Therapy in Infants: Pharmacologic Principles and Clinical Experience.* Philadelphia: Saunders, 1984.

Appendix 29
Dosages for Other Agents
for Term Infants

Drug	Dosage
Chloral hydrate	25–50 mg/kg (PO or rectally)
Furosemide	1–2 mg/kg (IV, IM, or PO); repeat as required, but no more often than q12hr
Morphine sulfate	0.1 mg/kg (IV); repeat q4hr usually
Prostaglandin E1 (PGE1)	0.1 μg/kg/min (IV)

Source: Adapted from R. J. Roberts. *Drug Therapy in Infants: Pharmacologic Principles and Clinical Experience*. Philadelphia: Saunders, 1984.

Appendix 30
Guidelines for Isolation

	Strict isolation	Contact isolation	Hepatitis B
Diseases	Viral pneumonia and/or meningitis, suspect sepsis, Chlamydia, syphilis, herpes simplex virus (HSV), varicella (VZV), rubella, cytomegalovirus (CMV).	Diarrhea of unknown etiology, Salmonella, Shigella, eye infections, wound infections, skin infections.	Definition: Infant of a known HB$_S$Ag + mother; infant with a + HB$_S$Ag.
Mode of transmission	Respiratory* and contact with oropharyngeal secretions, stool, skin lesions, urine, blood.	Contact with stool, secretions, or exudates.	Contact with blood and secretions.
Duration of isolation	Duration of hospitalization or until discontinued by consultation between the nursery and Infection Control Committee; or in suspect sepsis until cultures are negative.	Until cultures are negative or until discontinued by consultation between the nursery and Infection Control Committee.	None. Caution is advised in handling blood and body fluids.
Method of isolation	Incubator necessary, with at least 4 ft on either side of incubator; may be fed out of isolette.	Incubator optional; unnecessary to separate by space from other infants; may be fed out of isolette.	Incubator unnecessary; unnecessary to separate from other infants; may be fed out of isolette.

Appendix 30 (continued).

	Strict isolation	Contact isolation	Hepatitis B
Feedings	May breast-feed within patients' space in nursery; may not leave nursery to go to mother.	May breast-feed; may leave nursery to go to mother if she is still in-patient.	If infant is HB_sAg+, may breast-feed or may be fed own mother's milk; if infant is HB_sAg- or if status is unknown, may not breast-feed or be fed own mother's milk.
Gloves	Change with each patient contact.	Change with each patient contact.	Change with each patient contact.
Gowns	Separate gown must be worn for each infant. May use same gown more than once for same infant. Change when soiled.	Separate gown must be worn for each infant. May use same gown more than once for same infant. Change when soiled.	Separate gown must be worn for each infant. May use same gown more than once for same infant. Change when soiled.
Masks	Only when handling infant out of incubator.	Unnecessary.	Unnecessary.
Comments	For HSV, CMV, VZV, and rubella, assign nonpregnant personnel unless demonstrated immunity. Hand washing is the single most important infection control practice.	Hand washing is the single most important infection control practice.	Mothers who are HB_sAg+ may excrete HB_sAg in their milk. Hand washing is the single most important infection control practice.

*Close face-to-face contact is required for infants to transmit these diseases by the respiratory route.
Source: Adapted from procedures of the University of California, San Diego, Medical Center.

Appendix 31
Preparation of Infant Formula
from Formula Concentrate

1. Wash hands.
2. Wash all supplies—bottles, nipples, and so forth.
3. Boil all equipment for a full 10 minutes.
4. Boil water for formula and for baby's drinking water for a full 10 minutes. Cool.
5. Mix formula: Using concentrated formula, add equal amount of boiled water to canned concentrate.
6. Pour formula into bottles or bottle. If you have one bottle for formula, put as much of the mixed formula you think the baby will need in the bottle. The rest of the formula should be covered with a lid in a 1-qt jar and put in the refrigerator. If you have enough bottles for a day's supply, divide the supply of formula into your bottles. Keep the bottles of formula in the refrigerator.
7. Wash and boil the bottles and nipples each time you use them. It is better if you have a day's supply of nipples so that you need to boil nipples only once a day.
8. Put boiled water in at least two bottles and offer baby water between feedings of formula, especially in hot weather.
9. Formula must be kept cold until you warm it to feed the baby.

Appendix 32
Preparation of Infant
Formula from Evaporated Milk

1. Wash hands.
2. Wash all supplies—bottles, nipples, and so forth.
3. Boil all equipment for a full 10 minutes.
4. Boil water for formula and for baby's drinking water for a full 10 minutes. Cool.
5. Make the formula: You may use any brand of evaporated milk. Empty large can (13 oz) of evaporated milk into a 1-qt jar. A quart mayonnaise jar will do very well. Add 2 tablespoons corn syrup. (Corn syrup should not be put in the refrigerator because it becomes stiff and hard to pour. It should be left out at room temperature.) Fill quart jar with boiled water. You will then have almost 2 oz of boiled water to 1 oz of evaporated milk.
6. Pour formula into bottles or bottle. If you have one bottle for formula, put in the bottle as much of the mixed formula as you think your baby will need. The rest of the formula in the quart jar should be covered with the lid and put in the refrigerator. If you have enough bottles for a day's supply, divide the supply of formula into your bottles. Keep the bottles of formula in the refrigerator.
7. Wash and boil the bottles and nipples each time you use them. It is better if you have a day's supply of nipples so that you need to boil nipples only once a day.
8. Put boiled water in at least two bottles and offer baby water between feedings of formula, especially in hot weather.
9. Formula must be kept cold until you warm it to feed the baby.
10. Call your doctor if you decide to use a prepared formula. He will advise the proper way to prepare it.

Appendix 33
Making Formula Using a Sterilizer Set
(Terminal Method)*

1. Wash hands.
2. Wash and dry all equipment. Make sure nipple holes are open. Be sure all soap is rinsed out of bottles and nipples.
3. Mix formula following directions given for the type of formula you have chosen (evaporated milk or prepared formula). You do not need to boil water first when using a sterilizer.
4. Fill each of six or eight bottles with the amount of milk you think the baby will drink in one feeding.
5. Put 4 oz of water into each of two bottles.
6. Place nipples and rings on bottles, with nipples on the inside. Be sure the rings are not sealed tight.
7. Place bottles in rack and put into sterilizer. Add 1 in. of water to bottom of pan.
8. Place lid on sterilizer and turn on heat.
9. When water begins to boil, time for 25 minutes, then turn off heat. Leave lid on until sterilizer is completely cool.
10. Remove cool bottles, tighten rings, and place bottles in refrigerator until used. Water may be kept at room temperature.

IMPORTANT POINTS
1. Always have equipment clean.
2. Wash your hands.
3. Do not save milk left in the bottle at one feeding. It is not safe to give it to the baby later.
4. Always hold the baby for feeding.

---

*Using a sterilizer is worthwhile only if you have enough bottles for a full day's supply of formula.

Appendix 34A
Administration of Eye Prophylaxis*

I. Purpose

   To prevent conjunctivitis of the newborn caused by neonatorum gonorrheal ophthalmia and some bacteria.

II. Policy

   A. Eye prophylaxis is done within four hours of admission to the newborn intensive care unit or newborn nursery. If infants are not admitted to the nursery, it will be done in labor and delivery.

   B. The instillation is done by an RN or LPN.

   C. Do not rinse eyes with sterile water after instillation of an eye prophylactic agent.

III. General information

   A. Erythromycin ointment is used prophylactically to prevent eye infections in the neonate, especially neonatorum gonorrheal ophthalmia.

   B. To be most effective, treatment should be done within the first four hours of the infant's life.

   C. Eye prophylaxis is required by state law.

   D. Standing orders cover use of eye prophylaxis.

IV. Equipment

   A. 4 × 4 gauze sponges or cotton balls.

   B. Erythromycin ophthalmic ointment.

V. Procedure

   A. Separate eyelids until they are elevated from eyeball.

   B. Instill a dab of erythromycin ointment to each eye.

   C. Close eyelids. Wipe excess off skin.

VI. Charting

   Record time, date, agent, and dose given on the infant's medical record.

---

*Procedure of the University of New Mexico Hospital/Bernalillo County Medical Center Division of Nursing Service.

Appendix 34B
Administration of
Vitamin K to Newborns*

I. Purpose

   To supplement the infant's normally low supply of vitamin K.

II. Policy

   A. Only licensed nurses may administer medications.

   B. Vitamin K is to be administered to every neonate following birth unless otherwise ordered by the doctor.

   C. All intramuscular injections ordered for newborns are to be given into the anterolateral aspect of the thigh to avoid injury to the sciatic nerve and major leg vessels.

III. General information

   A. Absence of vitamin K leads to impaired synthesis of the clotting factors. This may increase the tendency to bleed.

   B. Vitamin K is used prophylactically against and in the treatment of hemolytic disease of the newborn.

   C. Natural causes of a low vitamin K level are:

      1. Antibiotic therapy eliminating the normal gastrointestinal flora.

      2. Diarrhea and malabsorption.

      3. Lack of vitamin K during prolonged parenteral fluid therapy.

      4. Deficient intake of vitamin K when fed formula without vitamin K supplements.

      5. Absence of vitamin K in breast milk.

IV. Equipment

   A. Vitamin K — 1 mg/0.5 cc

   B. Filter needle

   C. Tuberculin syringe and needle

   D. Alcohol swab

V. Procedure

   A. Draw up the ordered dose of vitamin K adhering to hospital medication procedure.

   B. Wipe the injection site with an alcohol swab.

   C. Pick up the tissue at the injection site between thumb and forefinger.

---

*Procedure of the University of New Mexico Hospital/Bernalillo County Medical Center Division of Nursing Service.

  D. Inject the medication at a right angle into the mid-anterolateral
     aspect of the thigh.
  E. Remove needle and discard.
VI. Charting
     Record the medication on the medication record.

Appendix 35
Using an Infant Safety Seat: Guidelines for Parents*

Automobile travel can and should be a safe, pleasant time for you and your baby. The safest mode of travel for your baby is in an infant safety seat, even for short trips.

1. When both parents travel in the car, one parent and the baby should ride in the back seat. Place the baby in the infant safety seat that is connected to the car with the seat belt so that the baby rides facing the back of the back seat.
2. When only one parent travels with the baby, place the baby in the front seat in the infant safety seat. Be sure the seat is connected to the car with the seat belt so that the baby rides facing the back of the front seat.
3. An infant seat is the most comfortable place for your baby to sleep, so let him sleep if possible.
4. When your baby is awake and behaving nicely (quiet, jabbering, or looking around), interact by singing, humming, or discussing where you are going and what you are going to do. In this way, your baby will learn to enjoy automobile travel. If your baby has a favorite blanket, place it within easy reach of the safety seat.
5. Provide one or two toys that your baby associates with quiet play, such as a stuffed animal or doll. Having special riding toys that are played with only in the car will help to decrease your baby's boredom. Remember that a young baby's attention span is extremely short. Do not expect a baby to stay occupied with a toy for more than a couple of minutes. Your anticipating a short attention span and acting accordingly will prevent your baby from throwing toys, crying, and fussing.
6. Many parents like to rest their elbow near the front of the safety seat so they can hold the baby's hand, rearrange the blankets, or play with the baby. Babies like this type of attention and will ride better for it; however, do not play with your baby if you are the driver.
7. On a long trip, plan for periodic rest stops to feed and change the baby. Plan to stop before the baby begins to fuss; do not form the habit of removing the baby from the safety seat if he cries.

---

*Reprinted with courtesy and permission of E. R. Christopherson.

8. When your baby travels in another person's car (grandparent or babysitter), insist that the driver use the infant safety seat correctly. You may wish to fasten the safety seat into the car yourself.

9. Remember that if you are pleasant and talk and interact with your baby during car rides, your baby will learn to enjoy traveling and will become accustomed to the safety seat.

10. When your baby is between 9 and 12 months of age, you will need to switch to a toddler safety seat or change the baby's riding position if your seat is a convertible style. Your pediatrician or nurse can tell you when it is time to switch.

11. Your child should continue to use a safety seat until age 8 to 10 years, or when the child can see out of the car window comfortably when restrained by a seat belt.

12. Older siblings should also be expected to behave appropriately. If the young child sees an older sibling climbing on the seat or hanging out the window, he will want to become a participant.

13. In many states, it is illegal for an infant or child to ride in the front seat of a car without being securely fastened into a restraint seat. The reason for these laws is to protect infants and children from injury and death. Please do what is best for your baby—use an approved safety seat during every car ride.

Appendix 36
Definitions of Terms*

LIVE BIRTH: The complete expulsion or extraction from the mother of a product of human conception, irrespective of the duration of pregnancy, that, after such expulsion or extraction, breathes or shows any other evidence of life, such as beating of the heart, pulsation of the umbilical cord, or definite movement of voluntary muscles whether or not the umbilical cord has been cut or the placenta is attached.

FETAL DEATH: Death of a product of human conception before its complete expulsion or extraction from the mother, irrespective of the duration of pregnancy; the death is indicated by the fact that, after such expulsion or extraction, the fetus does not breathe or show any other evidence of life, such as beating of the heart, pulsation of the umbilical cord, or definite movement of voluntary muscles. Fetal death is subdivided according to the timing and mode:

1. EARLY FETAL DEATH (ABORTION). The expulsion or extraction from the mother of a fetus or embryo weighing 500 gm or less (about 22 weeks' gestation). This definition excludes induced terminations of pregnancy.

2. LATE FETAL DEATH (STILLBIRTH). Death before expulsion, extraction, or delivery in which the fetal weight is greater than 500 gm or, if weight is unknown, the duration of the pregnancy exceeds 22 completed weeks' gestation. When neither birth weight nor gestational age is available, a body length of 25 cm (crown-heel) is considered equivalent to a 500 gm weight.

3. INDUCED TERMINATION OF PREGNANCY. The deliberate interruption of pregnancy—to produce other than a liveborn neonate or to remove a dead fetus—that does not result in a live birth.

TOTAL BIRTHS: The number of live births plus the number of deaths of fetuses weighing more than 500 gm (late fetal deaths).

NEONATAL DEATH: Death of a liveborn neonate before the neonate becomes 28 days old (up to and including 27 days, 23 hours, 59 minutes from the moment of birth). Neonatal deaths may be subdivided, qualified, or defined in other ways for various purposes:

1. EARLY NEONATAL DEATH. Death of a liveborn neonate during the first seven days of life (up to and including six days, 23 hours, 59 minutes from the moment of birth). These deaths have been described as hebdomadal. For early neonatal deaths, the time of death can be categorized further, using the following intervals or some combination thereof:
Birth to less than 60 completed minutes
One hour to less than 12 completed hours
12 hours to less than 24 completed hours
24 hours to less than 48 completed hours
48 hours to less than 72 completed hours
72 hours to less than 168 completed hours

---

*From *Guidelines for Perinatal Care*. Evanston, IL/Washington, DC: American Academy of Pediatrics and American College of Obstetricians and Gynecologists, 1983. With permission.

251

2. LATE NEONATAL DEATH.   Death of a liveborn neonate after seven completed days (168 hours) but before 28 days of life (27 days, 23 hours, 59 minutes).

Early and late neonatal death statistics are useful for international comparisons. They are terms recommended by the World Health Organization and by the International Federation of Gynecology and Obstetrics.

INFANT DEATH: Any death at any time from birth up to, but not including, 1 year of age.

BIRTH WEIGHT: The weight of a neonate determined immediately after delivery or as soon thereafter as feasible. It should be expressed to the nearest gram. Division into birth weight groups may be required; neonates with birth weights of 1000 gm or less may be categorized in 100-, 200-, or 250-gm intervals, and neonates with birth weights of 1000 to 2499 gm may be categorized in at least 250-gm intervals. Liveborn neonates have traditionally been classified according to weight at birth, and birth weight has been the most commonly used criterion for defining a neonatal population with special risks, as well as for developing uniform national and international vital statistics. Classification based on weight alone equates birth size to fetal age, however, and tends to obscure medically important differences between like-sized neonates of differing gestational age.

GESTATIONAL AGE: The number of completed weeks that have elapsed between the first day of the last normal menstrual period — not the presumed time of conception — and the date of delivery, irrespective of whether the gestation results in a live birth or a fetal death. All neonates can be defined in categories for birth weight-gestational age comparisons: appropriate for gestational age (AGA), small for gestational age (SGA), and large for gestational age (LGA). Graphs and tables of the normal distribution of birth weights over the latter half of gestation are used to classify each birth. Neonates whose birth weights are less than the tenth percentile or greater than the ninetieth percentile for their population are classified as SGA and LGA, respectively. The interval between death and delivery in cases of fetal death may significantly alter statistics related to gestational age and weight.

CONCEPTIONAL AGE: The number of completed weeks that have elapsed between the time of conception, when accurately known, and the date of delivery. Add two weeks to conceptional age to obtain gestational age.

LOW BIRTH WEIGHT NEONATE: Any neonate, regardless of gestational age, whose weight at birth is less than 2500 gm. A neonate weighing 1500 gm or less at birth is considered a very low birth weight neonate.

PRETERM NEONATE: Any neonate whose calculated gestational age from the first day of the last menstrual period is less than 37 completed weeks or 258 completed days.

TERM NEONATE: Any neonate whose gestational age is equal to or greater than 38 weeks but equal to or less than 42 weeks (259–294 days).

POSTTERM NEONATE: Any neonate whose gestational age is greater than 42 weeks (greater than 294 completed days).

Appendix 37
Statistical Evaluation of Mortality Rates*

Fetal mortality rate is computed by relating deaths of fetuses 500 gm and over to total births:

$$\text{Fetal mortality rate} = \frac{\text{Fetal deaths} \geq 500 \text{ gm} \times 1000}{\text{Total number of births} \geq 500 \text{ gm}}$$

Neonatal mortality rate is computed by relating deaths during the first 28 days of postnatal life to live births:

$$\text{Neonatal mortality rate} = \frac{\text{Neonatal deaths} < 28 \text{ days of age} \times 1000}{\text{Total number of live births} \geq 500 \text{ gm}}$$

Perinatal mortality rate is computed by relating deaths of fetuses 500 gm and over plus neonatal deaths during the first 28 days of postnatal life to total births:

$$\text{Perinatal mortality rate} = \frac{\text{Fetal deaths} \geq 500 \text{ gm} + \text{Neonatal deaths} \times 1000}{\text{Total number of births} \geq 500 \text{ gm}}$$

For international comparisons, the following formulas should be used:

$$\text{Perinatal mortality rate} = \frac{\text{Stillbirths} \geq 1000 \text{ gm} + \text{early neonatal deaths} \geq 1000 \text{ gm} \times 1000}{\text{Total births} \geq 1000 \text{ gm}}$$

$$\text{Early neonatal mortality rate} = \frac{\text{Early neonatal deaths} \geq 1000 \text{ gm at birth} \times 1000}{\text{Live births} \geq 1000 \text{ gm}}$$

$$\text{Fetal mortality rate} = \frac{\text{Stillbirths} \geq 1000 \text{ gm} \times 1000}{\text{Total births} \geq 1000 \text{ gm}}$$

*From *Guidelines for Perinatal Care*. Evanston, IL/Washington, DC: American Academy of Pediatrics and American College of Obstetricians and Gynecologists, 1983. With permission.

Index

Abdomen, 80–87, 144–145
  examination of, 29–31
  septicemia diagnosis, 124
Acid-base balance
  respiratory acidosis versus
    alkalosis, 72
  and respiratory distress, 75
  resuscitation of newborn, 14–15
Acquired immune deficiency
    syndrome (AIDS) and
    complex, 184
Acrocyanosis, 74. See also Cyanosis
Adaptation following birth
  assessment of, 12
  cardiovascular system, 9–11
  clinical behavior, 20
  pulmonary system, 6–8, 9
  role of other systems in, 11–12
  thermoregulation, 19, 21
  transition period, 19, 20
Administration. See Nursery, organi-
    zation and management of
Admission procedures
  bathing, 25–26
  eye care, 24
  vital signs, 23–24
  vitamin K prophylaxis, 24–25
Age, gestational, 1–2, 52–57, 58
Airway, obstruction of
  nasal abnormalities, 43
  neck mass and, 95
Amino acid disturbances
  screening for, 174–175
  and seizures, 96
Amnion nodosum, 62, 87
Amniotic fluid
  abnormalities of. See also
    Oligohydramnios
  in gastrointestinal obstruction,
    11, 82
  polyhydramnios, 11, 82, 188
  in urinary tract obstruction, 87
  assessment of, 4
  composition of, 6, 7
  pulmonary maturation and, 8
Anemia, 12, 22
Anencephaly, 131
Anesthesia, and respiratory
    depression, 13
Anoxia, and seizures, 96

Antibiotics
  dosages, 235–237
  in septicemia, 126–127
  with serology, positive, 112
Antibody screening test, 21, 111–
    112
Anticonvulsant dosages, 238
Anus
  examination of, 32–33
  imperforate, 82, 128
Apgar scores, 12, 16
Apnea
  hypoglycemia and, 120
  resuscitation indications, 12
  sudden infant death syndrome
    (SIDS), 171
Appendicitis, 124
Appropriate for gestational age
    infant
  defined, 57
  mortality and morbidity risk, 60
Apt test, 227
Arrhythmias, 74, 76, 78
Arthrogryposis, 92, 93
Ascites, 81
Asphyxia, 4, 94
  and hypoglycemia, 119–120
  postterm infant, 131
  and seizures, 96, 98
  sinus bradycardia after, 78
Aspiration pneumonia, 12
Assessment, initial
  adaptation, neonatal, 6–12
    cardiovascular, 9–11
    pulmonary, 6–8, 9
    role of other systems, 11–12
  delivery, normal, 4–6
  delivery room procedures, 15–16
  history, 1
  labor, normal, 3–4
  pregnancy, 1–3
  resuscitation, 12–15

Babinski reflex, 47
Babkin reflex, 46
Back, examination of, 38. See also
    Spine
Balanitis, 90
Ballard assessment, 52, 56
Barlow test, 34, 37, 38

Basal cell carcinoma, 104
Bathing, 25–26
Beckwith-Wiedemann syndrome, 120
Bednar's aphthae, 71–72
Behavioral states, 94–95, 139, 140
  characteristics, 43, 202–207
  hypoglycemia and, 120
  with increased intracranial
      pressure, 141
  parent preparation for discharge, 168
Bicarbonate
  body fluid composition, 6, 7
  in resuscitation of newborn,
      14–15, 128
Bilirubin. See also Hyperbilirubinemia/
      jaundice.
Bilirubin metabolism, 112–114
Birthmarks, 100, 104. See also Skin
Birth trauma. See Day one, common
      problems
Birth weight, 51
  conversion from gm to lb, 51, 211
  fetal growth measurements, 58, 59
  indications for transport, 189
  and mortality and morbidity risk, 60
Bladder
  exstrophy of, 85, 128
  suprapubic aspiration, 125, 230
Bleeding disorders. See Vitamin K
      prophylaxis; Hemorrhage;
      Coagulation factors
Blood count
  normal values, 221
  in sepsis, 125
Blood gases
  with cardiorespiratory symptoms,
      143
  hemoglobin oxygen dissociation
      curves, 73
  respiratory acidosis versus alkalosis,
      72
  in respiratory distress, 74
  in septicemia, 126
Blood group incompatibilities. See
      Coombs' test.
Blood pressure, 29. See also Vital signs
Blood volume
  normal values, 222
  with twin-to-twin transfusion, 133–
      134
Blood volume expanders
  in intestinal obstruction, 84
  in polycythemia, 117, 119
  Plasmanate, 79

preterm infant, 128
  in resuscitation, 13
  in systemic hypotension, 79
Bloody stools, 140, 145
Blueberry muffin baby, 106
Bohn's nodules, 43, 100
Bowel function
  adaptation, normal, 20
  parent instruction, 170
Bowel obstruction. See Gastro-
      intestinal system, obstruction
Brachial plexus trauma, 72, 95, 98
Bradycardia, sinus, 78
Brain abnormalities. See also Central
      nervous system
  and neonatal adaptation, 11
  and respiratory distress, 75
Breast, 27
  engorgement of, parent instruction,
      170
  gestational age assessment, 53, 56
  hypertrophy of, 143, 144
  supernumerary nipples, 100–101,
      102
Breast-feeding, 155–161, 162
  composition of breast milk, 156–
      158
  isolation guidelines, 241
  preterm infant, 130–131
Breast pump, 130–131, 161
Breathing. See also Respiration
  in utero, 6, 8
  respiration rate. See Respiration
      rate
Breath sounds, 28
Breech birth, 4
  cervical cord transection, 72
  genu recurvatum, 33, 36
  and posture, 95
Bruits, 39
Bullous dermatitis, 25
Buphthalmos, 67

Café au lait spots, 104
Calcium disturbances, 96, 122
Calcium levels, normal values, 216
Candidal infections
  diaper dermatitis, 151
  mouth, 143
Capillary hemangioma, 48, 104
Capillary refill time, 84, 125
Caput succedaneum, 38, 65, 140
Cardiac massage, 14
Cardiogenic shock, 78, 79

Cardiovascular system, 72–74, 75, 143–144. *See also* Heart
adaptation, normal, 20
chest examination, 27–28
medications, dosages for neonate, 239
and respiratory distress, 75
surgery, problems requiring, 128
syndrome complex with skin lesions, 104
Cataract, 67
Cavernous hemangioma, 72, 104
Cellulitis, periumbilical, 25
Centigrade-farenheit table, 210
Central nervous system, 94–99. *See also* Reflexes
and adaptation, 11, 12
examination of, 44–48
and gestational age, 54–55
hemorrhage of
and respiratory distress, 75
and seizures, 96
and irritability, 146
polycythemia and, 23
and postterm delivery, 131
and respiratory distress, 75
surgery, problems requiring, 128
Cephalhematomas, 38, 65, 140
Cerebrospinal fluid, 228
Cervical cord transection, 47–48, 72
Chest, 72–74, 75, 143–144
anomalies of, 198
initial examination of, 27–29
Chlamydial infections, 123, 141
Chloride
body fluid composition, 6, 7
normal values, 216
Choanal atresia, 69, 128
Chorioretinitis, 67
Chromosomal abnormalities
and hypoglycemia, 120
as intrinsic risks, 3
and seizures, 98
trisomies, 72, 199–200
Chylothorax, 12, 75, 128
Circulation, fetal, 9, 11
Circumcision, 89–90
care of, parent instruction, 169
risks and benefits, 234
technique for, 231–233
Clavicle, fracture of, 28, 91, 146
Cleft lip and palate, 42, 69–70
Cleidocranial dysostosis, associated with large fontanelle, 65

Coagulation factors, 226. *See also* Vitamin K prophylaxis
Coarctation of aorta, 120, 144
Cold stress, 25, 74
Collodion baby, 105
Color. *See also* Cyanosis
adaptation, normal, 20
Apgar scoring, 12
with cardiac abnormalities, 74
in drug withdrawal, 149
in methemoglobinemia, 79
physical examination, 29
resuscitation considerations, 12, 14
septicemia diagnosis, 124–125
Colostrum
defined, 160
neonatal (witch's milk), 100
Conceptional age, defined, 252
Congenital abnormalities. *See also* specific anatomic sites of lesions.
indications for transport, 190
minor, checklist of, 198–199
trisomies, major findings with, 200–201
Congenital adrenal hyperplasia, 88
Congenital heart disease
and hypoglycemia, 120
and respiratory distress, 75
ventricular hypertrophy in, 80, 81
Congenital hip dislocation, 34, 37, 38
Congenital ichthyosis, 105
Congenital methemoglobinemia, 79
Congestive heart failure. *See* Heart failure
Conjugate eye movement, 41
Conjunctiva
anomalies of, 104
hemorrhages, 66
inflammation, 66, 141
Constipation, 170
Contact dermatitis, 147
Contact isolation, 183–184
Conversion table
temperature, 210
weight, 51, 211
Coombs' test, 21, 111–112
Cord pulsation, 20
Cornea, 65–66. *See also* Eye
Cranial nerves
examination of, 44–46
facial nerve palsy, 99
Cranial sutures. *See* Sutures, skull
Craniosynostosis, 65

Craniotabes, 38
Crepitus, 146
Crossed extensor reflex, 47
Crown-rump length, 2, 52
Crying, 168, 208. *See also* Behavioral
    states
Cryptorchidism, 88, 201
Cutis marmorata, 100
Cyanosis
    of cardiac versus pulmonary origin,
        78, 79
    with chest abnormalities, 143
    conditions causing, 73–74
    with polycythemia, 117
    resuscitation considerations, 12, 14
Cycloplegia, 41, 67
Cystic adenomatoid malformation,
    128
Cystic hygroma, neck, 72
Cysts
    neck, 72
    oral cavity, 69, 70–71
Cytomegalovirus
    and blueberry muffin baby, 106
    cultures, 126
    isolation with, 184
    and jaundice, 115
    and seizures, 96

Daily routines, parent instruction, 170
Day one, common problems
    abdomen, 80–87
    birth trauma, 91
        and brachial plexus, 95–96
        and facial nerve palsies, 99
    chest, 72–74, 75
    ear, 68
    eyes, 65–68
    genitalia, 88–89, 90
    genitourinary tract, 87–88
    head, 65, 66
    heart, 74, 76–80
    mouth, 69–72
    neck, 72
    nervous system, 94–99
    nose, 68–69
    record of, 16
    skeleton, 91–94
    skin, 99–106
Day one, special problems
    calcium and magnesium
        disturbances, 122
    Coombs' test, 111–112

diabetic mother, 122
    hypoglycemia, 119–122
    jaundice, 112–117
    multiple births (twins), 131–132
    polycythemia, 117–119
    postterm infant, 131, 133
    preterm infant, 128–131
    septicemia, 123–127
    serology, positive, 112
    surgical emergencies, 127–128
Day two and beyond
    abdomen, 144–145
    chest, 143–144
    ears, 142
    eyes, 142
    general assessment, 139–140
    genitourinary system, 146
    head, 140–141
    mouth, 143
    neck, 143
    nervous system, 146, 148–149
    nose, 142–143
    skeleton, 146
    skin, 146–147, 150–151
Death
    definitions, 251–252
    of fetus or infant, 175–176
    in utero, of twin, 134–135
Deep tendon reflexes, 46
Defecation. *See* Stools
Dehydration, 124. *See also* Blood
        volume; Fluid balance
DeLee suction trap, 14
Delivery
    normal, 4–6
    transport, indications for, 188, 189
Delivery room, assessment procedures,
        15–16
Dermatitis
    contact, 147
    monilial, 106, 150, 151
Dermatoglyphics, 34, 201
Dermoerythropoiesis, 106
Development, normal embryonic and
        fetal, 194–197
Diabetes, 188
    and fetal maturation, 57
    infant of diabetic mother, manage-
        ment of, 122
    and polycythemia, 117
Diabetic cardiomyopathy, and
        respiratory distress, 75
Diaper dermatitis, 150, 151

monilial, 106
parent instruction, 169
Diaphragmatic hernia, 127, 128, 189
Diarrhea
with abdominal distention, 145
isolation with, 183
parent instruction, 170
Diastasis recti, 29
Digits, anomalies of, 91–92, 198
Discharge from hospital
anticipatory guidance, 167–171
fetal and neonatal loss, 175–176
metabolic disease screening, 173–175
procedures, 172–173
routine versus early, 171–172
after septicemia, 127
Disseminated intravascular coagulation, 134–135
Drug depression, neonatal, 94
Drug withdrawal, 146, 148–149
and failure to gain weight, 163
and seizures, 96
Drugs. See Medications
Dubowitz scoring system, 52, 53–55
Ductus arteriosus-dependent anomaly, 143–144
Duodenal atresia, 11
Dysmature infant
defined, 131
skin of, 105
Dysplasias, skeletal, 92
Dysraphism, occult spinal, 101

Ear, 68, 142
anomalies of, 198
cranial nerve function, 45
examination of, 41–43
as gestational age criterion, 53, 56
in trisomies, 200
Early discharge criteria, 171
Ecchymosis, head and face, 38–39
Edema
with heart failure, 78
scalp, 140
in Turner's syndrome, 93
Education, parent. See Discharge
Education, staff, 186–189
Electrocardiography, 80, 81
with arrhythmias, 76, 78
with cardiorespiratory symptoms, 143
normal values, 212–215

Electrolyte balance
body fluids, 6, 72
with congenital adrenal hyperplasia, 88
in gastrointestinal disorders, 81
intravenous, for surgical patient, 128
normal values, 216
and seizures, 96
Embryonic development, normal, 194–195
Emergencies, surgical, 127–128
Encephalocele, 99, 128
Endotracheal tube, 13, 129
Enteric infections, isolation with, 183
Epidermal nevi, 104
Epispadias, 89
Epithelial rests, 43
Epstein's pearls, 43, 100
Equinovarus malformation, 33, 35, 201
Erb's palsy, 95, 98
Erythema, toxic, 147
Erythroblastosis fetalis, 120
Esophageal atresia, 11, 82, 153, 189
diagnosis, 81–82, 83
surgery, 127, 128
types of, 84
Esophagus, development of, 154
Evaluation, initial. See Assessment, initial
Evaluation, routine, 21–23
laboratory procedures, 21–23
thermoregulation, 19, 21
transition period, 19, 20
Evaporated milk, preparation of formula from, 244
Examination. See Physical examination
Exchange transfusion
with jaundice, 114, 115, 117
with polycythemia, 117, 119
Expected date of confinement (EDC), 1, 2
Exstrophy of bladder, 85, 128
External cardiac massage, 14
Extremities
anomalies of, 11, 198
examination of, 33, 35, 36
fractures, 14, 91
in trisomies, 201
Eye, 65–68, 141–142
anomalies of, 104, 198, 200
cranial nerve function, 45
examination of, 40–41

Eye—*Continued*
  prophylaxis, 16, 24, 65, 141, 246
  in trisomies, 200

Facial nerve palsies, 99
Facilities. *See* Nursery, organization
      and management of
Familial disorders, 188. *See also*
      Genetic disorders
  hearing impairment risk, 42
  and jaundice, 115, 116
  retinoblastoma, 67
  and seizures, 98
Farenheit-centigrade table, 210
Fasciitis, 145
Fat necrosis, 140, 141
Feeding behavior
  with cardiac abnormalities, 74, 78
  cranial nerve function, 45, 46
  and hypoglycemia, 120
  near-term infant, 130
  with septicemia, 124
  with transient myasthenia gravis, 99
Feeding intolerance
  in drug withdrawal, 148, 149
  in gastrointestinal disease, 80
  with increased intracranial pressure,
      141
  and irritability, 146
Feet, anomalies of, 33, 35, 198, 201
Femoral pulses, 29, 31
Fetal breathing, 6, 8
Fetal circulation, 9, 11
Fetal development
  estimation of age, 1–2
  normal, 196–197
  and preterm delivery, 129
Fetal distress, 188, 189
Fetal growth measurements, 58, 59
Fetal heart tones
  decelerations, 4, 5
  gestational age assessment, 2
  monitoring, 4
Fetal hemoglobin, Apt test, 227
Fetomaternal transfusion, 79
Fetus papyraceus, 101, 103
Fever, 170. *See also* Temperature,
      body
First embryonic arch syndrome, 68
First trimester, 3
Fistulas, neck, 72
Flame nevus, 48, 104
Flea-bite dermatitis, 147

Fluid balance
  with cardiac abnormalities, 74
  preterm infant, 128, 130
  surgical patient, 127
Fluoride, 163
Fontanelle, 65, 141
  bulging, 141
  examination of, 38, 39, 40
  in septicemia, 124
Foremilk, 160
Foreskin
  circumcision. *See* Circumcision
  squamous cell inclusions, 100, 101
Formulas, 161, 163
  versus breast milk, 156–158
  preparation methods, 243–245
Fracture
  clavicle, 28
  humerus, 91
  skull, 140–141
Fungal infections
  monilial colonization of skin, 105–
      106
  mouth, 143
Fussiness, 140, 208
  parent preparation, 168

Gagging, 19, 153
Galant's response, 47
Gastrointestinal system
  and adaptation, 11, 20
  anomalies of, 81, 82, 144–145
  infection, 124, 127, 183
  initial assessment, 29
  obstruction, 81, 82–84, 153
    and abdominal distention, 145
    diagnostic algorithm, 86
    indications for transport, 190
    intubation for surgery, 127
    and jaundice, 115
    surgery, problems requiring, 128
Gastroschisis, 85, 128, 189
Gavage feeding, preterm infant, 130
Genetic disorders
  cleft lip and palate, 69–70
  retinal changes with, 67
  neural tube defects, 99
Genitalia. *See also* Circumcision
  anomalies of, 88–89, 199
  day one, 88–89, 90
  examination of, 31–32, 33
  as gestational age criterion, 53, 56
  in trisomies, 201

Genitourinary system, 87–88, 90, 146
  abdominal wall malformations, 85
  surgery, problems requiring, 128
Genu recurvatum, 33, 36
Gestational age assessment, 1–2, 52–57, 58
Glaucoma, congenital, 66
Glossoptosis, 71
Glucose levels. *See also* Hypoglycemia
  normal values, 23, 119
  preterm infant, 130
  routine admissions tests, 22–23, 120
Goiter, congenital, 72
Gonococcal infections. *See also* Eye prophylaxis
  conjunctivitis, 141
  and septicemia, 123
Grams, conversion, 211
Granuloma, umbilical, 145
Grieving, 175–176
Group B streptococcus, 123
Growth. *See also* Weight
  caloric requirements, 154
  intrauterine. *See also* Birth weight
    and adaptation, 11
    postterm infant, 13
    skeletal dysplasias, 92
  measurements of, 58, 59
Grunting, 72, 73
Guaiac test, 140, 145

Hair, anomalies of, 198
Hamartomas, 104
Hands
  anomalies of, 198
  in trisomies, 201
Hand washing
  family visits, 26
  instructions for, 181
  and prevention of infection, 123
Harlequin fetus, 105
Harlequin sign, 100
Head, 65–66, 140–141
  circumference of, 51, 141
  cranial nerve function, 45
  examination of, 38, 39
  fetal growth measurements, 58, 59
  hyperextension of, 95
  in trisomies, major findings with, 200
Hearing, 123, 167, 203
  risks, 42

Heart, 74, 76–80, 143–144
  abnormalities of. *See also* Electro-cardiography
  cyanosis with, 74–75
  and hypoglycemia, 120
  indications for transport, 190
  surgery, problems requiring, 128
  ventricular hypertrophy, 80, 81
  point of maximal cardiac impulse, 28
  in polycythemia, 118, 119
  and respiratory distress, 75
  in trisomies, 201
Heart block, 78
Heart failure
  anemia and, 12
  with blood group incompatibilities, 111
  feeding tolerance in, 78
  and hypoglycemia, 119–120
Heart rate. *See also* Vital signs
  adaptation, normal, 20
  Apgar scoring, 12
  assessment of response to resuscitation, 14
  fetal, decelerations, 4, 5
  hypoglycemia and, 120
  resuscitation indications, 12
  in shock, 78
  sinus bradycardia, 78
Heat loss, mechanisms of, 19, 21
Heat rash, 100
Hemangiomas, capillary, 48, 104
Hematochezia, 145
Hematocrit
  in gastrointestinal hemorrhage, 145
  with jaundice, 116, 117
  normal values, 221
  in polycythemia, 117
  routine admission procedures, 22–23
  with twin-to-twin transfusion, 133–134
  umbilical cord management and, 5
Hemoglobin
  in cyanosis, 73
  fetal, Apt test, 227
  normal values, 221
Hemolysis
  and bilirubin, 112, 114
  with blood group incompatibilities, 111
Hemorrhage. *See also* Vitamin K prophylaxis

Hemorrhage—*Continued*
  central nervous system. *See* Central
      nervous system, hemorrhage of
  conjunctival, 66
  cranial, 141
  gastrointestinal tract, 145
  and jaundice, 116
  and respiratory distress, 75
  scalp, 140
  and seizures, 97, 98
  and shock, 79
  skin, 100
  sternocleidomastoid, 72
  subgaleal, 38–39
  umbilical cord region, 84
Hepatitis, 115, 184
Hernia
  diaphragmatic, 127, 128, 189
  inguinal, 88
  omphalocele, 85
  umbilical, 29
Herpes infection, 188
  acquisition of, 123
  cultures in, 126
  encephalitis, 96
  and hearing impairment risk, 42
  isolation with, 184
  and jaundice, 115
  and seizures, 96
  skin, 100
Heteroclites, 100
Hexachlorophene, 25
Hindmilk, 160
Hip, examination of, 34, 37, 38
Hirschsprung's disease, 170
Horner's syndrome, 99
Horseshoe kidney, 104
Humerus, fracture of, 91
Hydranencephaly, 141
Hydration. *See* Fluid balance
Hydroceles, 32, 33
Hydrocephalus, 128, 141
Hydrometrocolpos, 89, 90
Hydronephrosis, 87
Hydrops fetalis, 61, 111, 188
Hyperbilirubinemia/jaundice, 112–
      117, 151
  and hearing impairment risk, 42
  sepsis and, 124–125
Hyperglycemia, 121
Hypermagnesemia, 122
Hypermetabolic states, 163
Hyperparathyroidism, maternal, 122

Hypertension, cerebral, 65, 124, 141
Hypertension, maternal, 188
  and fetal maturation, 57
  and hypoglycemia, 120
Hypertension, pulmonary, 75
Hyperthermia, 170
Hyperthyroidism, 163
Hyperventilation. *See also* Tachypnea
  in heart failure, 78
  and respiratory alkalosis, 72
Hyperviscosity, 117–119
Hypervolemia, and polycythemia, 23
Hypocalcemia
  and irritability, 146
  preterm infant, 129
  and seizures, 96, 97
  treatment of, 122
Hypoglycemia
  defined, 23
  with genital abnormalities, 88
  and irritability, 146
  management of, 119–122
  postterm infant, 131
  preterm infant, 129
  and seizures, 96, 97
Hypomagnesemia, 122, 146
Hypophosphatasia, anterior
      fontanelle and, 65
Hypoplasia, pulmonary, 11, 87
Hypoplastic left heart, 120, 144
Hypospadias, 88–89, 201
Hypotension. *See also* Shock
  causes and management of, 78–79
  fontanelle in, 124
Hypothermia, 25
  and cyanosis, 74
  and hypoglycemia, 119–120
Hypothyroidism, 65, 173
Hypotonia, 94
  differential diagnosis, 98
  resuscitation indications, 12
Hypovolemia
  and respiratory distress, 75
  and shock, 78
Hypoxemia
  airway suctioning and, 14
  and polycythemia, 23
  and seizures, 97

Ichthyosis, 105
Ileus, 81
  meconium, 128
Immune system, 123

Immunization, 75, 168
Immunoglobulin M, 21, 123, 126
Immunoglobulins, normal values, 218
Increased intracranial pressure, 65, 124, 141
Infant of diabetic mother, 122
Infection, 188
  eye, 65, 67, 141
  isolation guidelines, 241–242
  and jaundice, 115, 116
  placental signs, 61–62
  respiratory, 143
  and seizures, 96, 97, 98
  septicemia, 123–127
    acquisition of, 123
    diagnosis, 124–126
    response to, 123
    therapy, 126–127
  skin care, 25
  umbilical cord, 145
  urinary tract, 146
Infection, maternal
  as breast-feeding contraindication, 161
  eye prophylaxis. See Eye prophylaxis
  and preterm delivery, 129
Infection control, 183–184
Intrauterine growth retarded infant, 131, 188
Intravenous fluids
  hypoglycemia, 121
  preterm infant, 128
  surgical patient, 127–128
Intestinal obstruction. See Gastro-intestinal system, obstruction
Intubation
  in respiratory depression, 13
  surgery patient, 127
Irritability
  causes of, 146, 148–149
  characteristics of, 205
  hypoglycemia and, 120
  with increased intracranial pressure, 141
Isolation
  guidelines, 241–242
  infection control, 183–184

Jadassohn, sebaceous nevus of, 104
Jaundice. See Hyperbilirubinemia/ jaundice

Jaw abnormalities, 69, 71, 200
Jitteriness, 95, 120
Junctional nevus, 104

Kernicterus, 96
Kidney
  abdomen, examination of, 29
  anomalies of
    fetal, 87–88
    horseshoe, 104
    and neonatal adaptation, 11
  polycythemia and, 23
Klumpke's palsy, 95, 98–99

Labor
  indications for transport, 187–188
  normal, 3–4
Laboratory studies
  with cardiorespiratory symptoms, 143
  in cyanosis, 79
  in gastrointestinal disorders, 81
  in jaundice, 116, 117
  normal values
    blood chemistries, 216, 217
    cerebrospinal fluid, 228
    coagulation factors, 226
    hematologic, 221
    immunoglobulin and serum protein, 218
    reticulocytes, sedimentation rate, and blood volume, 222
    thyroid function tests, 219–220
    urinalysis, 229
    white blood cells, 223–224
  in respiratory distress, 74
  routine admission procedures, 21–23
  in septicemia, 125–126
Lactation, physiology of, 155, 159
Lamellar ichthyosis, 105
Lanugo, 48, 53, 56
Large for gestational age neonate
  defined, 57
  mortality and morbidity risk, 60
Laryngoscopy, 14
Last normal menstrual period (LNMP), 1, 2, 57
Low birth weight neonate, defined, 252
Lecithin to sphingomyelin ratio, 8, 9
Lentigines neonatorum, 48, 50
Length, growth measurements, 51–52, 58, 59

Let-down reflex, 159
Lethargy, 140
  with increased intracranial
    pressure, 141
  with septicemia, 124
Leukokoria, 67
Linear sebaceous nevus, 104
Liver
  with blood group incompatibilities,
    111
  determination of size, 29
  with heart failure, 78
Lumbar puncture, 126, 141
Lumbosacral pit, 104–105, 106
Lungs. *See also* Pneumonia;
    Respiratory system
  in polycythemia, 118, 119
  profile, 8, 9
  pulmonary hypoplasia, 11, 87

Macroglossia, 69
Magnesium, normal values, 217
Mandibular hypoplasia, 71
Mature milk, 160
Maturity rating, 56
  gestational age assessment, 1–2,
    52–57, 58
Measurements, 2, 49, 51–52
Meconium, 4, 140
  with abdominal distention, 145
  resuscitation procedures with, 14
  in transition period, 19
Meconium aspiration
  postterm infant, 131
  and respiratory distress, 75
Meconium ileus, 128
Meconium plug, 82, 85, 145
Medical conditions, maternal
  as breast-feeding contraindication,
    161
  and fetal maturation, 57
  in history, 1
  indications for transport, 187,
    188
  and preterm delivery, 129
Medications, 141
  dosages, 235–240
    antibiotics, 235–237
    anticonvulsants, 238
    cardiovascular agents, 239
    other agents, 240
  maternal
    and breast-feeding, 162

  in history, 1
  and neonatal depression, 94
  and respiratory distress, 75
  and seizures, 96, 98
  preterm infant, 128
  in resuscitation, 14, 15
Melanocytic nevus, 104
Melanosis, transient pustular, 48, 50
Melena, 140, 145
Membrane rupture, 188
  and preterm delivery, 129
  and sepsis, 124
Meningitis, 124, 141
  antibiotics in, 127, 235, 236, 237
  and hearing impairment risk, 42
  indications for transport, 190
  and seizures, 96
Meningomyelocele. *See*
    Myelomeningocele
Metabolic acidosis, 72, 75
Metabolic conditions and disorders
  and hypoglycemia, 120
  indications for transport, 190
  and jaundice, 115, 116
  preterm infant, 129
  and respiration, 72, 75
  screening, 173–175
  and seizures, 96, 98
Metabolism, caloric requirements, 154
Methemoglobinemia, 74, 79
Metric system. *See* Conversion table
Micrognathia, 69, 71, 200
Milia, 48
Miliaria, 100
Milk line, 100
Molding, cranial, 65
Monilial infections
  diaper dermatitis, 150, 151
  mouth, 143
Moro reflex, 47, 148
Mortality and morbidity risk
  birth weight and gestational age as
    factors, 60
  with seizures, 97
Mortality rates, evaluation of, 253
Mouth, 69–72, 143
  anomalies of, 198
  cranial nerve function, 45
  examination of, 43
  in trisomies, 200
Multicystic dysplasia of kidney, 87
Multiple births, 131–135, 188.
  and adaptation, 12

and hypoglycemia, 120
twin-to-twin transfusion, 133–134
Murmur, 74, 143
assessment of, 78
physical examination, 28
Myasthenia gravis, transient, 99
Mydriasis, 41, 67
Myelomeningocele, 99, 128
and seizures, 98
and sensory system, 47–48
Myocardial ventricular hypertrophy, 77, 80, 81

Naloxone, 15
Nasal flaring, 73, 149
Nasogastric intubation
with assisted ventilation, 13–14
surgery patient, 127
Near-term infant, 131
Neck, 72, 143
examination of, 43
Neck mass
airway obstruction, 95
surgery, problems requiring, 128
Necrotizing enterocolitis, 145
Neoplasia, 72, 104, 128
blueberry muffin baby, 106
and hypoglycemia, 120
nevi, 104, 105
Nervous system. See Neurologic system
Nesidioblastosis, 120
Neural tube defects, 99
Neuroblastoma, 106, 128
Neurofibromatosis, 104
Neurologic signs. See also Reflexes
in physical examination, 44–48
gestational age criteria, 54, 55
Neurologic system, 94–99, 146, 148–149
abnormalities of
and neonatal adaptation, 11
optic atrophy with, 67
adaptation, normal, 20
examination of, 44–48
in trisomies, major findings with, 200
Neutral thermal environment, 19, 21
Neutrophils, 223–224
Nevi, types of, 104, 105
Nipple, infant. See also Breast
as gestational age criterion, 53
supernumerary, 100–101, 102
Nipple, maternal, 161

Noonan's syndrome, 72
Nose, 68–69, 142–143
cranial nerve function, 45
examination of, 43
Nosebleeds, 143
Nuchal cord, 66
Nuchal rigidity, 124
Nursery, organization and management of
education, 185–186
facilities, 179–183
admission and observation area, 180
delivery room resuscitation area, 179–180
design and environmental control, 182–183
entry and scrub area, 181
equipment, 182
normal care area, 180–181
goals, 179
infection control, 183–184
personnel, 184–185
transport, 186–189
Nurses, 184–185
education and training, 185–186
observations of, 125, 139
Nutrition
breast feeding, 155–161, 162
first feeding, 153
formulas, proprietary, 161, 163
gastrointestinal tract development, 153, 154
requirements, 154–155
Nystagmus, 68

Obstetric history, 1
Obstipation, 170
Occult bleeding, 140, 145.
Oligohydramnios, 93
causes of, 11
placental signs, 61–62
and respiratory distress, 75
tetrad, 11
in urinary tract obstruction, 87
Omphalitis, 25, 127, 145
Omphalocele, 85, 128, 189
Ophthalmia neonatorum. See Eye prophylaxis
Ophthalmoscopy, 41
Optic atrophy, 67
Orange-peel skin, 140, 141

Organogenesis, 2–3
Ortolani test, 34
Osteogenesis imperfecta, 65
Osteomyelitis, 124, 127, 146
Otitis media, 124
Oxygen tension. *See also* Blood gases
  hemoglobin oxygen dissociation
    curves, 73
  in pulmonary versus cardiac shunt,
    79
Oxygen therapy, 12

Pacemaker, 78
Palate
  cleft of, 42, 69–70
  examination of, 43
  Pierre Robin syndrome, 71
Palmar reflex, 47
Panting, in heart failure, 78
Papilledema, 67
Paraphimosis, 90
Parents. *See also* Discharge
  behavioral states, 202–207
  delivery room procedures, 15–16
  family visits, 26
  near-term infant, 131
  observations of, 125
  safety seat use guidelines, 249–250
Paroxysmal atrial tachycardia, 76, 78
Patent ductus arteriosus, 78, 104
Penis. *See also* Circumcision
  anomalies of, 88–89, 199, 201
  care of, parent instruction, 169
  squamous cell inclusions, 100, 101
Peritonitis, 124
Petechiae, 100, 124–125
pH
  body fluids, 6, 7
  fetal scalp, 4
Phenylketonuria (PKU) screening,
    173, 174–175
Phimosis, 90
Phototherapy, 114, 115, 117
Physical examination
  abdomen, 29–31
  anus, 32–33
  chest, 27–29
  ears, 41–43
  eyes, 40–41
  genitalia, 31–32, 33
  gestational age assessment, 52–57,
    58
  head, 38–39
  history review in, 1

  measurements, 49, 51–52
  mouth, 43
  neck, 43
  neurologic system, 44–48
  nose, 43
  placenta, 61–62
  recording data, 57, 61
  skeleton, 33–38
  skin, 48, 50
Pits
  ear, 68
  lumbosacral, 104–105, 106
Placenta, 3
  amnion nodosum, 87
  examination of, 61–62
  labeling and storage of, 16
  in sepsis, 125
  with transient pustular melanosis, 48
  in trisomies, 200
  in twin-to-twin transfusion, 133
  uteroplacental insufficiency, 4, 5
Placental abnormalities, 188
  and hypoglycemia, 120
  and polycythemia, 117
  and postterm delivery, 131
  and preterm delivery, 129
Plantar creases, 53, 56, 201
Plantar grasp, 47
Plasma expanders. *See* Blood volume
  expanders
Platelet count, 81
Pneumatosis intestinalis, 145
Pneumonia
  antibiotic therapy, 127
  aspiration, 12
  respiratory distress, 74, 75
Pneumothorax, 127
  indications for transport, 190
  and respiratory distress, 75
  tension, 128
Point of maximal cardiac impulse
  (PMI), 28
Polycythemia-hyperviscosity syndrome,
  12
  and cyanosis, 74
  defined, 22–23
  management of, 117–119
  postterm infant, 131
Polyhydramnios, 11, 82, 188
Port wine stain, 104
Postmature infant, 131
Postterm infant
  defined, 252
  management, day one, 131, 133

mortality and morbidity risk, 60
skin of, 105
Posture
adaptation, normal, 20
breech presentation and, 95
gestational age assessment, 54, 55, 56
Potassium
body fluid composition, 6, 7
normal values, 216
Potter's facies, 11
Preauricular tags, 68, 69
Pregnancy, 1–3
Premature labor, 187–188
Prenatal care, 3
Preterm infant
defined, 252
management, day one, 128–131
mortality and morbidity risk, 60
Proctoscopy, 145
Prophylaxis. See Eye prophylaxis; Vitamin K prophylaxis
Prostaglandin E-1, 144
Protein
body fluid composition, 6, 7
serum, normal laboratory values, 218
Pseudoparalysis, 124, 146
Pulmonary circulation
assessment of, 28
with heart conditions, 76, 77
Pulmonary edema, 78
Pulmonary effusion, 78
Pulmonary fluid, composition of, 6, 7
Pulmonary hypoplasia, 11, 87
Pulses. See also Vital signs
assessment with heart conditions, 76
physical examination, 29, 31
resuscitation of newborn, 14
in shock, 78
Pupillary reflexes, 67
Pupils, dilation of, 41, 67
Purpura, sepsis and, 124–125
Pustular melanosis, transient, 48, 50

Quickening, 2, 3

Ranula, 70–71
Rectal temperature. See Temperature, body
Red blood cells. See also Hematocrit; Polycythemia-hyperviscosity syndrome

with blood group incompatibilities, 111
counts, normal values, 221
Red brick dust stains, 87, 170
Red reflex from the eye, 41, 66
Reflexes
adaptation, normal, 20
Apgar scoring, 12
cranial nerve function, 45
in drug withdrawal, 148
examination of, 46–47
eye, 41, 66, 67
Respiration
in heart failure, 78
neck malformations and, 72
onset of, 8
see-saw, 73
in transition period, 19
with urinary tract abnormalities, 87
Respiration rate. See also Tachypnea; Vital signs
Apgar scoring, 12
choanal atresia and, 69
in drug withdrawal, 149
physical examination, 28
resuscitation indications, 12
Respiratory acidosis, 14, 72
Respiratory alkalosis, 14–15, 72
Respiratory depression
causes of, 12–13
management of, 13–14
with transient myasthenia gravis, 99
Respiratory distress
choanal atresia and, 69
and hypoglycemia, 119–120
preparation for surgery, 127
Respiratory system, 72–74, 75, 143–144
adaptation, normal, 20
chest examination, 27–28
surgery, problems requiring, 128
Resuscitation, 12–15
equipment for preterm infants, 128
indications for transport, 189
Reticulocytes, 222
Reticuloendothelial system, 111
Retina, 41, 67
Retinoblastoma, 67
Retractions, 72, 73
with chest abnormalities, 143
Silverman score, 74
Rh incompatibilities, 188
and hypoglycemia, 120
management of, 111–112

Risk factors
  morbidity and mortality rates, 60,
    253
  in pregnancy, 3
Rooting reflex, 46
Rubella
  and blueberry muffin baby, 106
  and cataracts, 67
  and hearing impairment risk, 42
  isolation with, 184
  and jaundice, 115

Sacrococcygeal teratoma, 128
Safety considerations
  automobile travel, safety seat use,
    249–250
  parent teaching, 169
Salivary gland retention cysts, 70–71
Salmon patch, 104
Scalp edema, 140
Scalp pH, 4
Scapula, winged, 38
Scoliosis, 38
Screening, metabolic diseases, 173–175
Sebaceous nevus of Jadassohn, 104
Second heart sound, 28
Second trimester, 3
Sedimentation rate, 222
See-saw respirations, 73
Seizures, 95–97
  anticonvulsant dosages, 238
  in drug withdrawal, 148
  etiologies, 96
  hypoglycemia and, 120
  indications for transport, 190
  and irritability, 146
  outcome, 97
  with septicemia, 124
Sensory system
  cranial nerve functions, 44–46
  examination of, 47–48
  hearing, 123, 167, 203
Sepsis/septicemia, 74, 141
  and abdominal distention, 145
  antibiotic dosages, 235–237
  and failure to gain weight, 163
  and heart murmurs, 143
  and hypoglycemia, 119–120
  indications for transport, 190
  and jaundice, 116
  management of, 123–127
  and shock, 79

Serology
  positive, complications with, 111–
    112
  routine, 21
Shock
  causes and management of, 78–79
  etiology of, 79
  fontanelle in, 124
  and respiratory distress, 75
  septic, 125
Siblings, 170
Sickle cell hemoglobin screening, 173,
    174–175
Silverman score, 74
Silver nitrate. See Eye prophylaxis
Simian crease, 201
Sinus arrhythmia, 28
Sinus bradycardia, 78
Sinuses, skin, 104–105
Sinus tachycardia, 76, 78
Skeleton, 91–94, 146
  anomalies of, 187, 199
  examination of, 33–38
    extremities, 33, 35, 36
    hip, 34, 37, 38
  in trisomies, 201
Skin, 99–106, 150–151
  admission procedures, 25–26
  anomalies of, 198
  aplasia cutis congenita, 101, 102
  care of, parent instruction, 169
  in congenital methemoglobinemia,
    79
  examination of, 48, 52
  gestational age criteria, 53, 56
  septicemia diagnosis, 124–125
  webbed neck, 72
Skin perfusion, with heart conditions,
    76
Skull. See also Fontanelle
  changes in the first day, 65
  examination of, 38, 39, 40
  fractures of, 140–141
  in trisomies, major findings with,
    200
Sleep, 139
  characteristics of, 43, 206–207
  disturbed patterns of, 146, 148–149
  in drug withdrawal, 148
  in transition period, 19
Small for gestational age neonate
  defined, 57
  mortality and morbidity risk, 60

Sodium balance
  body fluid composition, 6, 7
  normal laboratory values, 216
  and seizures, 96
Spinal cord transection, 47–48, 72
Spinal dysraphism, occult, 101
Spine
  examination of, 38
  Klippel-Feil syndrome, 72
  lumbosacral dimples, 104–105
  neural tube defects, 99
  skin defects, 101
Spleen, 111
Squamous cell inclusions, 100, 101
Staphylococcal infections, 25
  conjunctivitis, 141
  umbilical cord, 145
Startle reflex, 47
Stepping reflex, 47
Sterilization, formula, 245
Sternocleidomastoid muscle, 143
Stools, 140
  with abdominal distention, 145
  adaptation, normal, 20
  culture of, 126
  in drug withdrawal, 149
  parent instruction, 170
  time of first defecation, 84
Strabismus, 67
Strawberry hemangioma, 104
Stress, and hypoglycemia, 119–120
Sucking, 167
  cranial nerve function, 45, 46
  and lactation, 159
Sucking blisters, 48, 49
Sucking reflex, 46
Suctioning, nose, 142–143
Sudden infant death syndrome (SIDS),
  170
Supernumerary digits, 91–92
Suprapubic bladder aspiration, 125,
  229
Surfactant, 8
Surgical emergencies
  and hypoglycemia, 119–120
  patient preparation, 127–128
Sutures, skull
  changes in the first day, 65
  examination of, 38, 39, 40
  increased intracranial pressure and,
  141
Swallowing, cranial nerve function,
  45, 46

Sweating
  in drug withdrawal, 149
  hypoglycemia and, 120
  in shock, 79
Syphilis, 112
  and nasal obstruction, 142
  and seizures, 96
Systemic lupus erythematosus, 78

Tachycardia
  hypoglycemia and, 120
  in shock, 79
Tachypnea
  with chest abnormalities, 143
  choanal atresia and, 69
  with respiratory distress, 75
  with septicemia, 124
Tags, skin
  back and spine area, 104–105
  preauricular, 68, 69
Tear duct obstruction, 141
Teeth, neonatal, 69, 70
Temperature, body. See also Vital
    signs
  adaptation, normal, 20
  delivery room records, 16
  gestational age assessment, 2
  parent instruction, 170
  in physical examination, 49
  preterm infant, 128, 129
  thermoregulation, evaluation of,
    19, 21
Temperature, environmental, 19–21,
    25, 182, 209
Tension pneumothorax, 127, 128
Terminal method, formula steriliza-
    tion, 245
Term infant
  defined, 252
  mortality and morbidity risk, 60
Testes, 32, 33, 88
Tetany, 95
Thermoregulation
  assessment of, 19, 21
  with septicemia, 124
Third trimester, 3
Thoracentesis, 127
Thoracic squeeze, 6
Thoracotomy, 127
Thrush, 143
Thumb sucking, 170
Thyroglossal duct cyst, 72

Thyroid function tests, 65, 173
  with jaundice, 114
  normal values, 219–220
  screening for metabolic diseases,
    174–175
Thyrotoxicosis, 188
Thyrotropin, 219
Thyroxine, 174–175, 219
Tone. *See* Tonus
Tongue, 69, 71
Tonus
  adaptation, normal, 20
  in drug withdrawal, 148
  hypoglycemia and, 120
TORCH complex, 184
Torticollis, 143
Toxic erythema, 147
Toxoplasmosis
  and hearing impairment risk, 42
  isolation with, 184
  and seizures, 96
Tracheoesophageal fistula, 128
Training, staff, 185–186
Transfusion, transplacental
  fetomaternal, 79
  and jaundice, 116
  placenta and, 133
  and polycythemia, 23, 117
  and respiratory distress, 75
  and shock, 79
  and transient myasthenia gravis, 99
  twin-to-twin, 133–134
Transfusions
  exchange, 114, 115, 117, 119
  in systemic hypotension, 79
Transient cutis marmorata, 100
Transient pustular melanosis, 48, 50
Transillumination
  head, 39
  testes, 32, 33
Transitional milk, 160
Transition period, 19, 20
Transport, 186–189
Transposition of great vessels, 144
Trauma
  airway suctioning and, 14
  and seizures, 96, 98
Trimesters, 3
Trisomies
  major findings with, 200–201
  webbed neck in, 72
Truncal incurvation reflex, 47
Tumors, 128. *See also* Neoplasia
  intraocular, 41

urinary tract obstruction, 88
Turner's syndrome, 72, 93, 95
Twin-to-twin transfusion. *See* Trans-
    fusion, transplacental
Tympanic membrane, 124

Ultrasonography
  craniospinal axis defects, 105
  gestational age assessment, 2
  head, 39, 141
  with heart conditions, 76
Umbilical cord, 84–85, 145
  assessment of, 5, 29
  care of, 25–26, 169
  clamping of, cardiovascular effects,
    9–10
  compression of, and fetal heart rate
    pattern, 5
  normal length, 61
  parent instruction, 169
  septicemia diagnosis, 124
Umbilical vessels
  catheterization, 119, 128
  pulsations, 20
  vasculitis, 25
Urachus, patent, 85
Urethral abnormalities, in males, 88–
    89
Urinalysis
  normal values, 229
  toxicologic, 146
Urinary tract. *See also* Genitourinary
    system
  anatomic abnormalities, 88–89
  infections, 146
  surgery, problems requiring, 128
Urine
  color of, parent instruction, 87,
    169–170
  in sepsis, 125
  suprapubic bladder aspiration, 125,
    230
  time of first void, 88
  with urinary tract abnormalities, 87
Uteroplacental insufficiency, 4, 5
Uvula, 43

Vacuum extractions, 4
Vaginal bleeding, 2
  infant, 170
  in labor, 189
Vascular nevus, 104
Vascular shunt, 79
Verrucous nevus, 104, 105

Vicarious menstruation, 170
Viral infections. *See also specific viruses*
  acquisition of, 123
  and blueberry muffin baby, 106
  and hearing impairment risk, 42
  isolation with, 184, 241
  and jaundice, 115
  and nasal obstruction, 142
  and septicemia, 126
Virilism, 88
Visual fixation, 41
Visual response, 201
Vital signs
  admissions procedures, 23–24
  with cardiac abnormalities, 74
  with increased intracranial pressure, 141
  in physical examination, 49
  preterm infant, 129
  resuscitation indications, 12
  in septicemia, 125
Vitamin K deficiency
  and bleeding (hemorrhagic disease of the newborn), 85
  and breast-feeding, 24
  and shock, 79
Vitamin K prophylaxis, 143, 145
  administration of, 16, 247–248
  admissions procedure, 24–25
  and bleeding, 85
Vitamin supplements, 163
Volume expanders. *See* Blood volume expanders
Vomiting
  with abdominal distention, 145
  in drug withdrawal, 149
  in gastrointestinal disease, 80
  with increased intracranial pressure, 141
  at time of nursery admission, 153

  in transition period, 19
  with upper gastrointestinal tract obstruction, 82

Waking state
  characteristics of, 43, 94–95, 207–208
  responses in, 202–208
Webbed neck, 72
Weight. *See also* Birth weight
  changes, 139, 140
  conversion table, 51, 211
  drug withdrawal and, 163
  of placenta, 62
  preterm infant, 130
White blood cells, 123
  normal values, 224
  in sepsis, 125
Wilms' tumor, 88
Winged scapula, 38
Witch's milk, 100
Withdrawal, drug. *See* Drug withdrawal

X-rays
  abdominal, in gastrointestinal disorders, 81
    bleeding, 145
    obstruction, 86
  chest
    with cardiorespiratory symptoms, 143
    with clavicular fracture, 91
    with gastrointestinal tract obstruction, 83, 86
    with heart conditions, 76
    with polycythemia, 118
    with respiratory distress, 74
  in septicemia, 126

Yeast infections, mouth, 143